Buyer's Price Guide

CHINESE PORCELAIN

by

Gordon Lang, Sotheby's

mJm
PUBLICATIONS
Pugin's Hall
Finchden Manor
Tenterden
Kent
telephone 058 06 2234

Pugin's Hall, Finchden Manor, Tenterden, Kent

Reprographic illustration work by
G.H. Graphics, St. Leonards-on-Sea, East Sussex

Photosetting by Ardek Photosetters
(division of Mainline Typesetters Ltd.)
Warrior Square Station Forecourt
St. Leonards-on-Sea, East Sussex

Made and printed in Great Britain by
Robert MacLehose, Scotland

The Publishers would like to acknowledge the great assistance given by:

Aldridges, 130-132 Walcot Street, Bath, Avon.
Anderson and Garland, Market Street, Newcastle-upon-Tyne NE1 6XA.
Bonhams, Montpelier Street, London, S.W.7.
Christie, Manson & Woods Ltd., 8 King Street, London SW17 6QT.
Christie, Manson & Woods International Inc., 502 Park Avenue, New York 10022.
Christie's East, 219 East 67th Street, New York 10021.
Christie's (International) S.A., 8 Place de la Taconnerie, 1204 Geneva.
Dacre Son and Hartley, 1-5 The Grove, Ilkley, Yorkshire.
Geering & Colyer, Hawkhurst, Kent.
Henry Spencer & Sons, 20 The Square, Retford, Notts.
Langlois, 10 Waterloo Street, Jersey, C.I.
Lawrences, South Street, Crewkerne, Somerset.
Louis Taylor & Sons, Percy Street, Hanley, Stoke-on-Trent.
Morphets of Harrogate, The Mart, 4 & 6 Albert Street, Harrogate, Yorks.
Neales of Nottingham, 192 Mansfield Road, Nottingham.
Peter Wilson, Market Street, Nantwich, Cheshire.
Phillips Auctioneers, Blenstock House, 7 Blenheim Street, London W1Y 0AS.
Sotheby Bearne, Rainbow, Torquay TQ2 5TG.
Sotheby Belgravia, 19 Motcomb Street, London SW1X 8LB.
Sotheby Beresford Adams, Booth Mansion, 28 Watergate Street, Chester CH1 1NP.
Sotheby King & Chasemore, Station Road, Pulborough, West Sussex RH20 1AJ.
Sotheby, Parke Bernet and Co., 34-35 New Bond Street, London W1A 2AA.
Sotheby Park Bernet Monaco S.A., P.O. Box 45, Sporting d'Hiver, Place du Casino, Monaco.

CONTENTS

PREFACE

It is hoped that this book will prove to be of value, not only as a guide to the current prices of antique Chinese porcelain, but also as a useful introduction to the subject generally. With this in mind, its illustrations (almost four hundred in all) have been arranged in roughly chronological order, spanning the period from the 14th to 20th centuries, allowing the reader to trace the development of structural and decorative styles. Occasionally, and to demonstrate stylistic development more clearly, some pieces have been inserted anachronistically through the text for comparative purposes.

Each illustration is accompanied by a concise, descriptive caption and an up to date valuation of the item illustrated in the condition described. Since condition is of paramount importance, this must be borne in mind when using the information herein as a basis for negotiating the purchase or sale of any similar piece. In order to add to the value of the book as an informative source of reference, many captions are concluded by footnotes (printed in italic type).

The compiler of this Buyer's Price Guide to Chinese Porcelain is Gordon Lang, a leading specialist in Chinese export and Imperial porcelain, and Annamese and Korean ceramics. For eighteen years, he has been cataloguing ceramics and works of art for the great auction houses of the world, including Bonhams, Phillips and Sotheby's, beside writing many commissioned articles and book reviews. He is also a regular contributor to the BBC Antiques Roadshow, and is at present head of Sotheby's ceramics department in Sussex.

Introduction

Chinese porcelain was first produced in an identifiable form during the ninth or tenth centuries. The earliest wares were manufactured in the Northern Provinces and are a white bodied cream glazed porcelain. From the tenth through to the fourteenth century, the different regions of China made their own characteristic wares, such as Dingyao and Xingyao in the north, and Shufu and Yingqing in the south. These latter two types are closely related in both composition and form to the earliest pieces of porcelain, decorated in either underglaze copper red or cobalt blue. We shall confine ourselves to porcelain manufactured from the early fourteenth century up to items dating from the beginning of the twentieth century.

The earliest pieces consist of a series of small water droppers, cuboid vessels, oil jars or bowls, which were tentatively painted with simple floral sprays (see p. 10). These wares have been excavated in some considerable quantity in the Philippines, Indonesia and other areas of South-east Asia during the last twenty or thirty years. Although they perhaps seem unsophisticated, they can be directly linked to the famous pair of vases dated 1351 housed in the Percival David Foundation of Chinese Art in London. These two vases are important for our understanding of the decorative development in the fourteenth century. Many vessels and plates decorated in similar style are to be found both in India and the Middle East, doubtless because of the close trading ties between China, which was governed at this time by the Muslim Yuan dynasty, and their Islamic cousins further west. The somewhat crowded decoration of this period (see p. 11) gave way in the fifteenth century to a more controlled and spacious style evident on the wares of Yongle and Xuande (see p. 12 meiping), and to an even greater extent on the porcelain of Chenghua, epitomised by the celebrated 'palace' bowls.

A gradual deterioration in the quality of the brushwork can be noted towards the end of the fifteenth century, and even the attractive porcelains produced for the use of the Muslim eunuch scholars or officials during the reign of Zhengde are afforded a fairly cursory treatment when compared with the earlier fifteenth century blue and white. It was during the following reign of Jiajing that a distinctive vibrant purplish cobalt blue, imported from the Middle East and termed Mohammedan blue, appeared. This reign was also noted for the greater use of figural subjects, a theme not popular during the major part of the fifteenth century, with the obvious exception of the more spontaneous 'windswept scholar' school of wares. Another, perhaps slightly curious, decorative feature during this period was the use of the Taoist shou characters, sometimes incorporated as the twisted branch of a tree (see p. 15 lower right). Taoist motifs remained popular throughout the latter two-thirds of the sixteenth century; particularly common are deer, crane and pine. With greater production required for export, quality naturally declined in the late Ming dynasty. The painting is casually executed and the wares are poorly finished, often with sand adhering to the base or footrim. It was during the reign of the Emperor Wanli that the Dutch literally captured the exportware market from the Portuguese and many thousands of pieces of 'kraakporselein' (Dutch for ship porcelain) found their way into Europe. This type is characterised by the use of compartments enclosing flowers or precious objects (see pp. 21-24). The subsequent reign of Tianqi is noteworthy for a series of blue and white and polychrome wares made for the Japanese market called 'kosometsuke'. Some pieces of this type were designed specifically for the Tea Ceremony. They are freely drawn, perhaps with only an isolated scholar meditating on a riverbank, or an asymmetrical arrangement of flowers or shrubs, and occasionally utilising variegated diapers or brocades (see pp. 25 and 26).

The Transitional period covers the fall of the Ming dynasty and the first troubled years of the Manchu or Qing dynasty. It was at this time that there appeared a highly attractive group of wares which were painted in an academic style with figures in idyllic cloud-lapped landscapes. Typical of this group is the frequent use of banana plantain to interrupt the scene and method of depicting grass by a series of arc-like brush strokes (see pp. 28-30). Another feature of this group is the *anhua* (secret) borders of scrollwork or hatching sometimes so lightly incised as to be almost invisible.

The Emperor Kangxi ascended the Dragon throne as a minor in troubled rebellious times. The kilns were seriously disrupted during the early years of his reign, and it was not until Cangying Xuan was made director of the kilns in 1683 that production was stabilised. Quality improved and the repertoire of types expanded. The 'famille verte' palette replaced the Ming *Wucai* enamels (see p. 32 and p. 45). New monochromes were introduced and old techniques revived. The former included 'peach bloom', a derivative of copper (see p. 33, lower right), various green glazes, mirror black and 'clair-de-lune' (a subtle pale blue glaze). Towards the end of this reign, pink (purple of Cassius) was included in the range of enamels to become the famous 'famille rose', a term coined by Jacquemart and other French connoisseurs in the middle of the nineteenth century in an attempt to classify Chinese porcelain (see p. 53). By this time the export of Chinese ceramics and works of art was a major industry and large orders for porcelain were placed, including porcelain bearing the coats-of-arms of European and American families (see p. 62). Many of these wares were based upon contemporary European designs or forms (see p. 59, tureen top left). Alongside this huge export trade, the Chinese manufactured items for their own consumption, namely the so-called 'Chinese taste' pieces, rarely seen in Europe at that time (see p. 76).

The Qianlong period witnessed a decline in the quality of the wares, both in technique and decoration. Although the beginning of the reign was noted for several innovations, particularly with respect to monochromes, there was a tendency to over-elaboration in the latter part of the reign. This decline continued in the nineteenth century probably reaching its lowest aesthetic appeal during the third quarter of the century. Under the influence of the Empress Dowager Tzu chi, there was a limited revival in quality, confined mainly to non-export wares and utilising retrospective designs. There were many fine examples of 'Chinese taste' wares produced at this time and in the early years of the present century, which have occasionally proved difficult to distinguish from their eighteenth century originals.

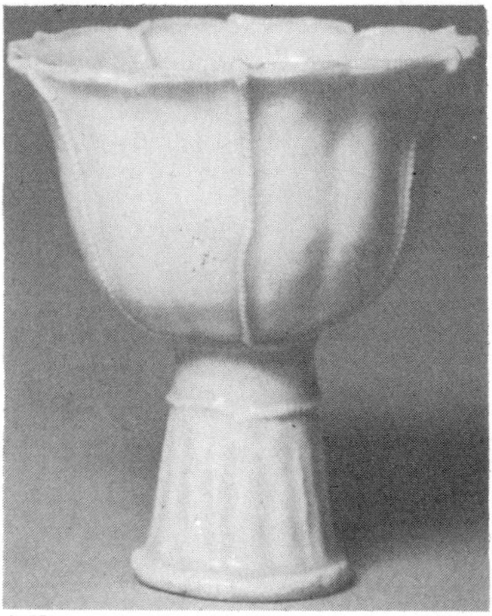

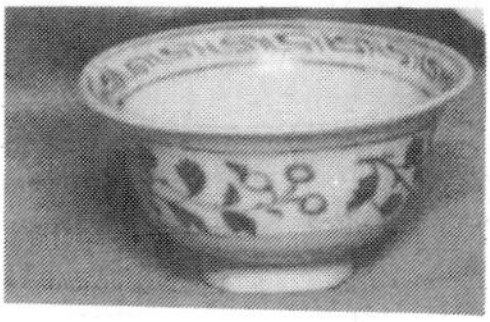

A rare Yuan blue and white wine cup, the interior painted in a dark grey blue with a chrysanthemum branch within a border of *leiwen,* the outside with two chrysanthemum branches in bud and flowers, one small hair crack, slightly irregular, 8 cm. diam., early 14th C., on a wooden stand. **£1,500-2,000**

A Yingqing stem-cup, the deep bowl with six ribs of beads radiating from a central rosette to form a hexafoil headed petal-shaped rim, the exterior with parallel beaded ribs, all under a translucent pale bluish glaze, diam. of bowl 8.5 cm., overall height 9 cm., early 14th C.
£8,000-12,000
This forms part of the well known Yuan group, which are variously moulded and applied with beading and figural decoration.

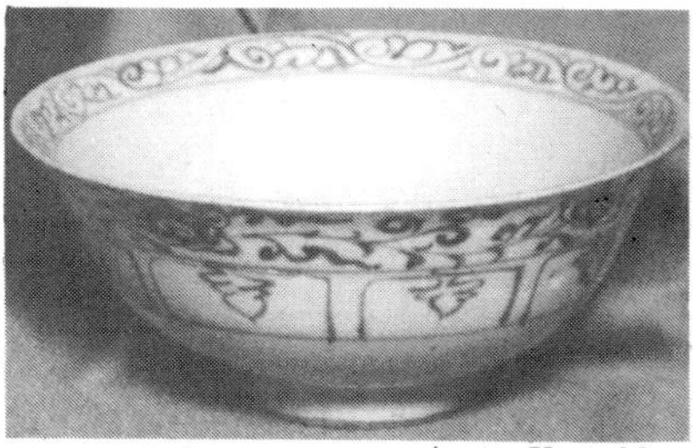

A rare Yuan blue and white bowl, painted in a dark grey blue with a pearl within a foliage border to the interior, the outside with flowering foliage, the glaze a fine clear grey blue, 16.5 cm. diam., early 14th C.
£5,000-7,000

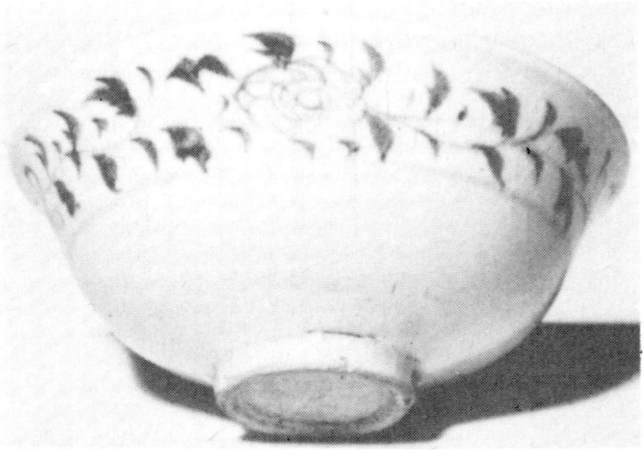

A blue and white shallow bowl, painted with a shou character below a band of stylised wave pattern on the interior, chrysanthemum on the exterior, cracked, fitted box, mid 14th C., 12 cm. diam. **£500-800**

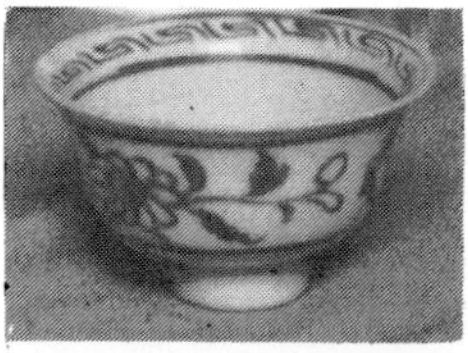

A rare Yuan underglaze copper red wine cup, the colour on the inside a smoky grey pink and on the outside a fine dark cherry red, the foot recessed unglazed and cut into a shallow cone, two haircracks, 8 cm. diam., on a wooden stand. **£2,500-4,000**

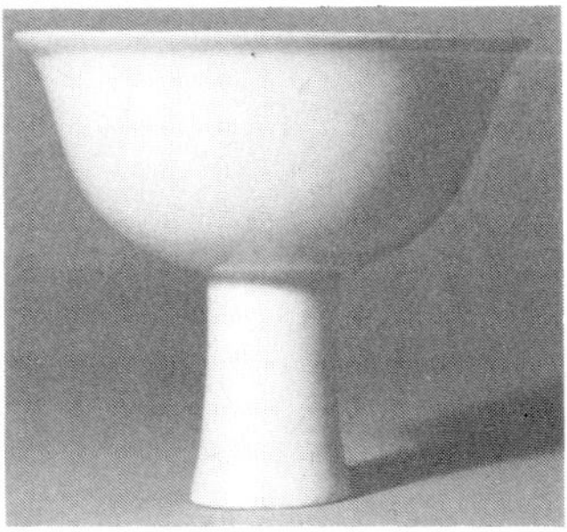

An early Ming white glazed stem-cup, decorated in anhua with two dragons amongst the clouds in the interior around a central incised S-shaped cloud, the exterior with a single iron spot, early 15th C., 5½ in. diam., 4½ in. high. **£8,000-12,000**

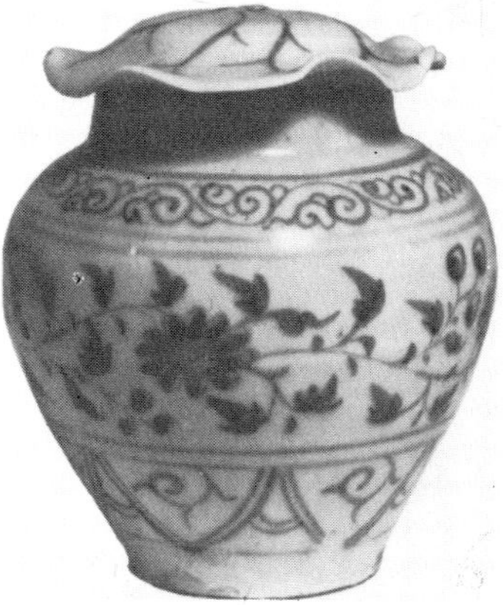

A blue and white jar and cover, painted with four chrysanthemum heads on a band of foliage around the centre above overlapping petals descending towards the base, the shoulder with a band of classic scrolls, the glaze pooling irregularly on and around the shallowly cut pale biscuit foot, 14th C., 11.5 cm. high. **£2,000-£3,000**
The overlapping petals encircling the base and the foliate scroll on the shoulders are features of 14th C. blue and white.

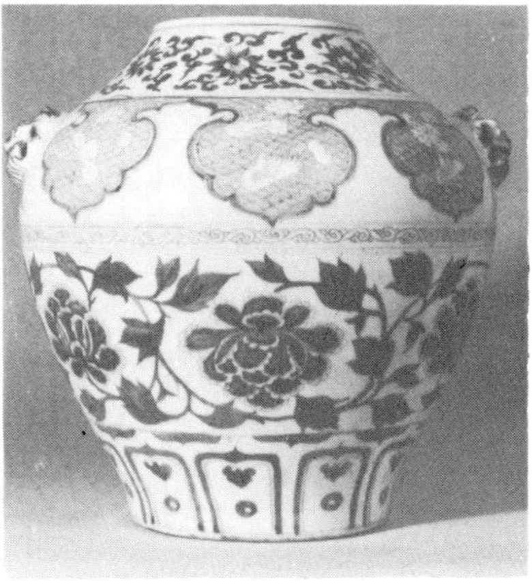

An important Yuan blue and white wine jar, painted with six large 'normal' peony heads below a narrow band of scrolls, the shoulder with six cloud collar lappets painted with ducks and a heron swimming, and lotus floating on the sea, with two lion mask handles, with typical early rectangular lappets above the flat foot, neck reduced, small chips on the handles, 33.5 cm. high, overall width 35.5 cm., mid 14th C. **£25,000-30,000**
This forms part of a group of large early blue and white jars used either for wine or for storage. See the Cleveland Museum example illustrated by Dr. Sherman Lee and Wai-kam Ho, 'Chinese Art Under the Mongols, The Yuan Dynasty (1279-1368)' fig. 156, which has both phoenix and geese, and Sir Harry Garner, 'Oriental Blue and White', pls. 20, 21, for the jars from the Hobart and Museum of Eastern Art, Oxford, collections.
The Cleveland example is much closer to the wine jar illustrated, particularly in the careful way in which the cloud collar lappets are spaced exactly as the six large peony heads in the meander below.
The central zone of peony in the present example has fully blown blossom giving an almost three dimensional appearance, which along with the thickly washed spiky leaves, are typical of the mid and third quarter of the 14th C. Also typical are the formal petal panels enclosing thin pendant lobed leaves and suspended 'O' motifs, which encircle the base. On the shoulders the barbed panels contain wave diaper decoration which were characteristic of the late 14th C. and early 15th C.

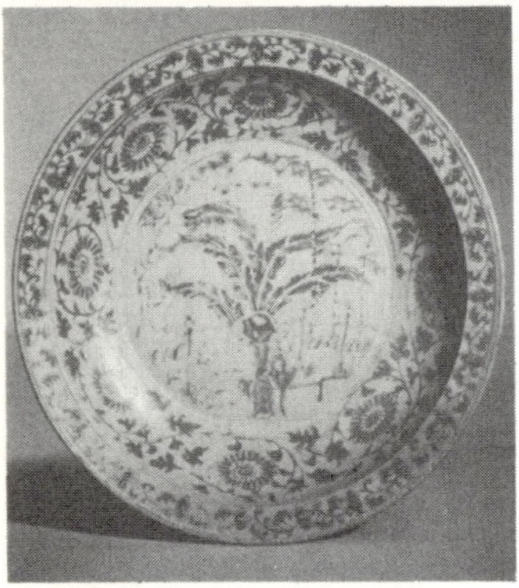

An underglaze copper and red and white deep dish, the copper red of a rich dark colour at the border and less strong at the centre, the translucent overglaze with areas of milky-white colour forming irregular pools and leaving small areas of unglazed biscuit, especially on the upper rim, shallow chips, mid/late 14th C., fitted box, 45 cm. diam. **£90,000-110,000**
Underglaze copper red is very rare. Early examples rarely fired the correct colour and many transmuted to a mushroom pink or even a greyish liver colour. The close almost crowded appearance is typical of the style fashionable under the Mongols during the Yuan dynasty. Perhaps the most recognisable and characteristic decorative motif on the present dish is the chrysanthemum scroll following the cavetto (or well). This is seen on both copper red and cobalt blue wares of this period. A slightly earlier and less sophisticated version of this chrysanthemum scroll is to be seen on the blue and white jar and cover illustration on p. 11.

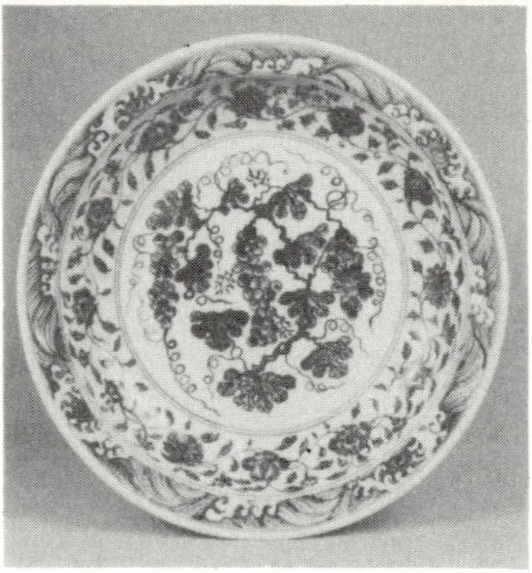

An early Ming blue and white deep dish, painted with three bunches of grapes on a vine, the well and reverse each with 12 flower-heads on continuous foliage meanders including peony, chrysanthemum, camellia, hibiscus, lotus, gardenia and dog rose, the cobalt blue of vivid deep colour with extensive 'heaping and piling', minutely fritted, Yongle, 14¾ in. diam. **£30,000-40,000**
A fine example of early 15th century blue and white porcelain. Noteworthy are the brilliantly painted comb-like wave borders, the scrolling foliate cavetto- executed with great control — and in the centre, the fruiting vine and tendrils. Every aspect of this plate is characteristic of the period.

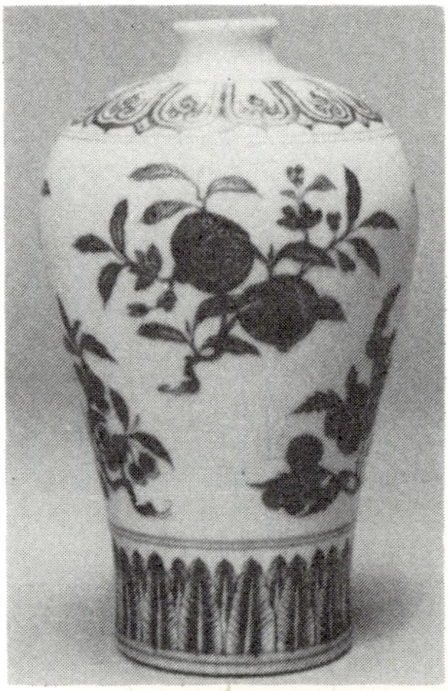

An early Ming blue and white meiping, painted in two registers with sprays of peaches, pomegranates and cherries above similar fruit sprays, the base unglazed below a band of tall overlapping leaves, the surface with extensive natural craque-lure, with slight related brown staining, 29.5 cm. high, mid 15th C. **£10,000-15,000**

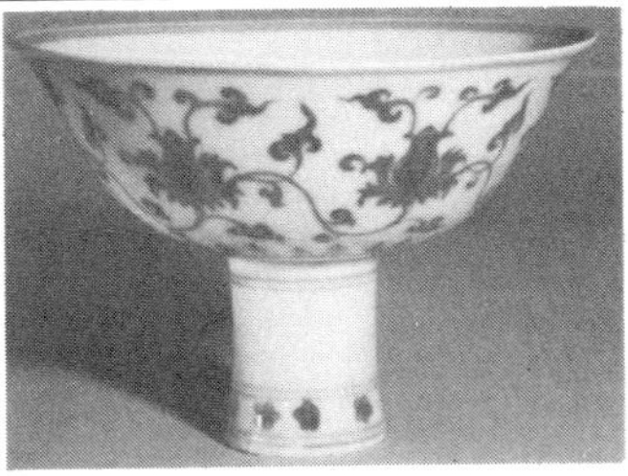

An early Ming blue and white stem-cup, with a peony spray at the centre of the interior, early/mid 15th C., 17.6 cm. diam., with fitted box. **£25,000-40,000**

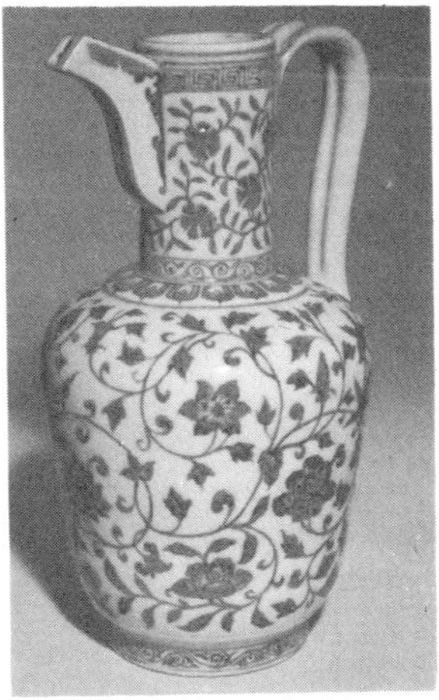

An early Ming blue and white ewer (*zhi hu*), painted with peony, camellia gardenia, lotus, chrysanthemum, hibiscus and other flowers and buds, the cobalt with extensive 'heaping and piling', Xuande or slightly earlier, the spout incised with a Persian inscription in a small cartouche, 33 cm. high, 18 cm. diam. **£50,000-80,000**

The inscription on the spout may be read as: 'Az Jehankar Shah Akbar Shah from Jehankar Shah Akbar Shah, 1038 A.H.' (1628 A.D.). This is a superb example of early 15th C. blue and white porcelain. There are four published ewers of similar shape which are slightly larger and have a different design, the chief difference being that the floral decoration on the body is contained in panels. The form is in fact derived from a Persian metal form. The strong floral painting manifests the heaped and piled effect so typical of Yongle and Xuande wares. The cobalt has oxidised through the glaze where the pigment has been too heavily loaded on the brushes.

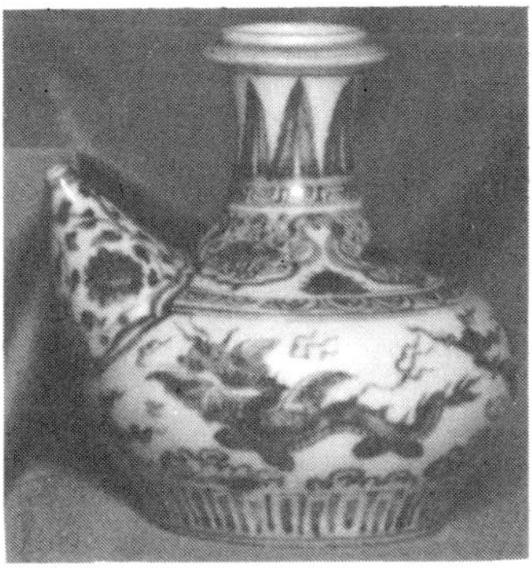

A Ming blue and white kendi, painted in a washy blue with three flying dragons, the waisted neck with lingzhi lappets, key pattern and stiff leaves, 15.5 cm. high, late 15th C. **£1,500-2,500**

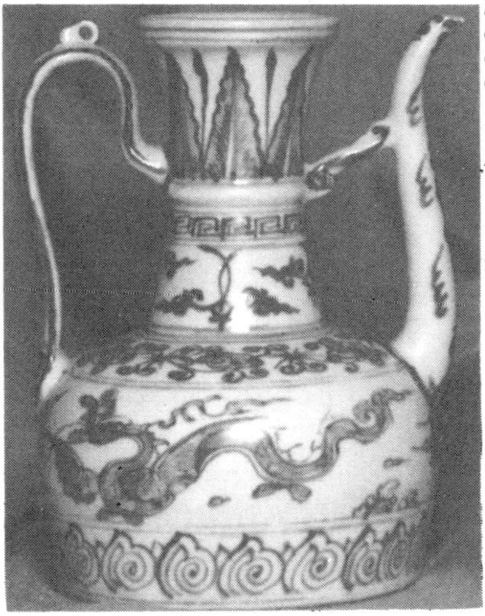

A rare Ming blue and white ewer, painted with two dragons in mutual pursuit, with an extended firing crack at the neck end; the spout with a restored chip at the end, 25 cm. high, late 15th C. **£7,000-10,000**

The shape is of Middle Eastern metalwork inspiration.

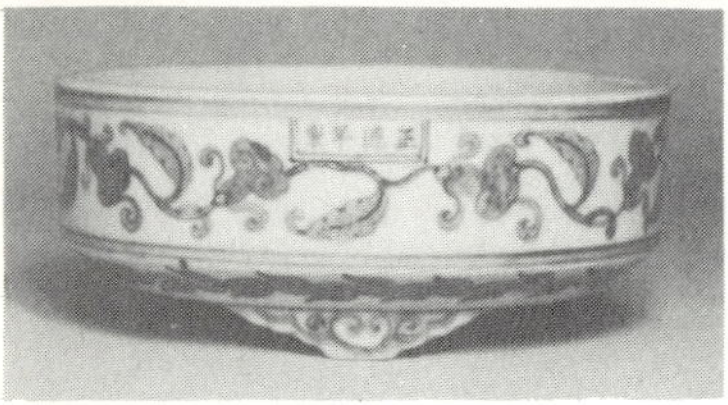

A rare Doucai shallow cylindrical narcissus bowl, enamelled with yellow lappets and scrolls, the chamfer with a green leaf scroll, 24 cm. diam., 9.5 cm. high, Zhengde four character mark in underglaze blue horizontally below the rim and of the period. **£8,000-11,000**
Doucai wares of this period and the subsequent Ming reigns are extremely rare.

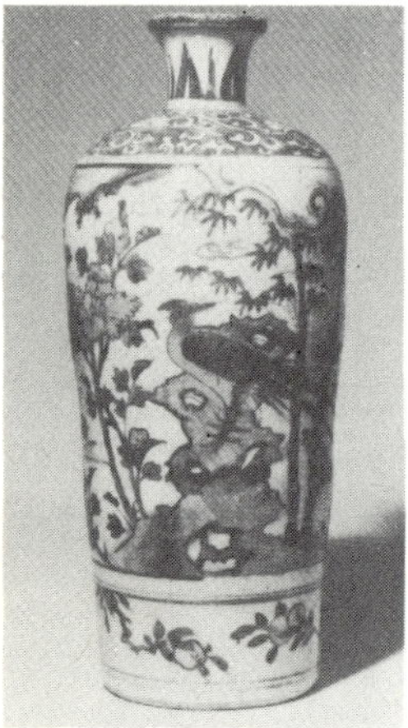

A pair of late Ming blue and white sleeve vases, painted with pheasants amongst peony and bamboo in rocky landscapes above fruit sprays at the foot, restored, early 17th C., 17 in. high. **£650-750**

Right
A Ming blue and white bowl, painted with the eight precious emblems amongst scrolling lingzhi and foliage, the interior with emblems and foliage at the centre, damaged and riveted, unencircled Jiajing six-character mark and of the period, 13 in. diam. **£300-400**
Note the thick-outlined and washed stems characteristic of the late 15th century and first half of the 16th century blue and white.

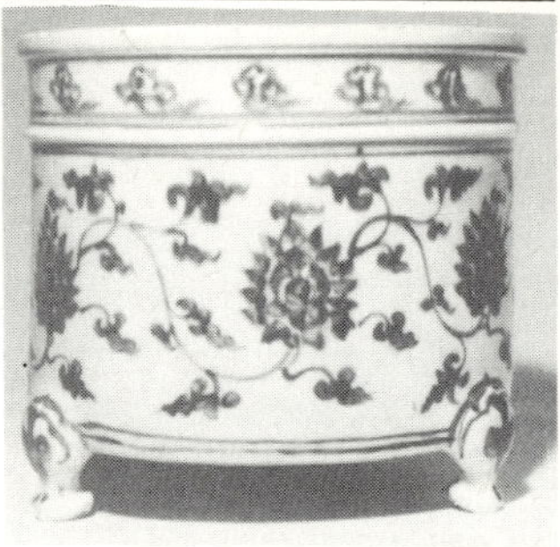

A Ming blue and white Censer, painted with a band of scrolling chrysanthemum, the cabriole feet each with a ruyi head, minor frits, c. 1500. **£3,000-4,000**
The scrolling lotus is painted in a manner idiosyncratic of the second quality blue and white produced during the later years of the 15th and the early years of the 16th centuries. Note especially the somewhat crudely painted lotus blossoms and small tightly curled leaves.

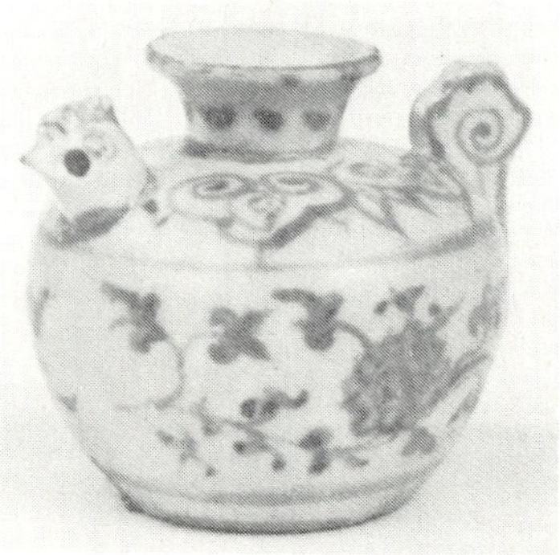

A Ming blue and white chicken-head ewer, painted with two peony sprays on the body below a band of ruyi heads on the shoulder, chipped, the neck cracked, 16th C., 3¾ in. wide. **£150-200**
Compare the painting on this early 16th C. chicken ewer with the tripod censer above.

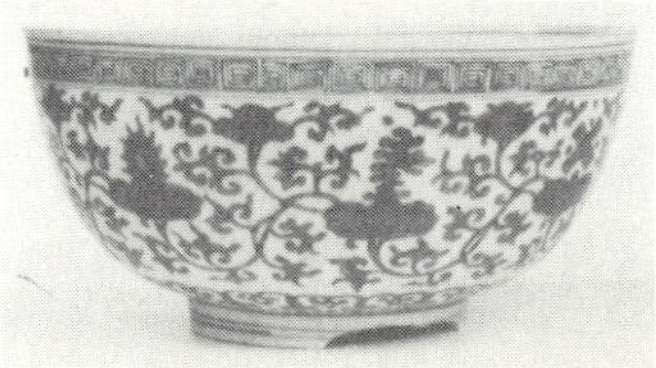

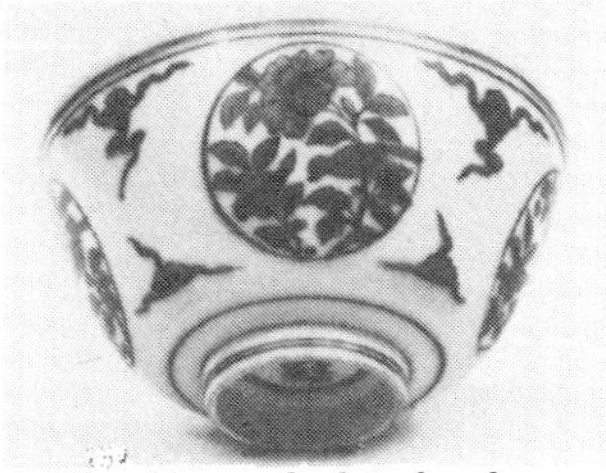

A Ming blue and white bowl, painted with four roundels of a bird perched on a peony branch, and a peony roundel at the centre of the interior, minor base underside chip, encircled Jiajing six-character mark and of the period, 4¾ in. diam. **£400-700**
The isolated stylised cloud scrolls which divide the four roundels on the exterior are characteristic of the late Jiajing period.

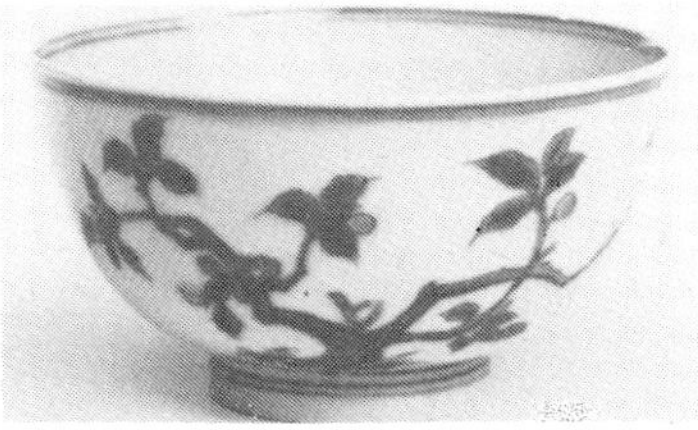

A blue and white bowl, painted with a fruiting peach tree and a branch of similar foliage amongst clouds in a roundel at the centre of the interior, encircled Jiajing six-character mark, Ming Dynasty, in fitted box, 5½ in. diam. **£2,500-3,800**

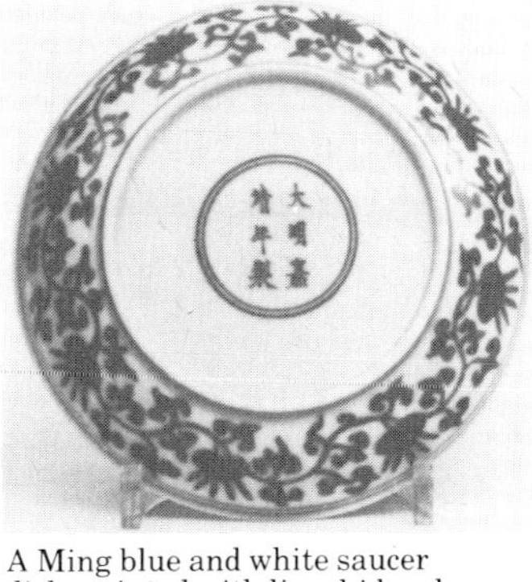

A Ming blue and white saucer dish, painted with lingzhi heads forming a cruciform pattern at the centre of the interior, under a widely crackled glaze, cracked, encircled Jiajing six-character mark and of the period, in fitted box, 5¾ in. diam. **£1,300-2,000**

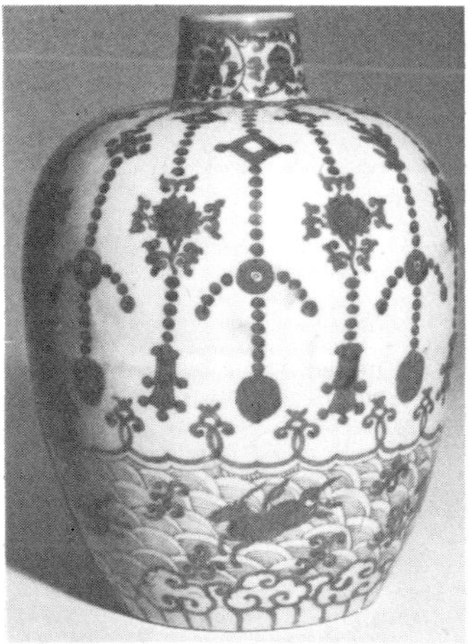

A Ming blue and white jar, painted with five horses leaping over swirling and breaking waves above a band of cloud-shaped lappets issuing from the foot, all below the eight precious emblems, alternating with lotus sprays suspended from a band of ruyi lappets around the shoulder, chipped, unencircled Jiajing six-character mark and of the period, in a wood box, 26 cm. high. **£6,000-9,000**
The tasselled decoration is a typical theme of this and the following reigns of Longqing and Wanli.

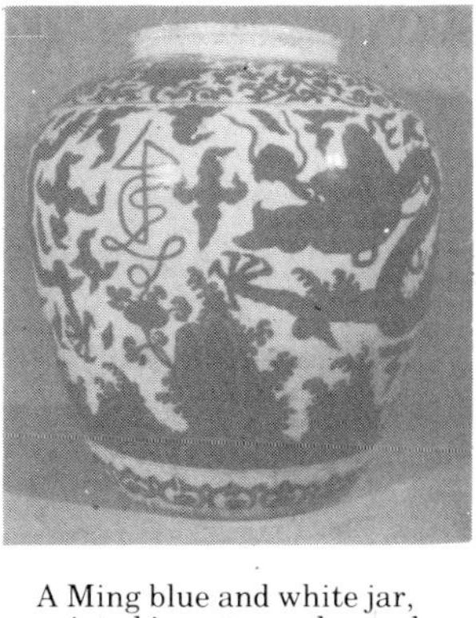

A Ming blue and white jar, painted in a strong deep colour with two dragons, amongst clouds divided by a shou character, unencircled Jiajing six-character mark and of the period, 21¾ in. high. **£10,000-£15,000**

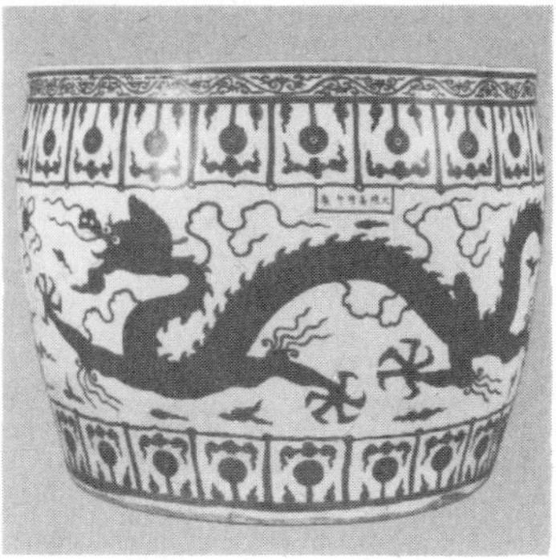

A massive late Ming blue and white fish bowl, with two five-clawed dragons between flaming pearls, between bands of large lappets centred with hanging bi discs, rim crack, large base firing star crack extending up the side, now cleaned, stabilised and restored, 74 cm. diam., Jiajing horizontal six-character mark on the body and of the period.
£10,000-14,000

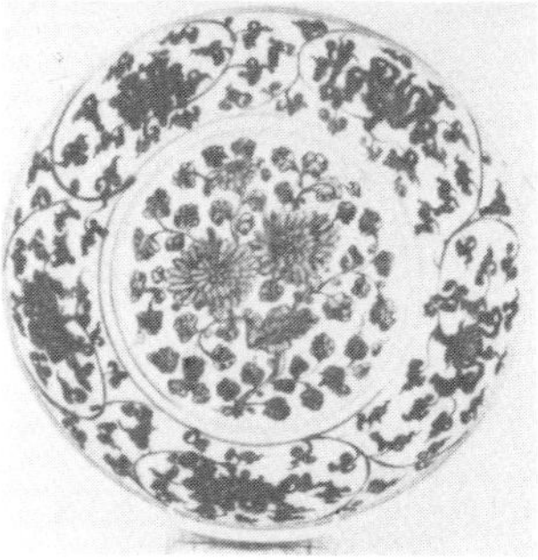

A Ming blue and white deep bowl, painted in inky blue with scrolling chrysanthemum between bands of formal scrolls and lappets, the interior with a chrysanthemum roundel, cracked, 12½ in. diam., 16th C.
£300-500
Heavily potted bowls of this type were frequently made for export to the Middle East.

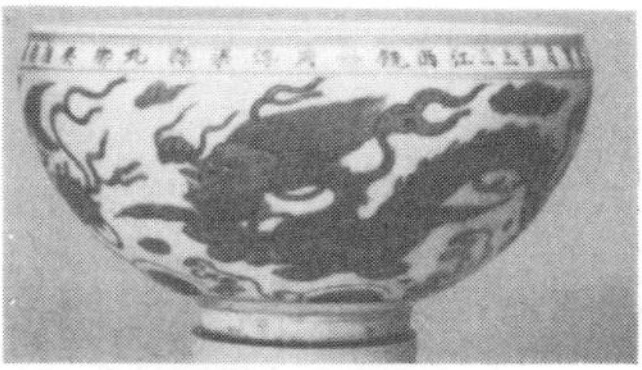

A documentary late Ming blue and white deep bowl, painted in a typical washy late Ming blue on the exterior, the rim with a long inscription, the centre of the interior with a Buddhist conch shell, slight sanding in the centre of the interior, firing crack within the footrim only on the exterior, 25.5 cm. diam., Longqing, dated 1572 and of the period. **£3,000-4,000**

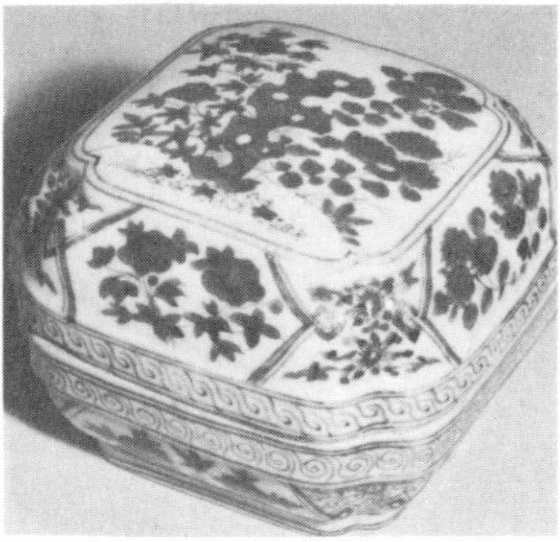

A Ming blue and white square box and cover, painted with peony and chrysanthemum issuing from rockwork, unencircled Jiajing six-character mark and of the period, 13 cm. square. **£6,000-10,000**

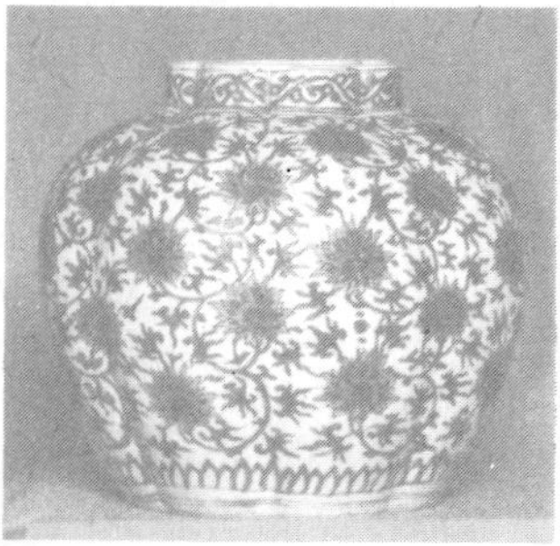

A late Ming blue and white jar, painted with scrolling lotus headed foliage above a band of overlapping petals, in a typical blackish-blue, one inch neck crack, rim slightly chipped, 19.5 cm. high, Wanli. **£3,500-£5,000**

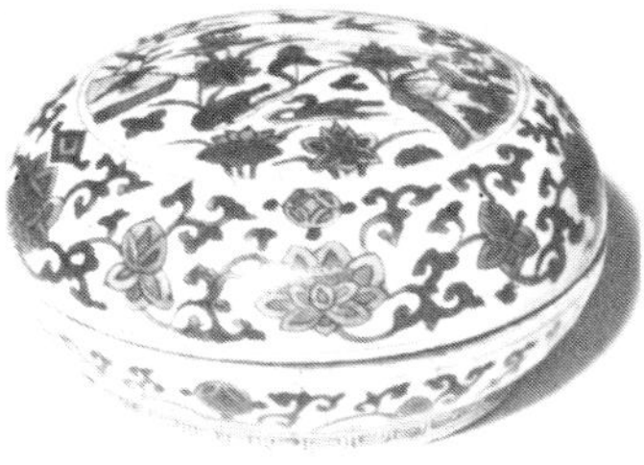

A late Ming blue and white box and cover, painted with a central panel of ducks swimming amongst lotus beneath a stork and birds in flight, cover with body crack, box compartments reduced, encircled Wanli six-character mark and of the period, 6 in. diam. **£900-1,100**
Domed circular boxes were popular during the 16th century reigns of Jiajing and Wanli.

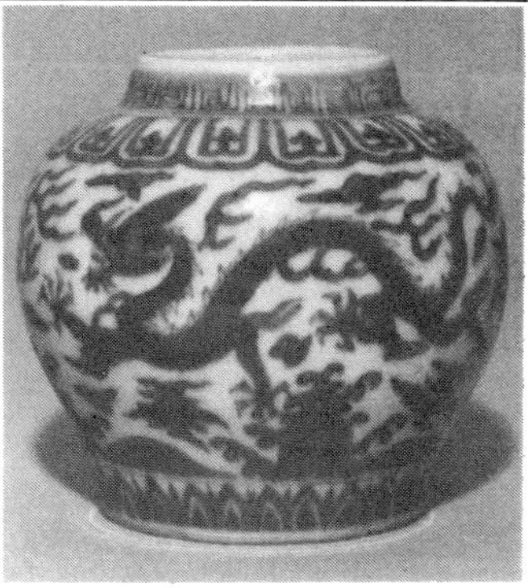

A late Ming blue and white jar, painted in a bright blue with two five clawed dragons, the glaze in unusually pristine condition, 10 cm. high, ivory cover formed as a domed lotus leaf. **£10,000-£12,000**

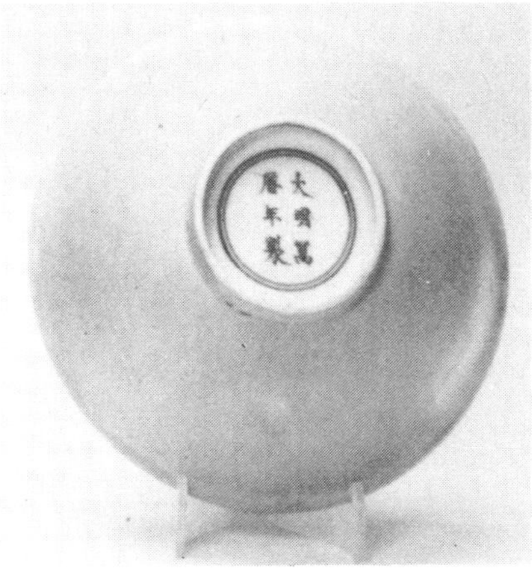

An Imperial yellow bowl, the exterior incised with five peony heads in a meander, all under an olive yellow glaze, 18 cm. diam., Wanli six-character mark and probably late in the period, damaged. **£300-500**
Imperial yellow (derived from iron and antimony) appears from the late 15th century through both Ming and Qing dynasties. Most periods have a characteristic tone, but perhaps the richest and finest colours were obtained during the reign of Kangxi.

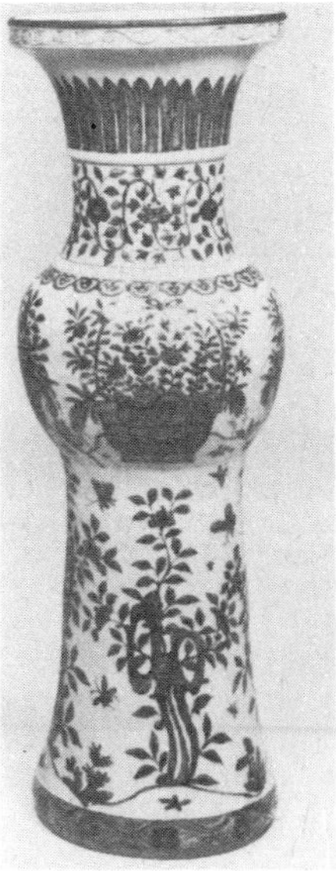

A large Ming blue and white vase, painted with baskets and bowls of peach, pomegranate, peony, chrysanthemum and other flowers below a band of ruyi lappets, the lower part with butterflies and a dragonfly in flight above foliage, the base rim reduced to fit in to a stand, long body crack, Wanli six-character mark on the rim bound in metal, 74 cm. high. **£8,500-10,000**

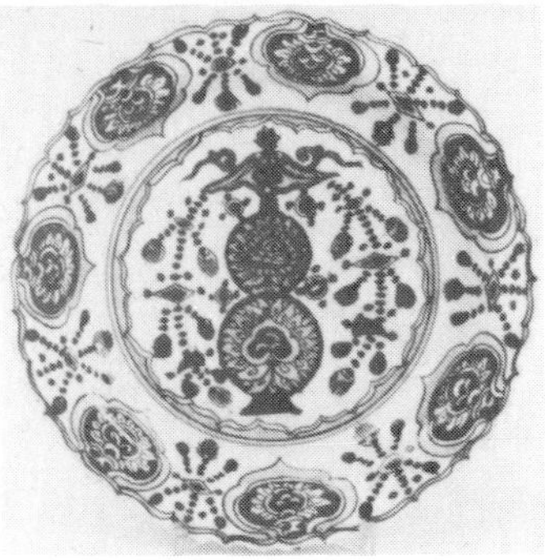

A late Ming blue and white plate, with foliate rim, painted with pendant precious emblems beside a double-gourd vase within a border of seven floral lappets, chipped, Wanli, 8¾ in. **£200-300**

Barbed forms borrowed from Islamic metalwares were common in the 14th century but seemed to lose favour after the Xuande period until the middle of the 16th century. The tasselled motifs on the rim first appear on wares of the Jiajing reign (1522-66).

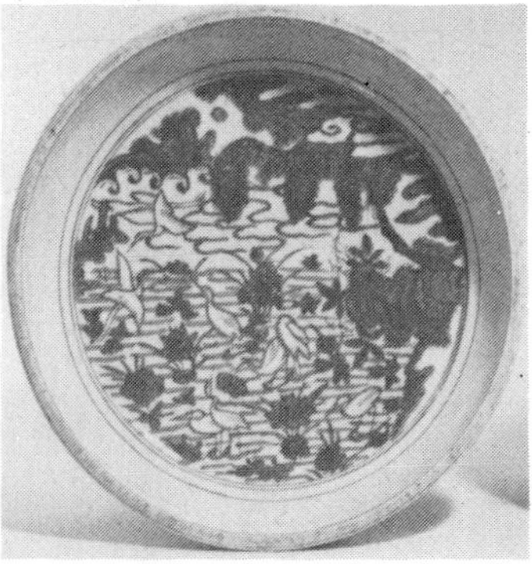

A dated Ming blue and white shallow bowl, painted with two storks in flight and six others wading amongst lotus and rippling water below pine, rockwork and clouds in the interior, unglazed rim, the centre of the mark erased, mark Wanli dinghai nien zao, 1587 A.D. and of the period, 29 cm. diam. **£1,000-1,500**

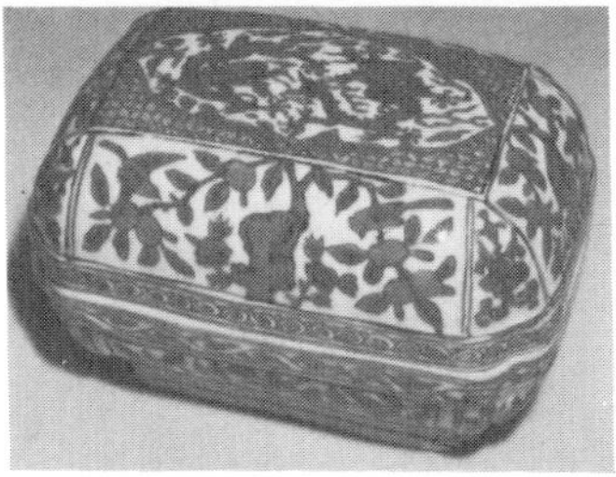

A Ming blue and white box and cover, painted with two five-clawed dragons, in confrontation amongst clouds within an oval quatrefoil panel on a trellis-pattern ground, chipped, unenclosed Wanli six-character mark and of the period, 18.8 cm. long. **£8,000-12,000**

This box belongs to a distinctive group in which the borders of the bases and covers are different. Another example of this is at the National Palace Museum, Taiwan.

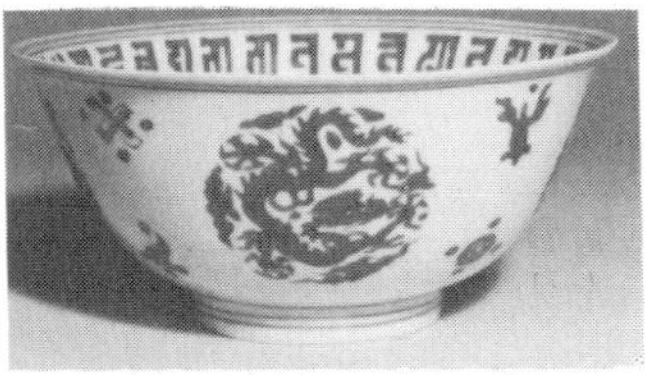

A Ming blue and white bowl, painted with four roundels of five-clawed dragons pursuing sacred pearls divided by pairs of eight precious emblems, with three rows of lhantsa characters above a similar character at the centre of the interior, slightly chipped, encircled Wanli six-character mark and of the period, fitted box, 21 cm. diam. **£6,000-10,000**

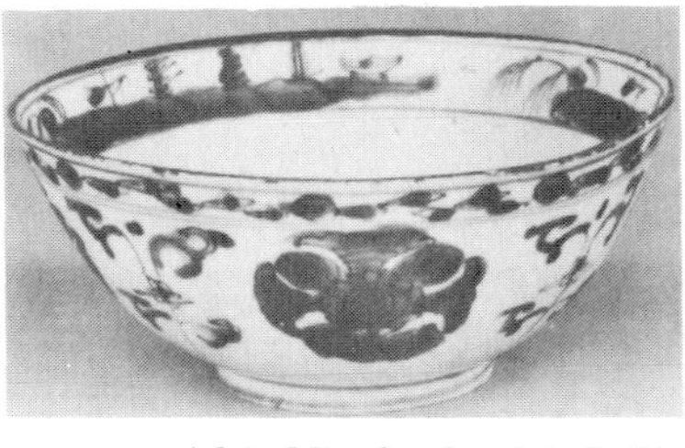

A late Ming bowl, painted with rosettes of flowers, 21.5 cm. diam., Wanli, minimal rim chips. **£200-300**

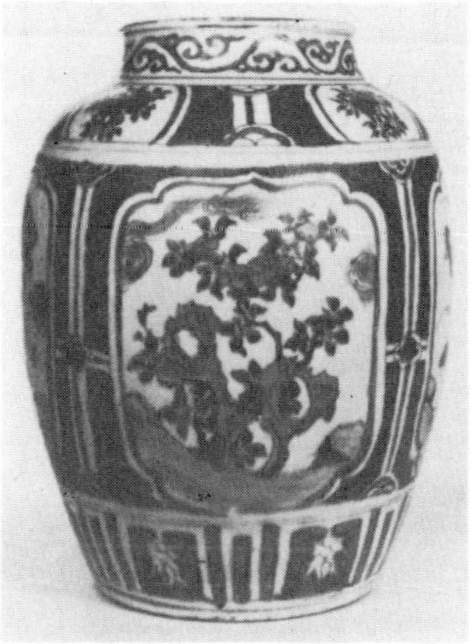

A late Ming blue and white oviform jar, painted with panels of peony, peach, camellia and lotus on a blue key-pattern ground, repaired, Wanli, 16 in. high. **£200-300**

If perfect: £800-1,200

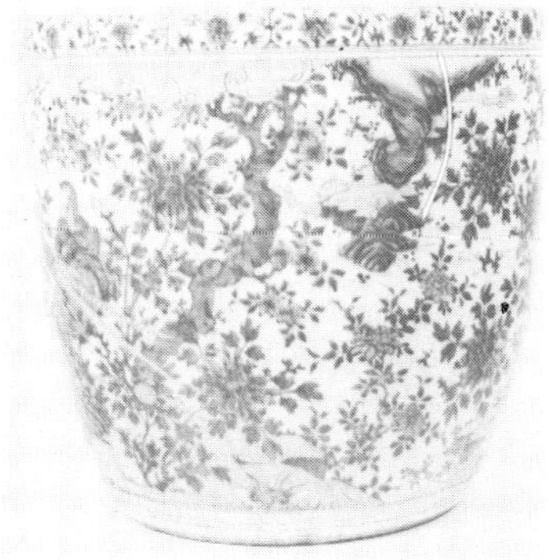

A massive Ming blue and white fish bowl, painted with pheasants and duck standing on rockwork amongst peony, daisy, camellia, prunus and peach on riverside terraces, the base with a repaired crack along the luting line and associated restored rivet holes, 63 cm. diam., 55 cm. high, late 16th C. **£9,000-11,000**

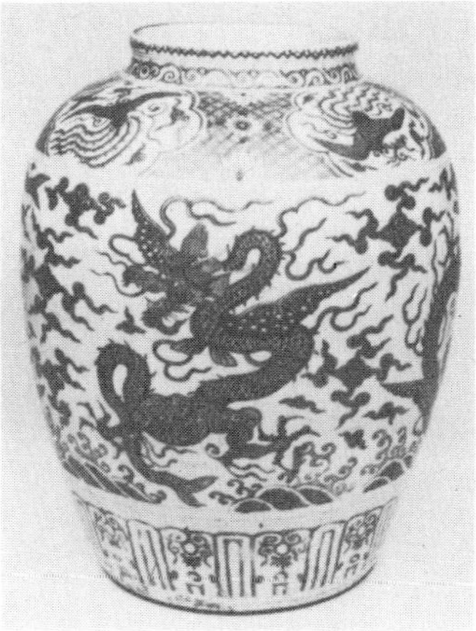

A late Ming blue and white oviform jar, painted with four winged four-clawed dragons, the shoulder with four ogival panels of phoenix alternately ascending and descending in flight, damaged, Wanli, 22½ in. high. **£1,500-2,000**

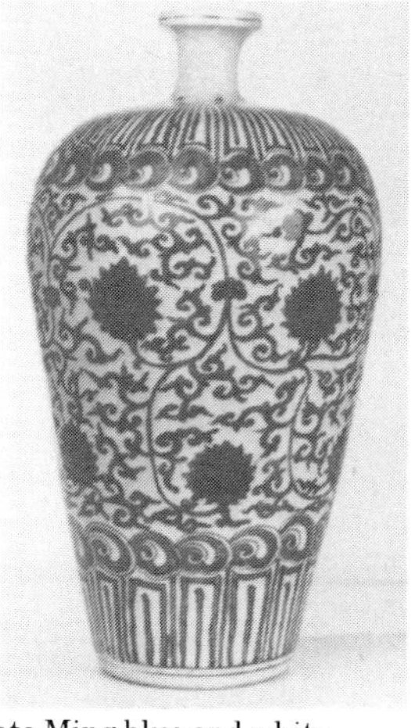

A late Ming blue and white baluster vase (meiping), painted with two bands of peony heads on scrolling foliage, the neck made up, Wanli six-character mark around the shoulder and of the period, overall height 19 in. **£1,500-2,500**

An example of a late Ming meiping. The sides are almost straight with no suggestion of a curve as would be found on 14th, 15th or early 16th century vases.

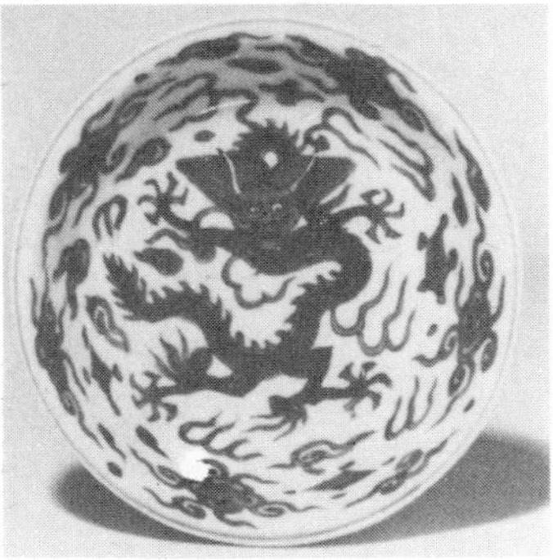

A late Ming blue and white bowl, painted with a writhing five clawed dragon, the exterior with birds and branches, some restoration, encircled Wanli six-character mark and of the period, 14.5 cm. diam. **£300-600**

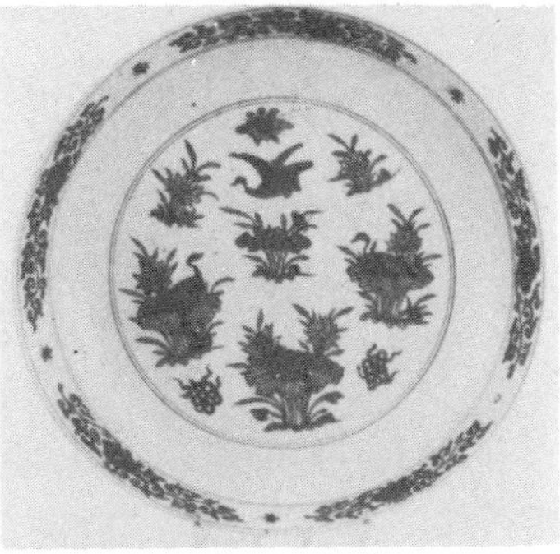

A late Ming blue and white saucer dish, painted with a duck in flight above three others standing on lotus clusters, within a border of insects in flight between five floral sprays, the exterior with three vine branches, chipped, late 16th/early 17th C., 17 in. diam. **£350-550**

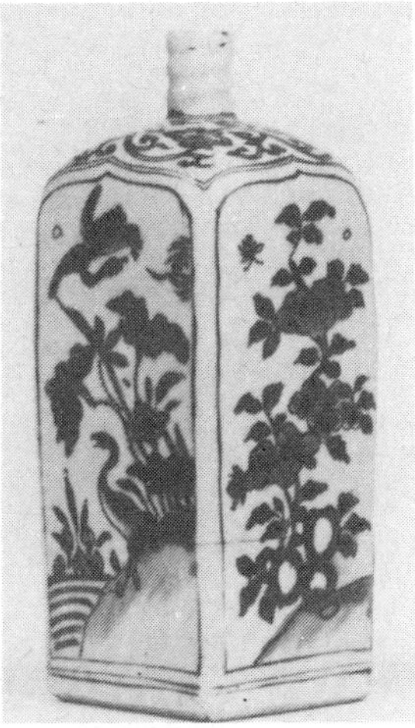

A late Ming blue and white square bottle, alternately painted with an insect above camellia and a goose in flight above another, minute rim cracks, late 16th/early 17th C., 10¼ in. high. **£600-900**

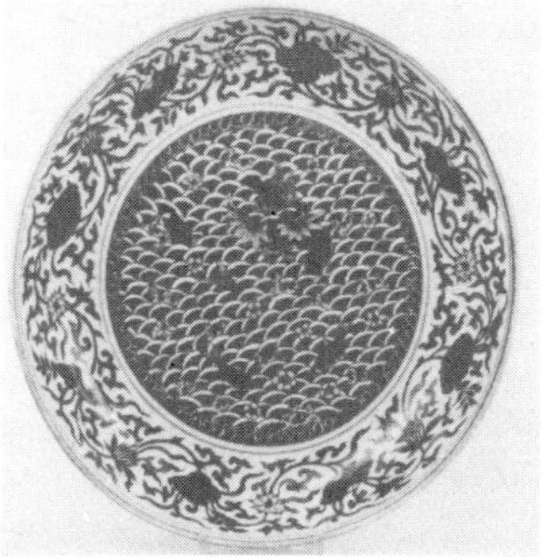

A Ming blue and white saucer dish, painted with a carp and a winged dragon leaping from waves amongst scattered lotus and prunus heads above two confronted fish, the exterior with four cranes in flight between cloud scrolls, chipped, encircled Chenghua six-character mark, Wanli, 13½ in. diam. **£1,500-2,000**

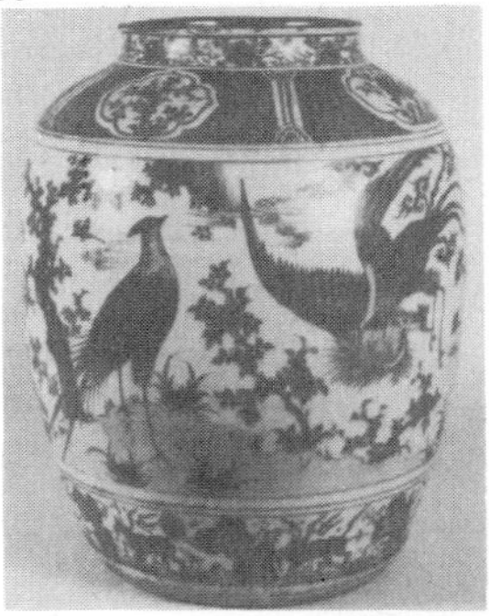

A late Ming blue and white oviform jar, painted with small birds and a phoenix in flight between a pheasant and another phoenix, above a band of horses and mythical beasts, the shoulder with four ogival panels, some neck restoration, Wanli, the rim and neck interior lined in copper, 60 cm. high. **£4,000-7,000**

KRAAK PORSELEIN

The designs found on Kraak porselein are frequently compartmented, especially on dishes, the centres being painted with birds on rocks, vases of flowers or even Buddhist lions, the rims being decorated with petal panels enclosing large sunflower like blooms, alternating with precious objects, often of Buddhist significance. Characteristic of these dishes and accompanying vases is the crudely knife-pared footrim, partially covered in sand from the kiln.

The dishes were copied not only by the Japanese when they temporarily captured the exportware market in the latter part of the 17th century, but also by Dutch, German, Spanish and English potters on tin glazed wares of the same era.

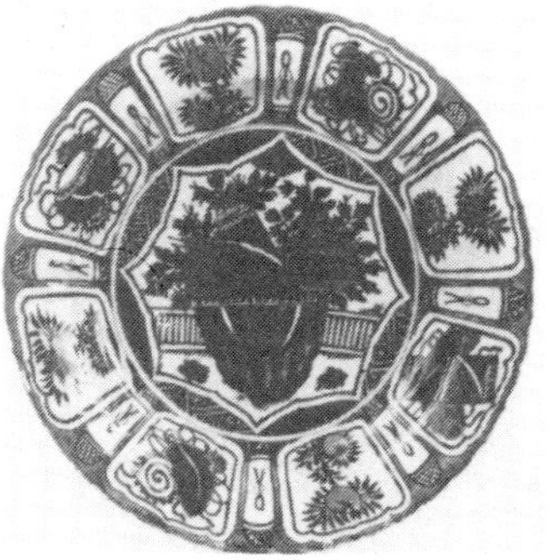

A late Ming blue and white Kraak porselein deep dish, painted with a scroll amongst chrysanthemum in a jardinière, with lappets of precious emblems and fruit sprays at the foliate rim, fritted, Wanli, 14½ in. diam. **£800-1,200**

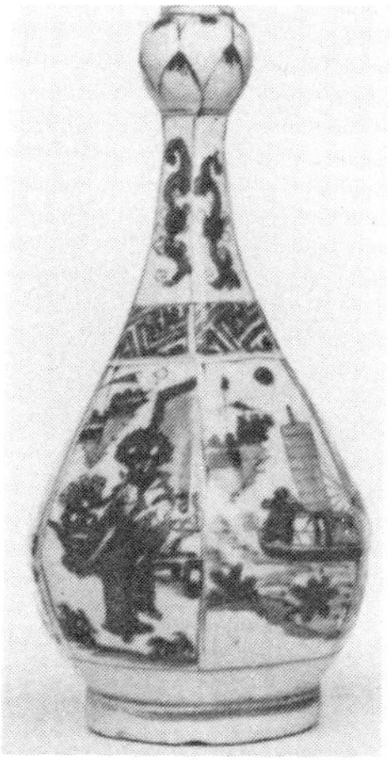

A late Ming blue and white hexagonal bottle, painted with panels of scholars in a boat and at leisure on rocky terraces, with overlapping lotus leaves on the garlic neck, cracked and chipped, late 16th/early 17th C., 11½ in. high. **£300-400**

A late Ming exportware bottle of Near Eastern metalware form. The irregular trellis about the shoulder is typical of the Wanli and Tianqi periods.

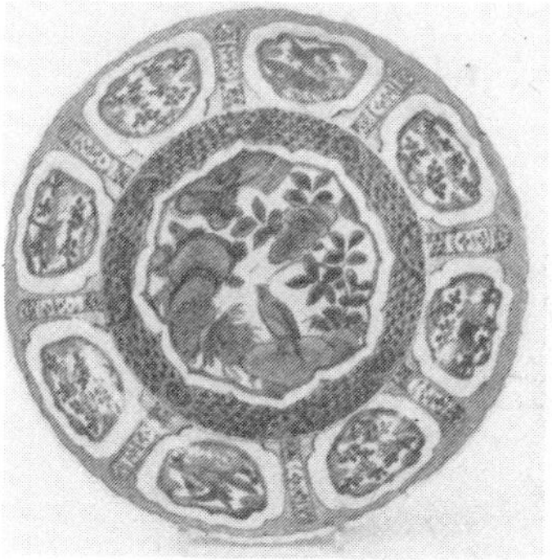

A late Ming blue and white Kraak porselein saucer dish, painted with lappets of geese in flight above lotus, insects and foliage, enclosing a central panel of two birds beside peony and rockwork, minor frit chips, Wanli, 10½ in. diam. **£350-450**

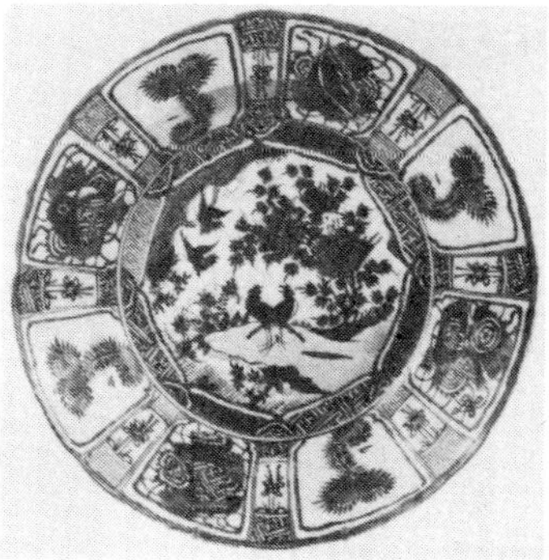

A late Ming blue and white Kraak porselein dish, painted with lappets of peach and Daoist Immortals' attributes around a central panel of two birds in flight above two others, chipped, Wanli, 19 in. diam. **£900-£1,200**

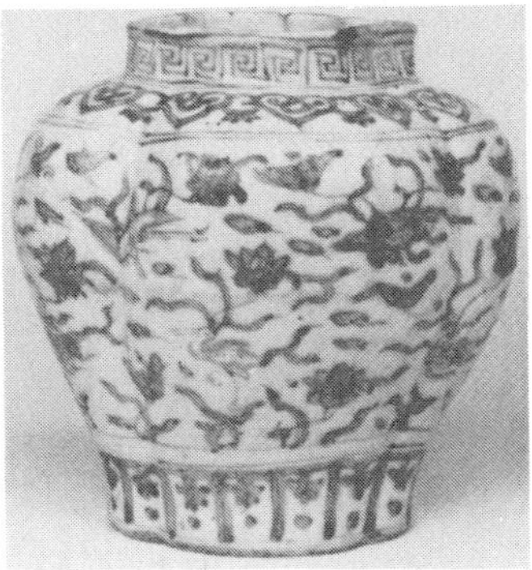

A Ming blue and white quatrefoil baluster jar, painted with cranes and ducks amongst lotus, below bands of ruyi lappets at the shoulder and key-pattern at the rim, chipped and cracked, Xuande four-character mark in a double square, 16th C., 6 in. high. **£250-400**

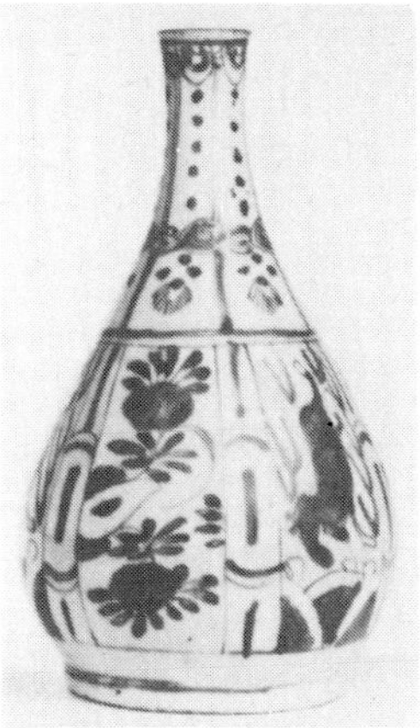

A late Ming blue and white Kraak Porselein bottle vase, painted with panels of horses amongst fire-scrolls and flower sprays, below pendant beads on the slender neck, Wanli, 11 in. high. **£400-500**

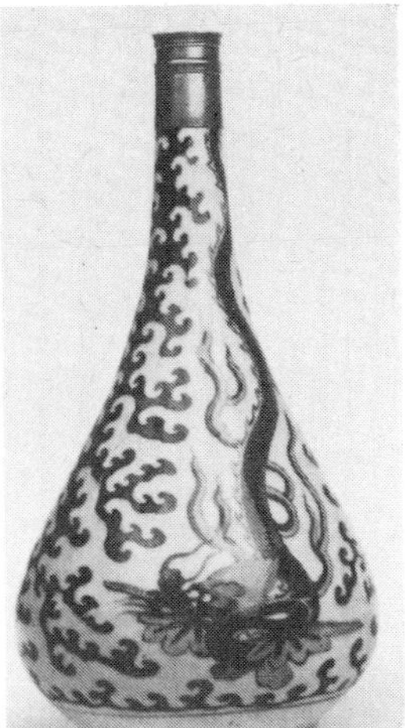

A mounted late Ming blue and white pear-shaped bottle, painted on each side with a winged dragon descending amongst flames, the rim possibly reduced, mounted with silvered metal collar and screw cover, mid 16th C., overall height 12¼ in. **£250-400**

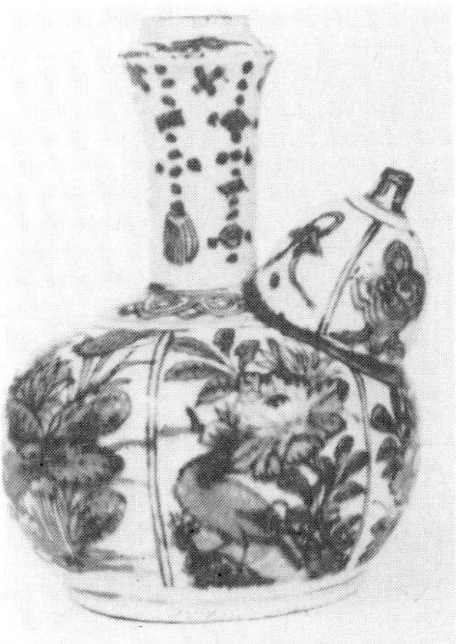

A late Ming blue and white kendi, painted with panels of lingzhi, bamboo, lotus, peony and precious emblems, fritted, the lip cracked, Wanli, 8 in. high. **£150-200**

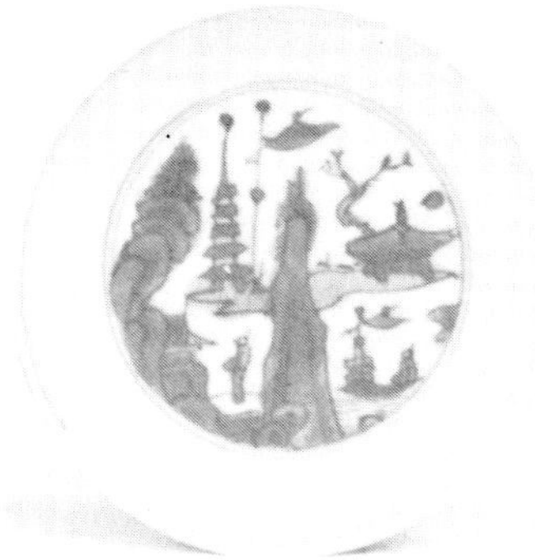

A pair of small late Ming blue and white saucer dishes, each painted with a scholar and a fisherman in his boat, one slightly fritted, mid 16th C., 3¾ in. diam. **£150-250**
This sketchily drawn riverscape typifies late 16th century blue and white. Note the tall, finger-like rocks, the 'xylophonic' pagoda and the trading station banner or flag.

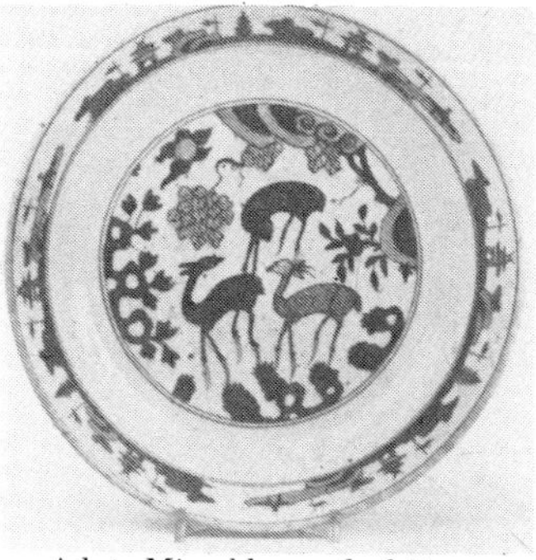

A late Ming blue and white saucer dish, painted with three deer amongst leaves and pierced rockwork below a band of landscape at the rim, late 16th/early 17th C., 10¼ in. diam. **£300-400**
Note the free cartoon-like treatment of the deer (symbolic of longevity). The style of the border is typical of late 16th century blue and white.

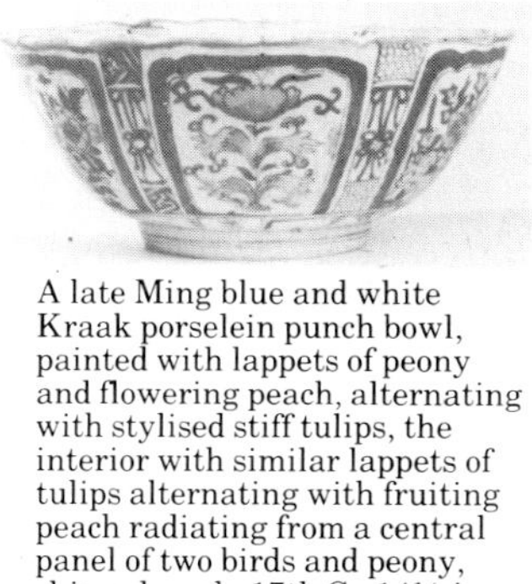

A late Ming blue and white Kraak porselein punch bowl, painted with lappets of peony and flowering peach, alternating with stylised stiff tulips, the interior with similar lappets of tulips alternating with fruiting peach radiating from a central panel of two birds and peony, chipped, early 17th C., 14½ in. diam. **£900-1,200**

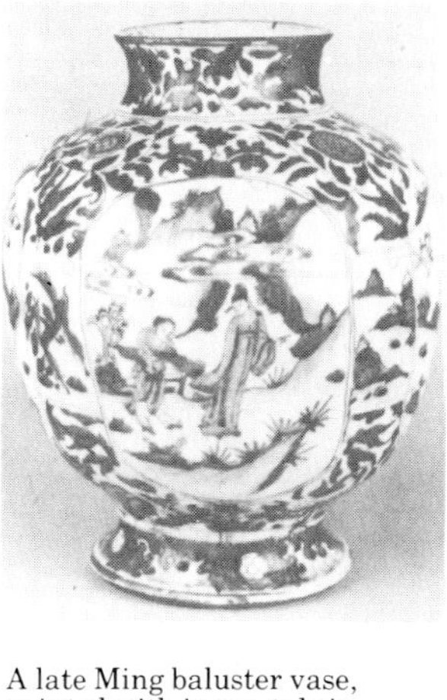

A late Ming baluster vase, painted with immortals in panels between scrolls of leaves and flowers, 33 cm., Wanli. **£600-£1,000**

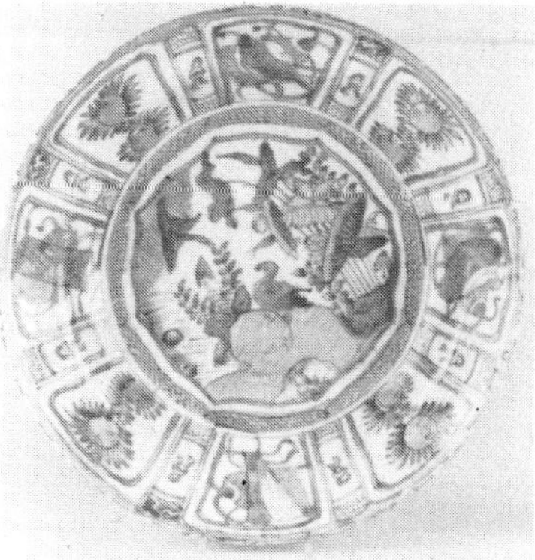

A Kraak porselein dish, painted with geese and plants near a brook, rim chipped, Wanli, 36.5 cm.
£300-400

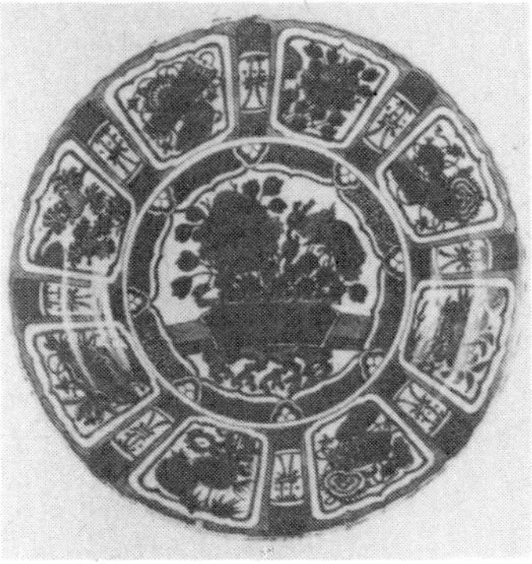

A late Ming blue and white Kraak porselein deep dish, painted with chrysanthemum issuing from a square jardinière, with petal-shaped panels of precious emblems of flower and fruit sprays at the foliate rim, chipped, Wanli, 19½ in. diam. **£1,200-1,500**

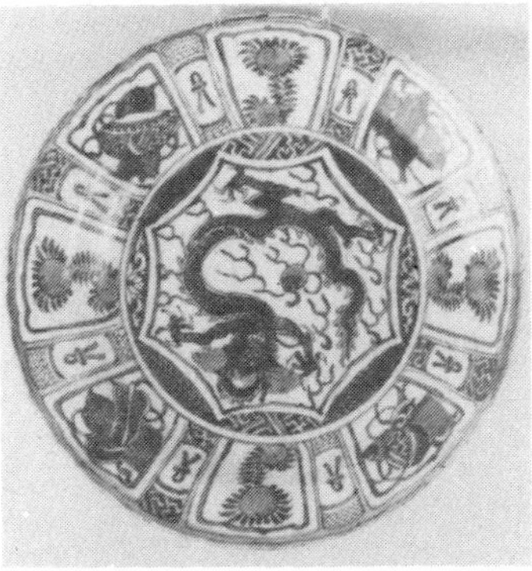

A Kraak porselein dish, painted with a four-clawed dragon and flaming pearl in octagonal panel, 35 cm. diam., Wanli, slight damage. **£300-400**

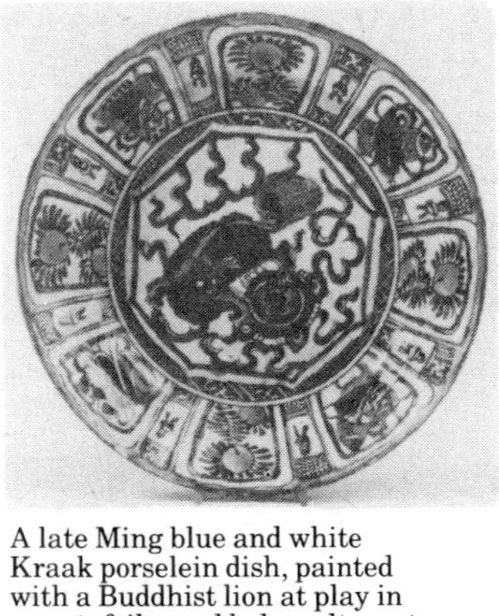

A late Ming blue and white Kraak porselein dish, painted with a Buddhist lion at play in an octafoil panel below alternate petal-shaped lappets of emblems and flowers, chipped, Wanli, 14 in. diam. **£250-400**

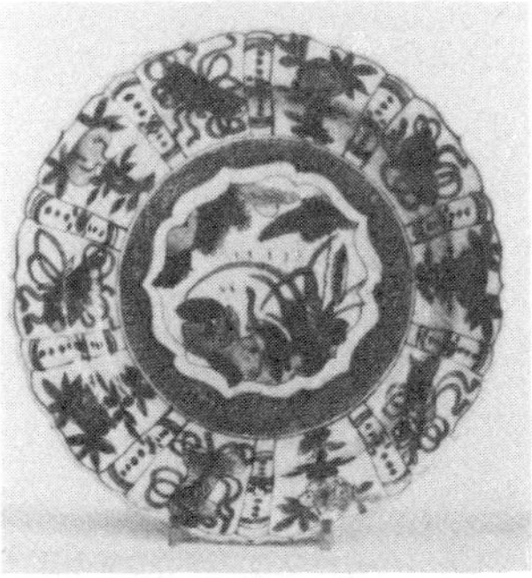

A late Ming blue and white dish, the rim painted with panels of peach and pomegranate alternating with Daoist Immortals' attributes, the central panel of a goose on rockwork amongst lotus, fritted, Wanli, 10¼ in. diam. **£250-350**

A late Ming blue and white lotus dish, with a central pine within two bands of moulded lotus petals decorated with pine, prunus, flower sprays, and scholars, the reverse with long life swastika symbols, rim extensively fritted on the points, 20.5 cm. diam., c. 1600. **£750-£1,250**

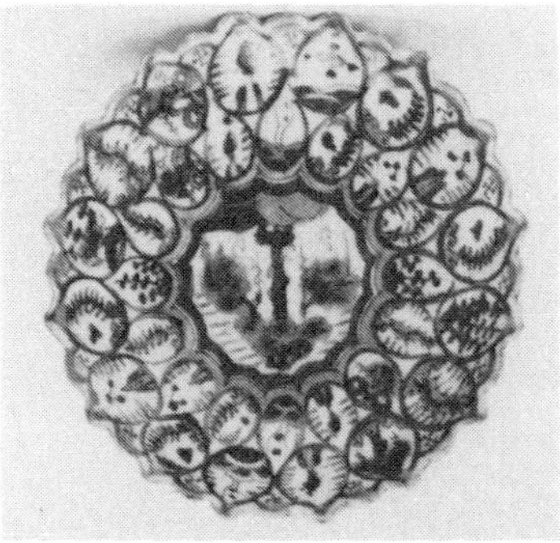

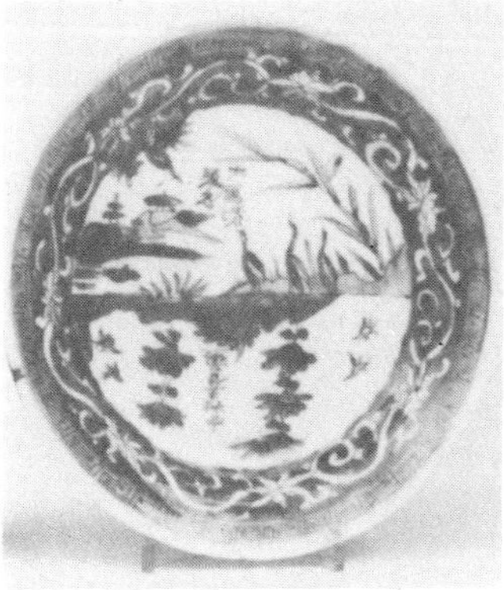

Two late Ming blue and white dishes, made for the Japanese market, painted with borders of key-pattern and scrolling lotus around central panels of geese on rocky river banks and birds in flight around inscriptions, chipped, one cracked, Tianqi/Chongzheng, 8½ in. diam. **£250-£350**

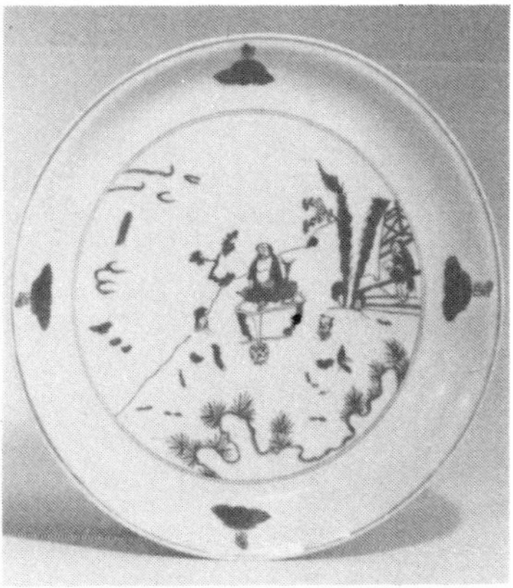

A Ming blue and white saucer dish, painted with a servant approaching an Immortal above a censer with the heads and arms of scholars at either side, within a border of four shou character with eight groups of leaves on the exterior, cracked and chipped, encircled Wanli six-character mark and of the period, 31 cm. diam. **£700-1,000**
This was clearly originally intended to be enamelled, since the bodies of the scholars are left white without being outlined.

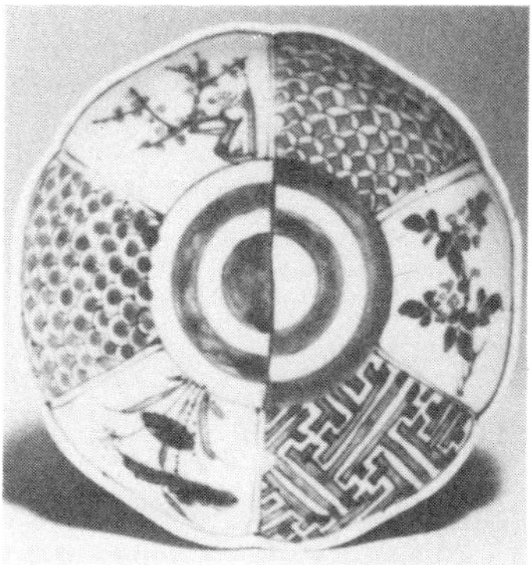

Two late Ming hexafoil dishes, painted in underglaze-blue and copper-red with panels of prunus, tree peony and lotus alternating with scale and key patterns radiating from central triple rings, frit chips, one foot crack, Tianqi/Chongzheng, 14.5 cm. wide. **£350-500**
A good example of the wares, esteemed by Japanese collectors for use in the Tea Ceremony. Note the use of variegated diapers and especially the irregular trellis found slightly earlier on Wanli wares.

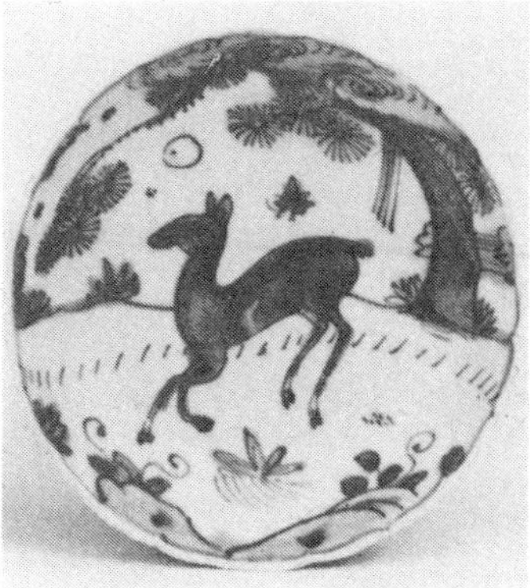

A pair of Ming blue and white saucer dishes, each painted with a deer walking below a pine and clouds in a rocky landscape, one chipped, Wanli/Tianqi, 5¼ in. diam. **£150-200**

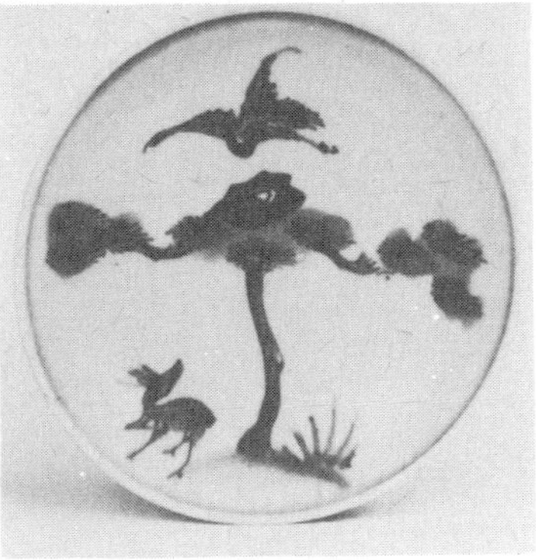

A late Ming blue and white saucer dish, painted with a spotted deer looking up at a crane in flight over a T-shaped pine, slightly fritted, ya (elegant) mark, Tianqi, 6 in. diam. **£150-£250**
Another charming example of Tianqi, beloved of Japanese collectors. The crane, pine and deer all being auspicious emblems of longevity.

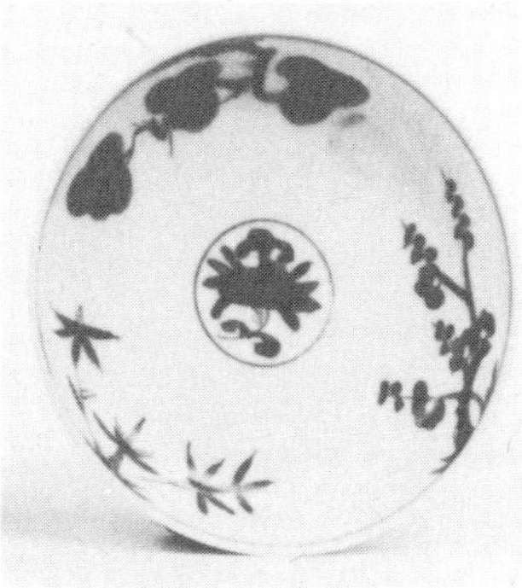

A Ming blue and white saucer dish, painted with the three friends, pine, prunus and bamboo descending towards a central floral roundel, minutely fritted, base underside chipped, unencircled Longqing six-character mark and of the period, in a fitted box, 5 in. diam. **£600-1,000**
A rare piece from this short reign, but displaying the more careless drawing of the second half of the 16th century, found on so many blue and white pieces.

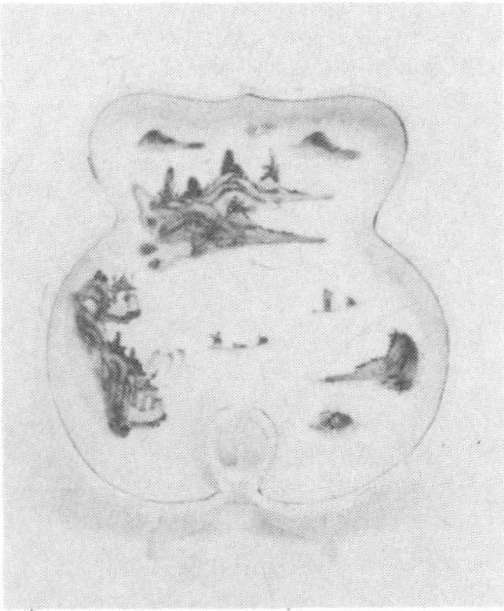

A rare late Ming blue and white ko-sometsuke dish, unusually shaped as a half gourd, standing on three D-shaped feet, the interior pencilled with two rafts in a riverscape, the exterior of the sides with breaking waves, edges fritted, 15.5 cm. wide, c. 1630. **£500-700**
Ko-sometsuke is the Japanese term for old Chinese blue and white porcelain admired by them and often used in the Tea Ceremony. It is somewhat cursorily painted and has a great appeal.

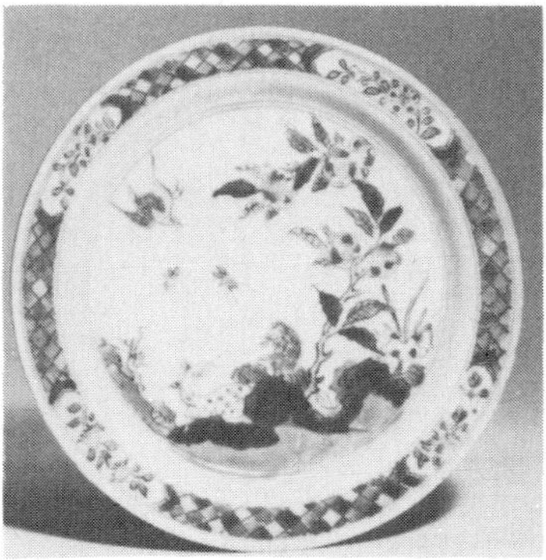

Two late Ming Wucai dishes, each painted with a bird in flight above insects, a recumbent deer and a monkey, within a harlequin trellis-pattern border divided by four floral panels, minor chips, encircled Chenghua six-character marks, Tianqi/ Chongzheng, 20.5 cm. diam. **£1,900-2,500**

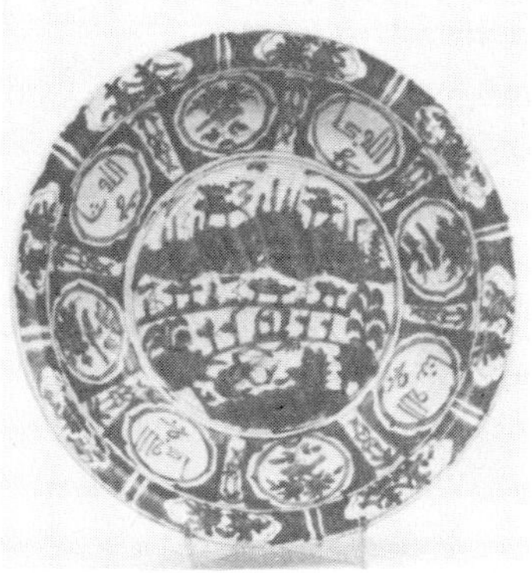

A Swatow blue and white deep dish, cracked and chipped, 17th C., 16¾ in. diam. **£450-500**
Inscribed with Arabic characters, probably intended for export to the Middle East.

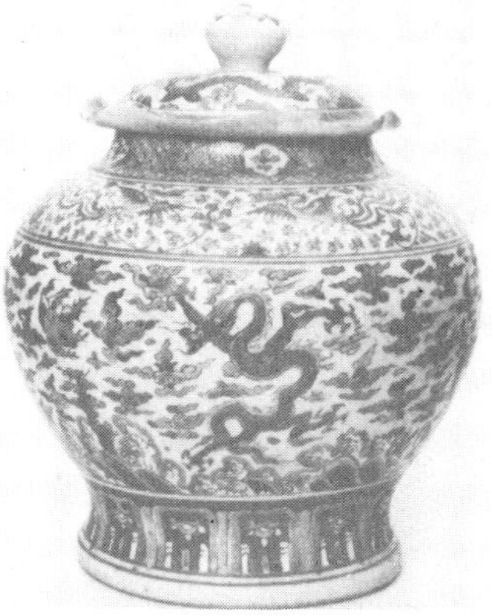

A rare late Ming polychrome storage jar and a cover, enamelled in green, iron red and yellow with four dragons flying above breaking waves amongst fire scrolls, the shoulder with a phoenix confronted in flight, the cover formed as a lotus leaf, neck reduced, body cracks, cover rim chips restored, 37 cm. high, decorated in Swatow, c. 1600. **£1,500-2,500**
This jar and cover appear to be one of a small group that were probably potted at Ching-tê Chên but decorated in Swatow.

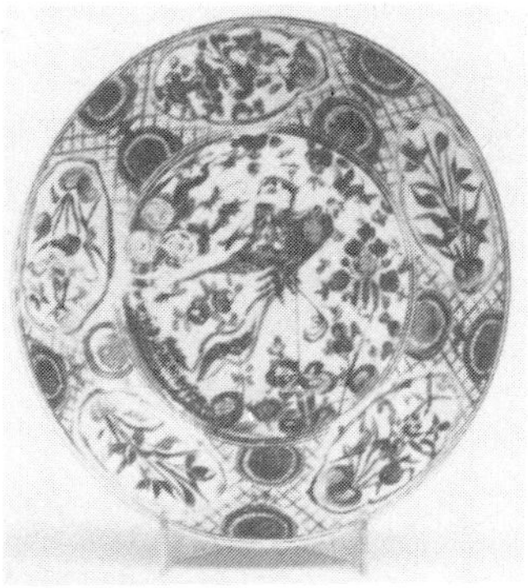

A Swatow polychrome dish, painted in iron-red, green and turquoise enamels with a phoenix in flight amongst foliage, the border with panels of lotus and a bird on a peony branch, chipped, 17th C., 14¼ in. diam. **£300-450**
Polychrome decoration on Swatow wares (from Fujian province) is boldly executed with much use of the trellis and roundel ground displayed here.

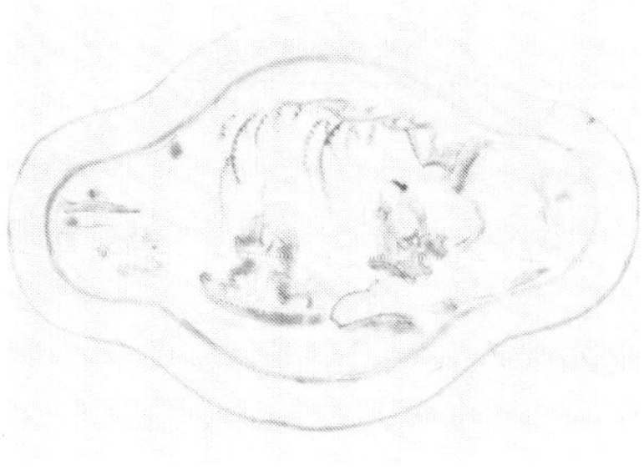

A pair of late Ming Wucai dishes, each with a boatman beside a bearded sage seated on a riverbank below willow, one chipped, 18.5 cm. wide, c. 1650. **£400-500**

TRANSITIONAL WARES

- These wares are readily identifiable both by their form and by their style of decoration.
- Forms: sleeve vases, oviform jars with domed lids, cylindrical brushpots and bottle vases are particularly common.
- The cobalt used is a brilliant purplish blue, rarely misfired.
- The ground colour is of a definite bluish tone, probably because the glaze is slightly thicker than that of the wares produced in the subsequent reigns of Kangxi and Yongzheng.
- The decoration is executed in a rather formal academic style, often with scholars and sages with attendants in idyllic cloud-lapped mountain landscapes.
- Other characteristics include the horizontal 'contoured' clouds, banana plantain used to interrupt scenes, and the method of drawing grass by means of short 'u' shaped brush strokes.
- In addition, borders are decorated with narrow bands of scrolling foliage, so lightly incised as to be almost invisible or secret *(anhua)*.

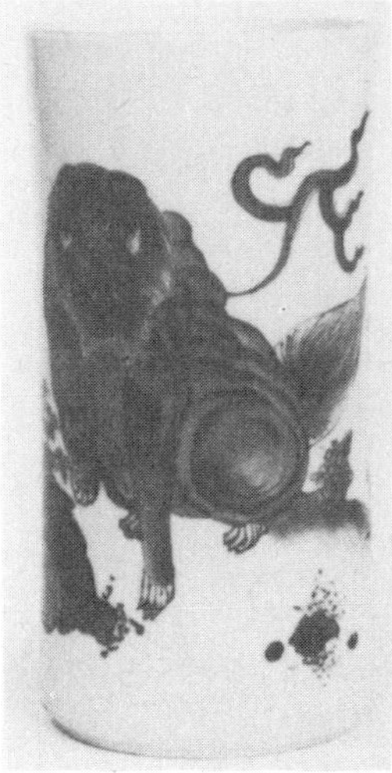

A Transitional blue and white slender brush pot, painted with a Buddhist lion seated beside plantain and rockwork, chipped, c. 1640, 6½ in. high. **£300-400**

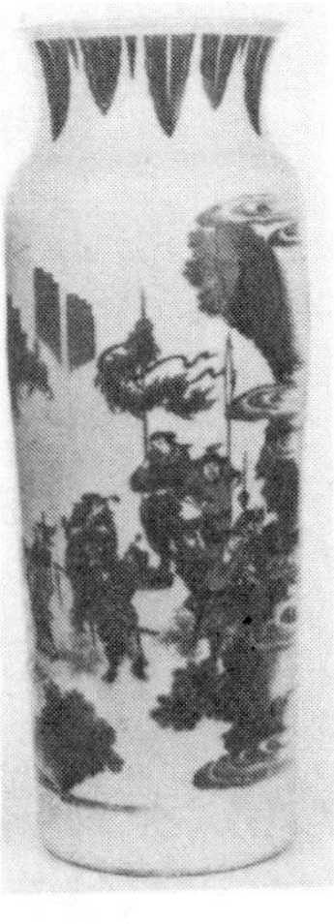

A Transitional blue and white sleeve vase, painted with a scene from a romance, a scholar with warrior attendants and bannermen, standing before a kowtowing boy at the entrance to a rustic villa in a mist-enshrouded mountainous landscape, fritted, c. 1640, 18¼ in. high. **£900-1,200**

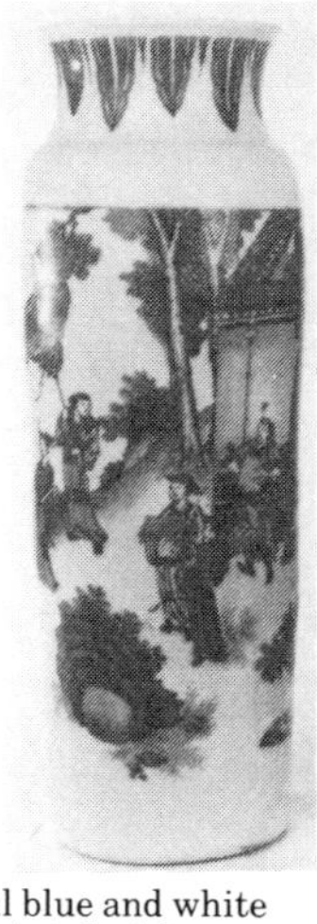

A Transitional blue and white sleeve vase, painted with a scene from a romance, with a servant offering an arrow vase to a scholar, fritted, c. 1640, 18¼ in. high. **£1,100-1,400**

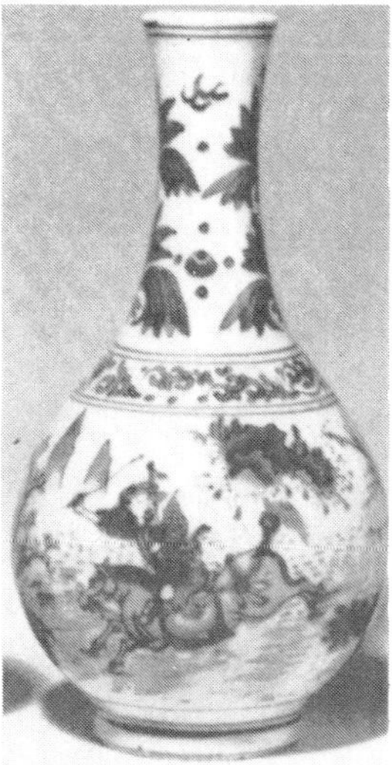

A Transitional blue and white bottle vase, painted with a scene from a romance, two soldiers attacking a mounted gentleman in a river landscape, c. 1650, 25.5 cm. high. **£900-1,100**

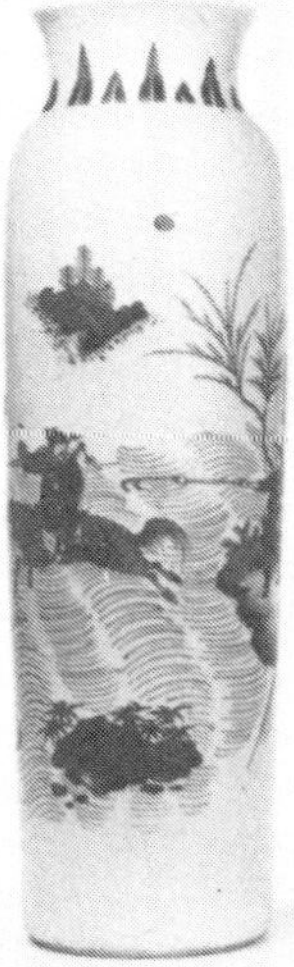

A Transitional blue and white sleeve vase, painted with a mounted warrior holding a whip and leaping across a turbulent river, his three pursuers brandishing swords, c. 1640, 17¼ in. high. **£1,000-1,400**

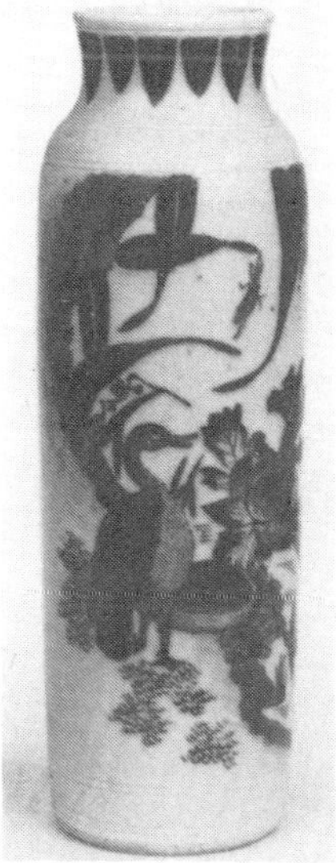

A Transitional blue and white sleeve vase, painted with a bird in flight above a goose standing upon a river bank beside lotus clusters below a band of incised scrolling foliage on the shoulder, c. 1640, 10½ in. high. **£450-600**

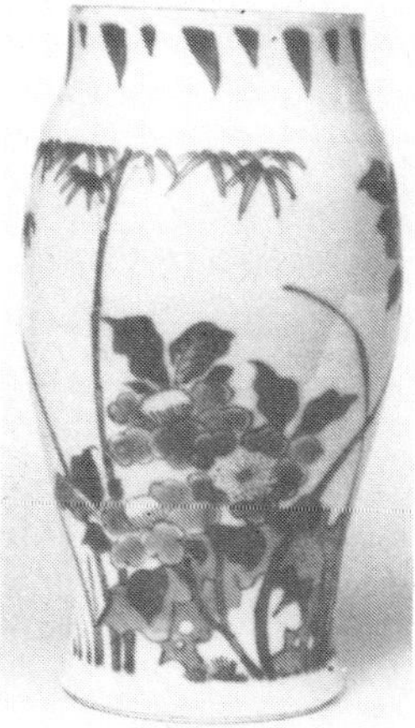

A Transitional blue and white vase, painted with a bird in flight between bamboo, camellia and rockwork, chipped, c. 1650, 7 in. high. **£150-200**

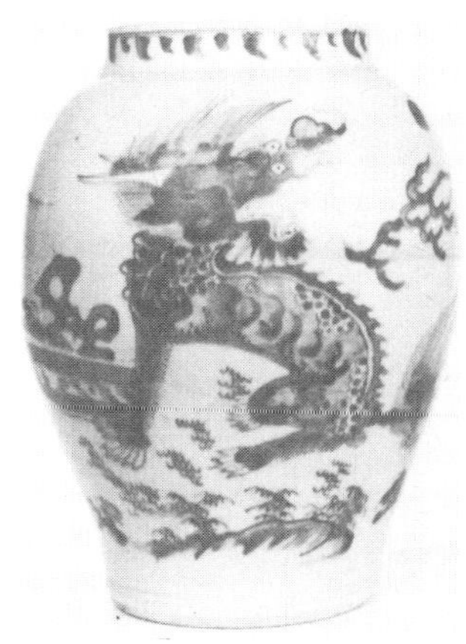

A Transitional baluster jar, painted with a qilin seated beside plantain on a garden terrace, c. 1640, 12½ in. high. **£400-500**

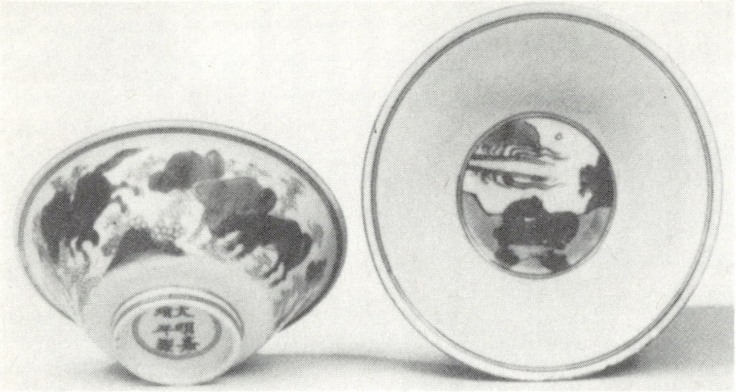

Two Transitional blue and white shallow conical bowls, each painted with the eight horses of Muwang in rocky landscapes, seven on the exterior and one seated in a roundel in the interior, one cracked, one chipped, encircled Jiajing six-character marks, mid 17th C., 6¾ in. diam. **£250-350**

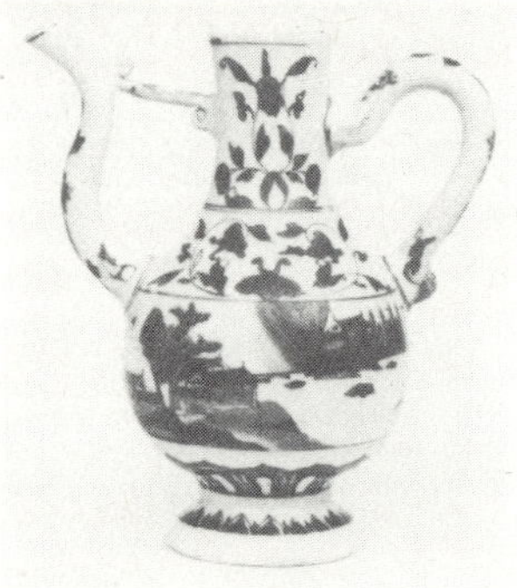

A Transitional blue and white pear-shaped ewer, painted with a band of river landscape below formal scrolling foliage, the base with bands of petals and stiff leaves, fritted, c. 1640, 6¾ in. high. **£350-450**

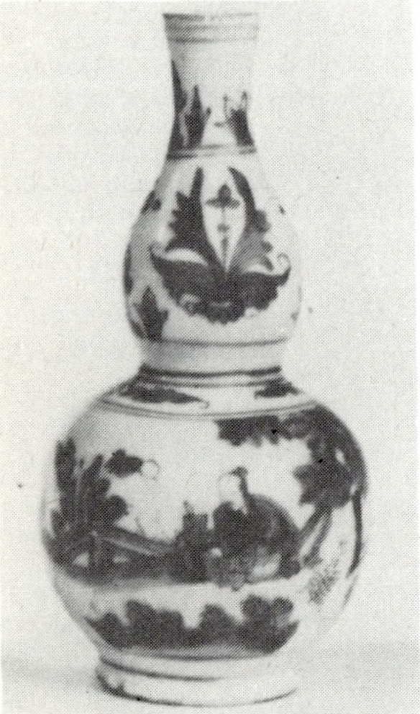

A Transitional blue and white double-gourd bottle, painted with a boy attendant and a scholar seated beside pine and plantain on a rocky terrace, fritted, c. 1650, 7¾ in. high. **£300-400**

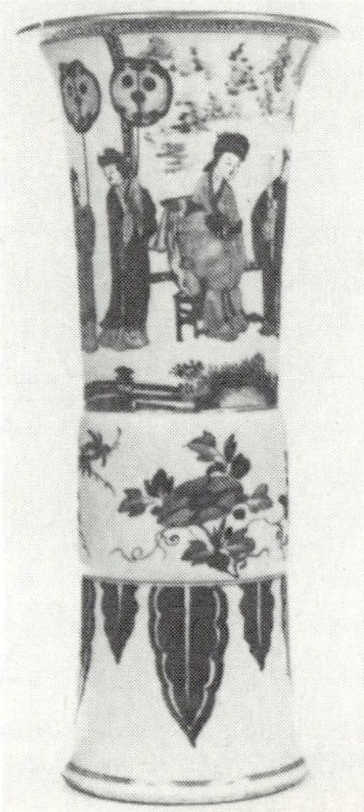

Right
A Transitional blue and white gu-shaped beaker vase, painted with a seated lady giving an audience to a scholar standing before a window beside plantain above convolvulus and grasses, rim slightly chipped, c. 1640, 20 in. high. **£1,000-£1,300**

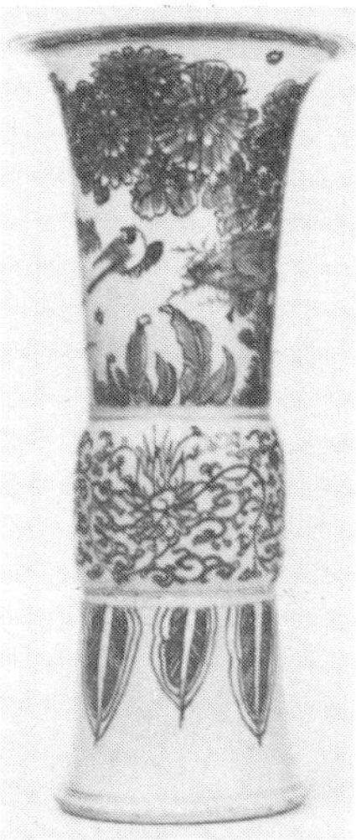

A Transitional blue and white beaker vase, painted in a pencilled style with stiff leaves on the lower section below scrolling lotus at the centre and birds in flight beside chrysanthemum and bamboo issuing from rockwork on the neck, cracked, the rim slightly reduced, mid 17th C., 16 in. high. **£200-300**

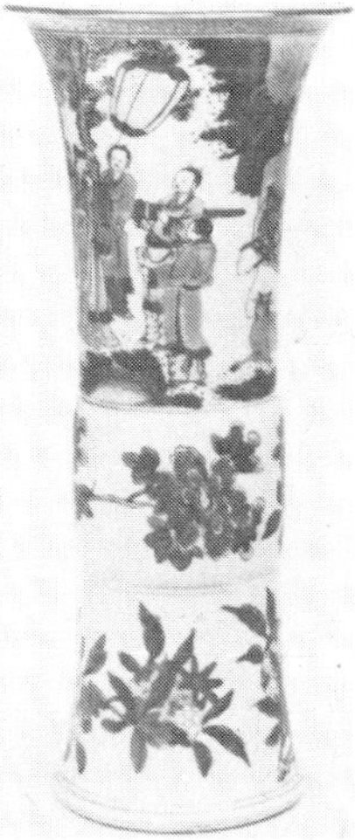

A Transitional Wucai beaker vase, painted with peach and pomegranate sprays, below peony and rockwork at the centre, the upper section with a scholar with warriors, a fan-beater and servants in attendance and a water-buffalo recumbent beside a chariot in a rocky landscape, chips restored in gold lacquer, 16 in. high, c. 1660. **£500-800**

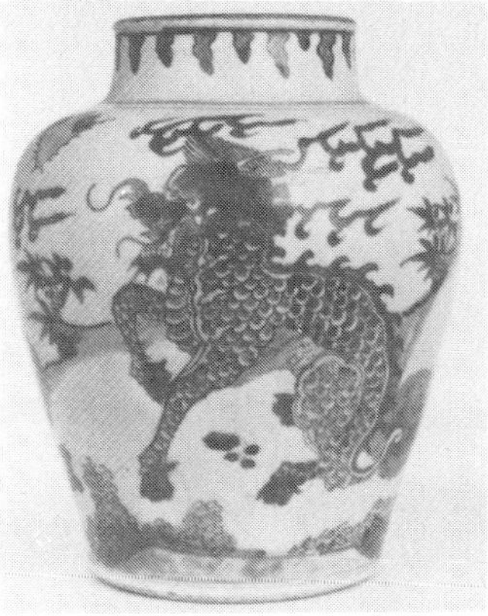

A blue and white baluster jar, painted with a qilin seated beside plantain and rockwork below a band of wavy petals on a short neck, Transitional/early Kangxi, 11¼ in. high. **£280-450**
The irregular wavy leaves around the neck are frequently found as a decorative theme on Transitional wares.

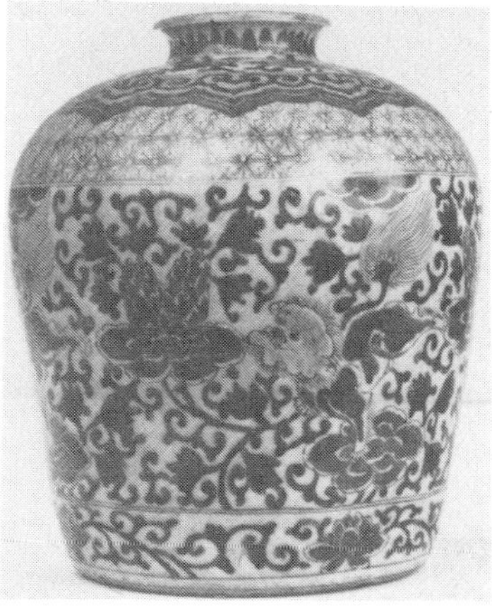

A vase, painted in iron-red, green and yellow enamels with four Buddhistic lions amongst scrolling peony below a band of ruyi heads on the shoulder and petals on the short flaring neck, cracked, Transitional/early Kangxi, on a wood stand, 10¾ in. high. **£150-250**

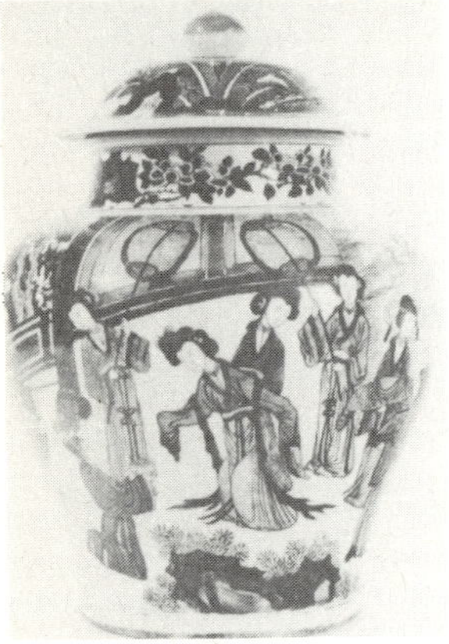

A very fine blue and white jar and cover, decorated with a kneeling servant offering a bowl to a court lady, surrounded by other standing ladies holding banners, lanterns and tea ceremony items, 46 cm. high, Transitional/early Kangxi. **£2,500-3,500**

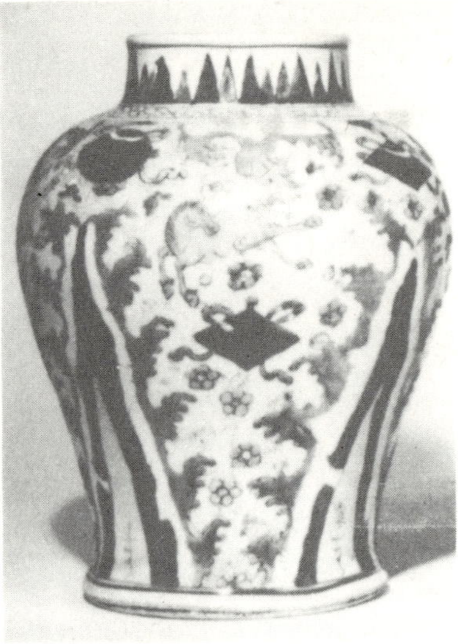

A Transitional Wucai baluster vase, painted with four horses, in yellow and pale aubergine, leaping amongst lotus and prunus heads on an iron-red whorl pattern ground, surmounted by the eight precious emblems below cracked ice pattern at the shoulder, fritted, mid 17th C., 32 cm. high. **£600-800**

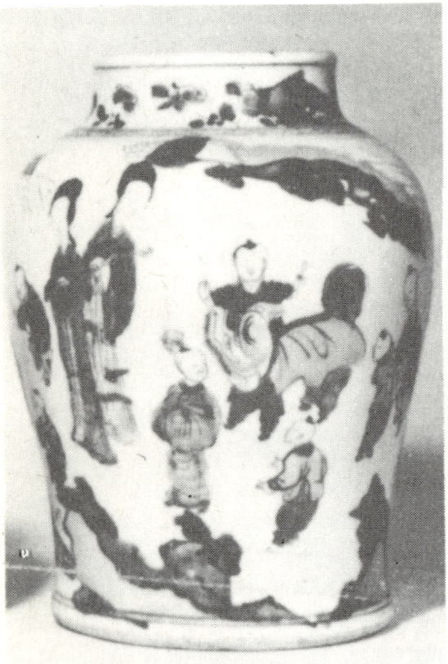

A Transitional Wucai baluster vase, painted with four ladies and small boys at play, two forming the front and back of a Buddhist lion, rim chips and short cracks, mid 17th C., 31.5 cm. high. **£800-1,000**

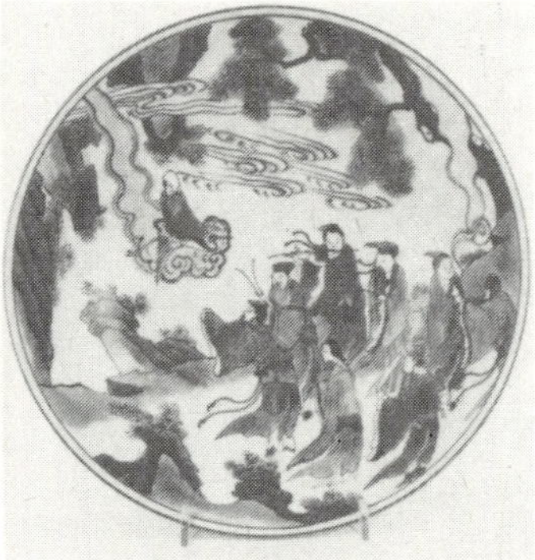

A Transitional blue and white saucer dish, painted with Shoulao seated upon a crane above the Eight Daoist Immortals, cracked, encircled four-character commendation mark, c. 1640, 14 in. diam. **£250-£300**

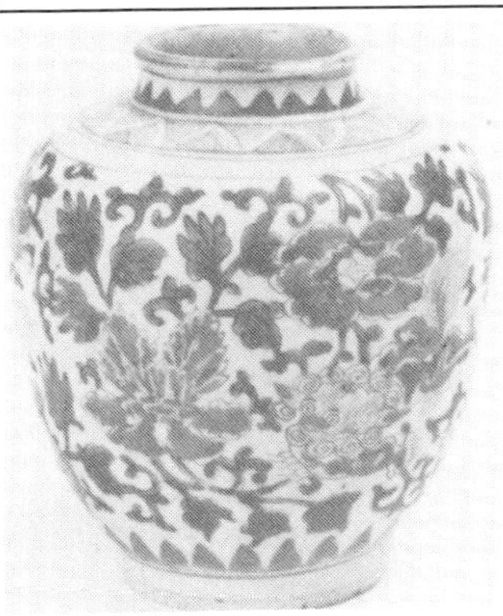

A small Transitional polychrome jar, painted on the sides in iron-red, green, yellow and black enamels, 13.5 cm., mid 17th C. **£150-180**

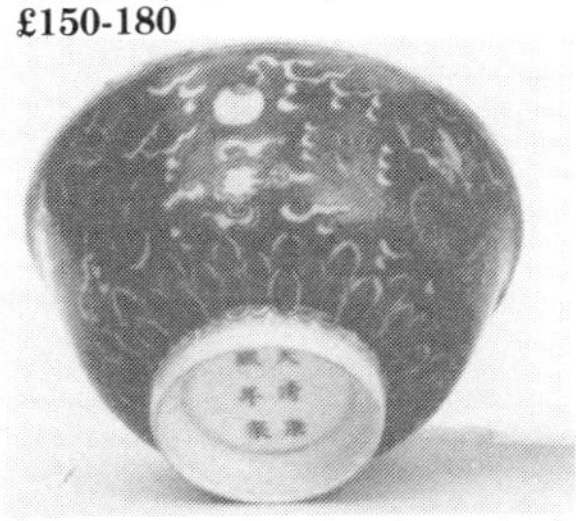

A blue and yellow bowl, cracked and chipped, encircled Kangxi six-character mark, 5½ in. diam. **£200-250**

Dragons disputing the 'flaming pearl' is a traditional design found on ceramics from the 14th century onwards.

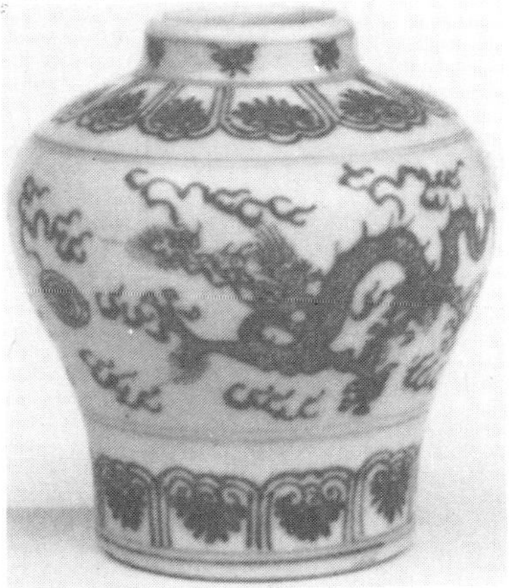

A blue and white jar, Tian mark, Kangxi, 4 in. high **£390-450**

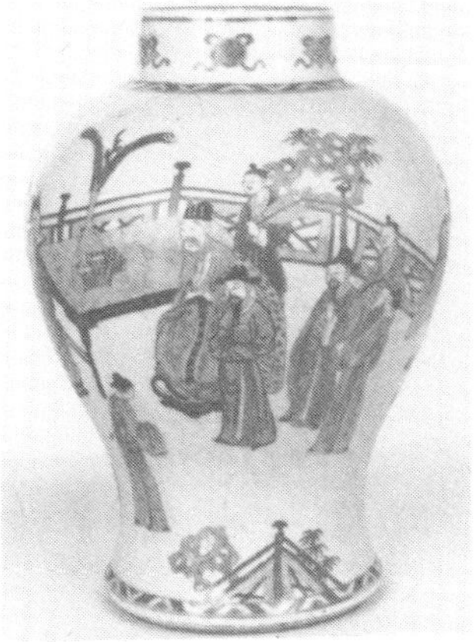

A Doucai vase, cracked, encircled Chenghua six-character mark, Kangxi, 14 in. high. **£330-400**

Doucai (meaning clashing or contrasting colours) is a palette revived in the Kangxi period. It was first utilised on Chenghua porcelain, a fact not missed by their Qing descendants who copied the Ming reign mark of that emperor. It largely fell into disuse during the subsequent Ming dynasty.

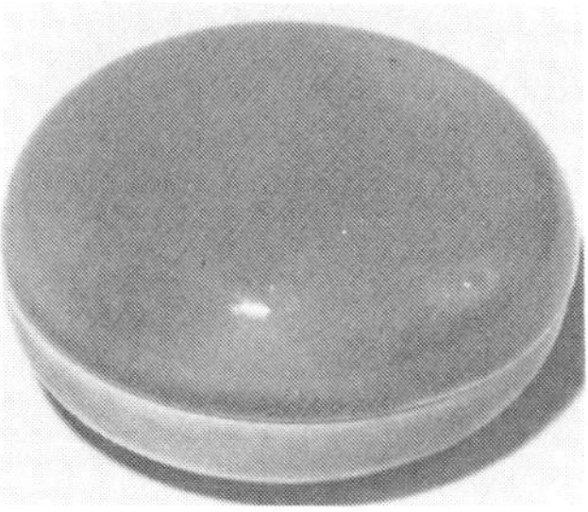

A 'peach bloom' circular cosmetic box and related domed cover, the top under a red glaze with green inclusions and the base with red inclusions on a green ground, the foot neatly trimmed, unencircled Kangxi six-character mark and of the period, fitted box, 2¾ in. diam. **£1,200-1,600**

Authentic peach bloom wares are extremely rare. A fairly limited repertoire of shapes was made and consisted mainly of wares which were probably intended for the scholar's table. These include amphora-shape vases, brush-washers and beehive-form brush pots.

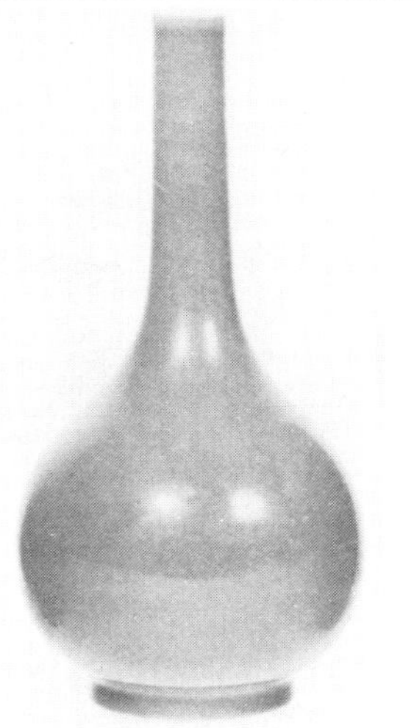

A Sang de Boeuf bottle, under an even rich glaze firing white on the lip and inside the foot rim, 20 cm. high, Kangxi six-character mark and of the period. **£1,000-1,500**

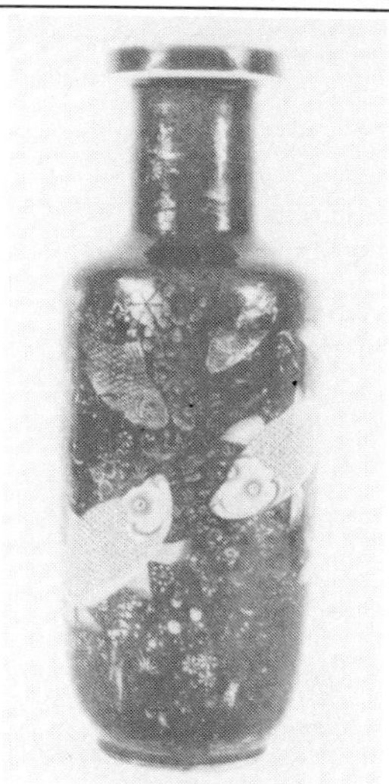

A powder blue ground carp vase, enamelled with four iron-red carp swimming on a mottled blue ground enriched with gilt carp, flowerheads and aquatic plants, gilding typically rubbed, Kangxi, 18½ in. high. **£1,500-£2,500**

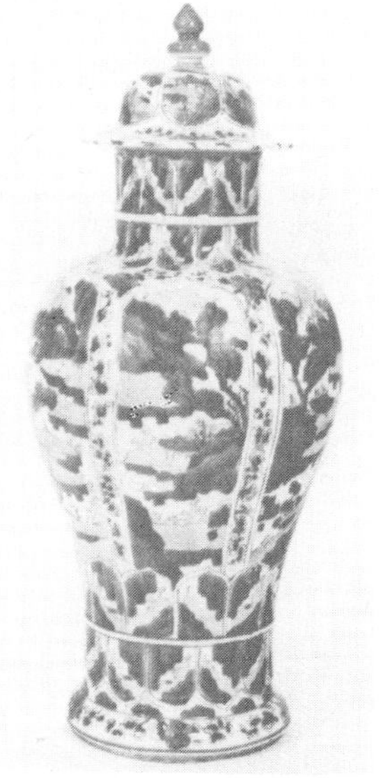

A pair of blue and white vases and covers, moulded and painted with panels of mountainous riverscapes on scrolling prunus grounds, finials repaired, rims fritted and slightly chipped, Kangxi, 48.5 cm. high. **£1,000-£1,250**

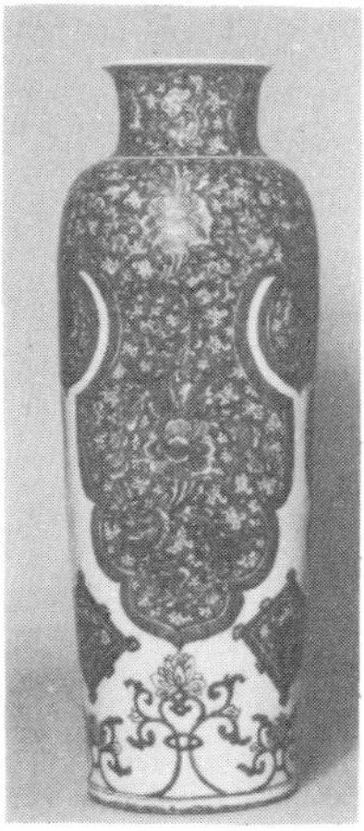

A blue and white and underglaze copper red tall Rouleau vase, painted in a dark cherry red with scrolling tree peony flowers, on brilliant washed blue grounds, Kangxi, 66 cm. high. **£3,500-£5,000**

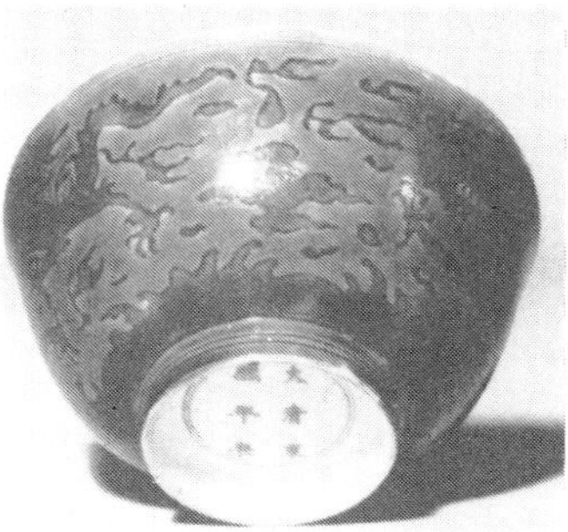

A green and aubergine bowl, incised and painted in aubergine with two five-clawed dragons pursuing flaming whorls, on a green ground, cracked, encircled, Kangxi six-character mark and of the period, 5¼ in. diam. **£600-£700**

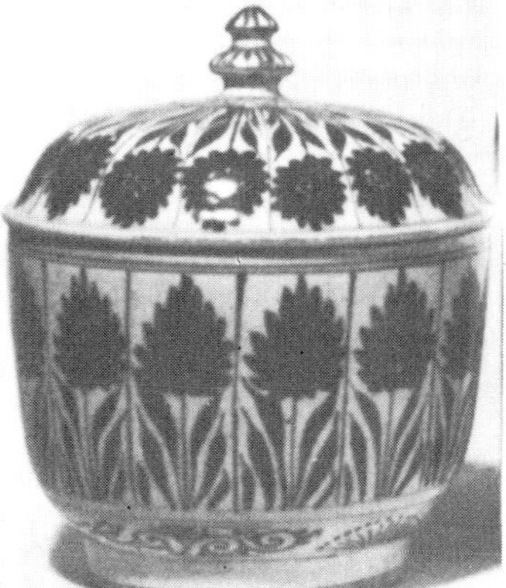

A blue and white 'Aster Pattern' deep bowl and domed cover, painted with flower sprays in vertical panels above a band of scrolling foliage, finial fritted, Kangxi, on wood stand, 23 cm. high. **£400-600**

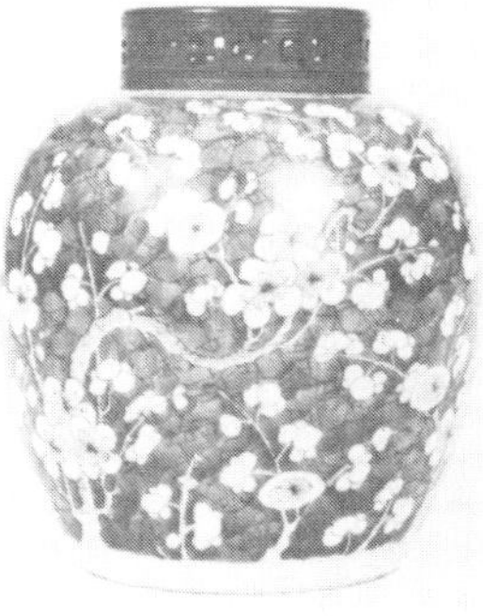

A fine blue and white hawthorn jar, densely painted with long flowering prunus branches on a cracked-ice ground, Kangxi, 22.5 cm. high. **£250-400**

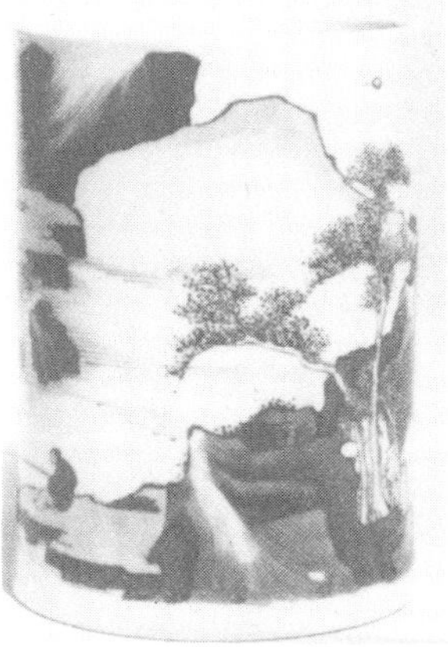

A blue and white brush-pot, painted with a solitary fisherman holding out his rod, Kangxi, 14 cm. high. **£700-1,000**

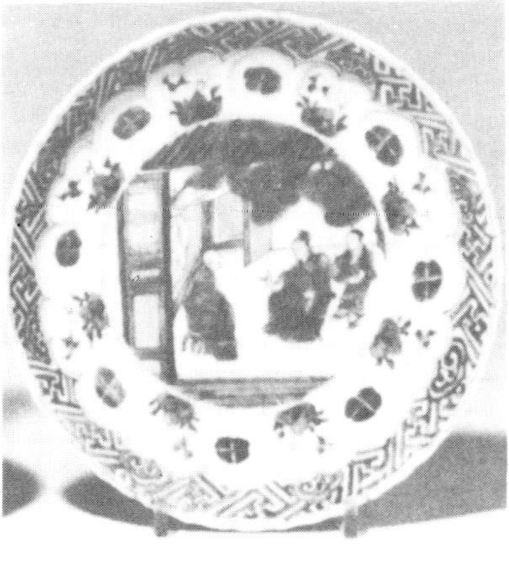

Two blue and white saucer dishes, each moulded and painted at the wells with flower sprays below key pattern, one with a mounted warrior at the centre, the other with a monk and a scholar, encircled Chenghua six-character marks, Kangxi, 20.5 cm. diam. **£500-800**

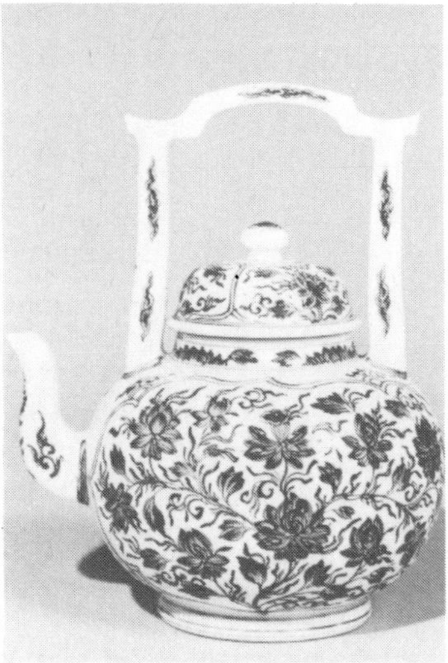

A blue and white wine ewer and cover, painted with two panels of scrolling lotus-headed foliage, spout end restored, 10 in. high, early Kangxi. **£150-200**

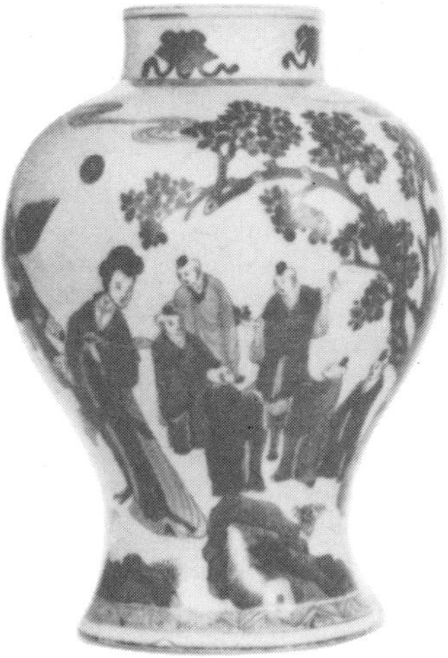

Two Qing blue and white baluster jars, with emblems on the necks, one with base chip repaired, Kangxi, 12¾ in. high. **£800-1,000**
Tall elegant ladies, so-called Long Elizas or Langelijsen, are often featured on Kangxi porcelain.

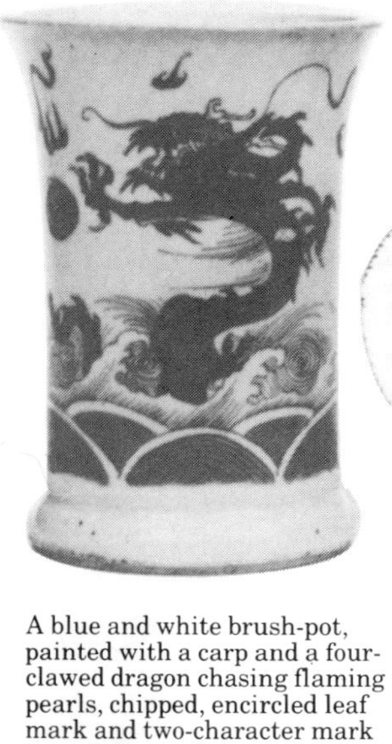

A blue and white brush-pot, painted with a carp and a four-clawed dragon chasing flaming pearls, chipped, encircled leaf mark and two-character mark hong ji, Kangxi, 5¼ in. high. **£200-350**

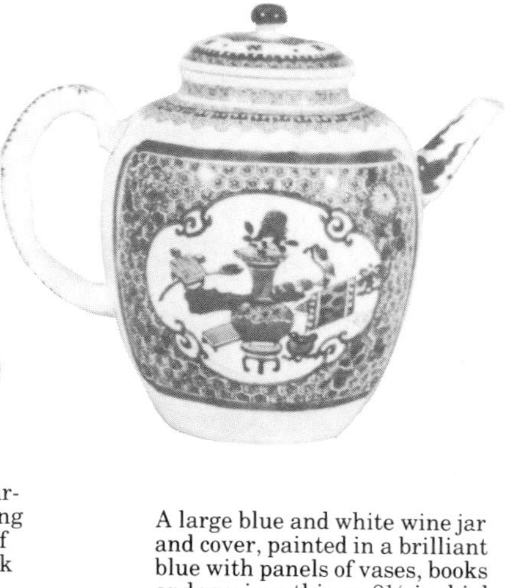

A large blue and white wine jar and cover, painted in a brilliant blue with panels of vases, books and precious things, 8¼ in. high, Kangxi. **£1,250-1,500**

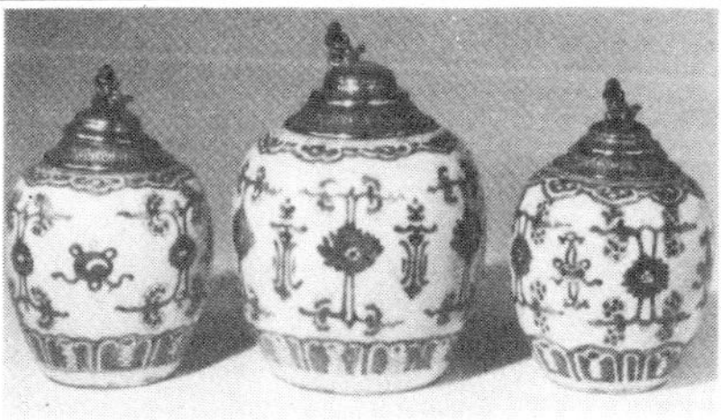

A garniture of three ormolu-mounted Chinese blue and white porcelain vases, decorated with stylised flowers and foliage, the porcelain Kangxi, 10¼ in. and 12 in. high. **£550-650**

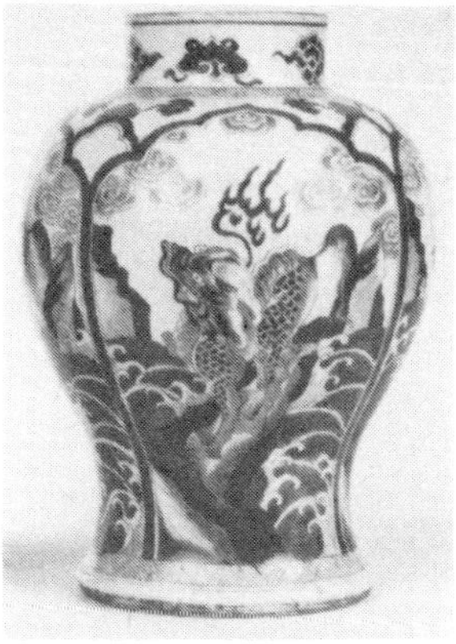

A Qing blue and white baluster vase, painted with emblems at the cylindrical neck, Kangxi, 13 in. high. **£400-500**
The herringbone frieze is a decorative border found frequently on Kangxi porcelains.

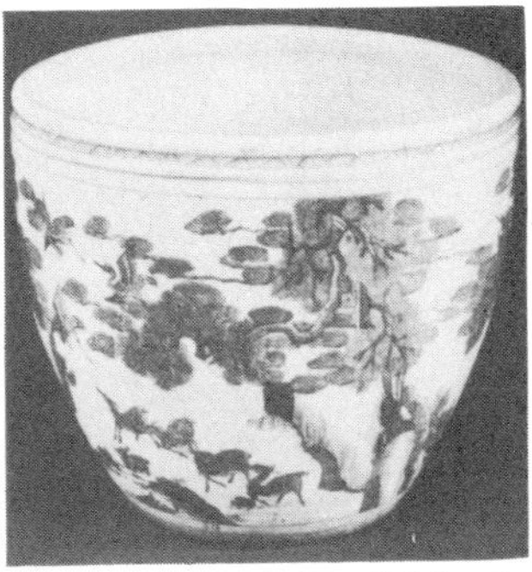

A large blue and white fish bowl, in cobalt underglaze blue, Kangxi, 55 cm. wide and 49 cm. deep. **£2,700-2,900**
Crane, deer and pine are all symbolic of longevity, a theme commonly found on 16th and 17th century wares.

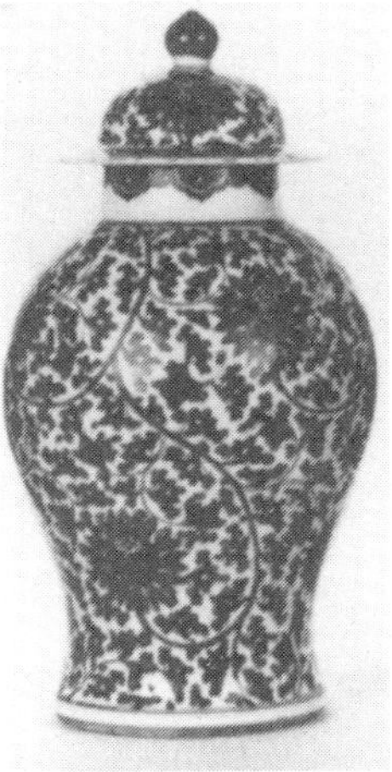

A pair of blue and white vases and covers, chipped, Kangxi, 18 in. high. **£1,100-1,300**
A popular theme on Kangxi is scrolling lotus (or chrysanthemum).

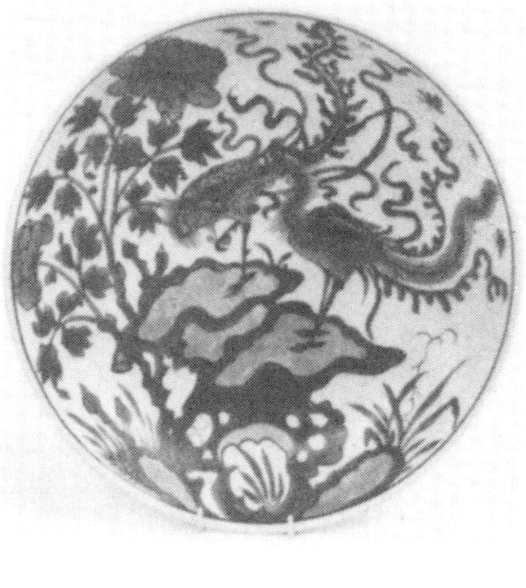

A blue and white saucer dish, 33.7 cm., Kangxi. **£120-150**
Decorated with phoenix symbolic of the Emperor and Empress, a common theme on Chinese porcelain of the 17th, 18th and 19th centuries.

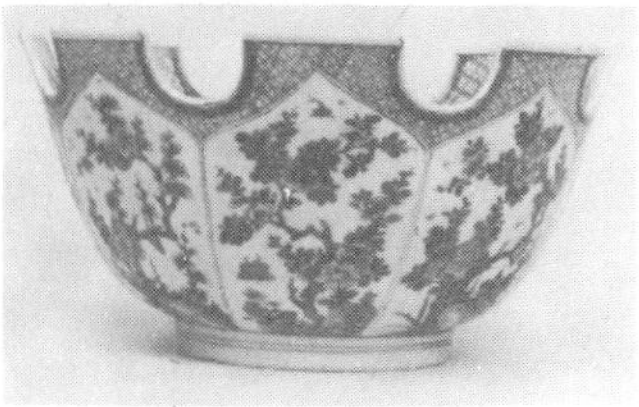

A blue and white monteith, slightly chipped, encircled zhi (made to order) mark, Kangxi, 12¾ in. diam. **£1,200-1,400**
This monteith or wine glass cooler is a good example of an idea borrowed from the West. Cross-hatched diaper grounds became popular in the Kangxi period and remained as such until the mid 18th C.

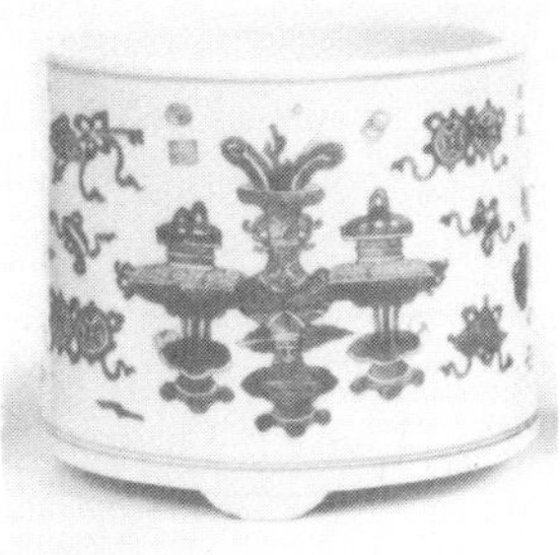

A Qing blue and white tripod cylindrical brush-pot, feet fritted, Kangxi, 7¾ in. diam. **£350-450**
The precious objects and archaic vessels seen on this brush-pot are a common decorative motif on Kangxi wares.

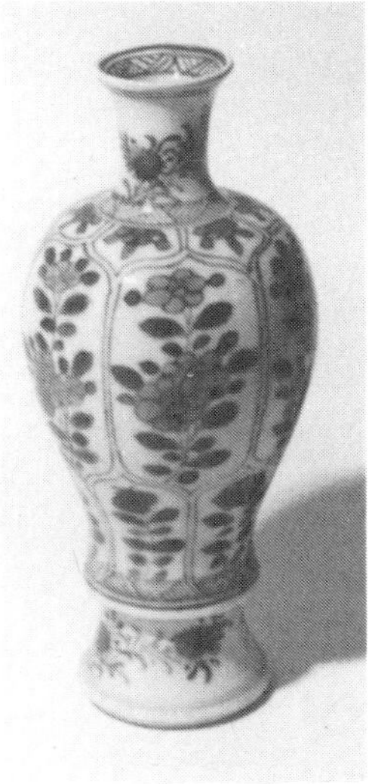

A Kangxi blue and white spill vase, 5½ in. high. **£30-40**
The compartmented design is a common layout to be found on wares of this period.

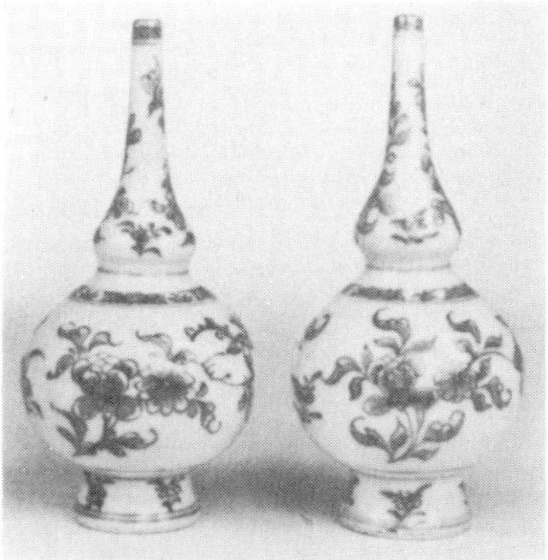

Two blue and white double-gourd sprinkler bottles, painted with peony, chrysanthemum and lingzhi sprays. Kangxi, 7 in. high. **£200-300**

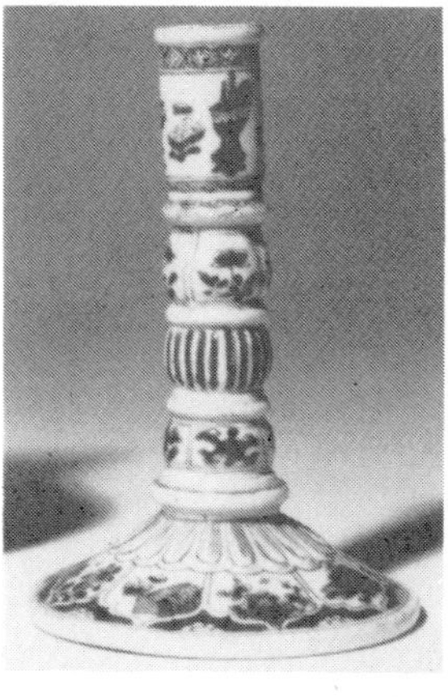

A blue and white candlestick, after a European silver shape, painted on the cylindrical nozzle with scholars' utensils above flower sprays on the knopped stems and moulded petal-shaped lappets descending on to utensils and flower-heads on the widely flaring conical foot, fritted, Kangxi, 16.5 cm. high. **£500-700**

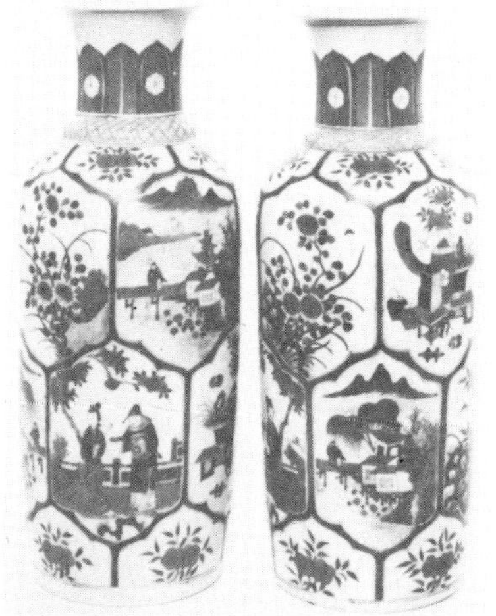

These vases are very good examples of 19th century copies of Kangxi blue and white.

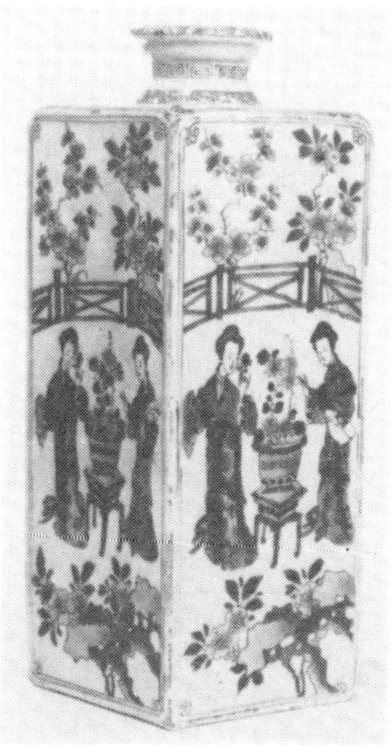

A blue and white square bottle vase, painted on each face with two ladies beside a jardinière on a rocky terrace below cracked-ice, key and trellis-pattern on the waisted neck, chipped, the base with a square recessed HM mark, Kangxi, 11½ in. high.
£150-250

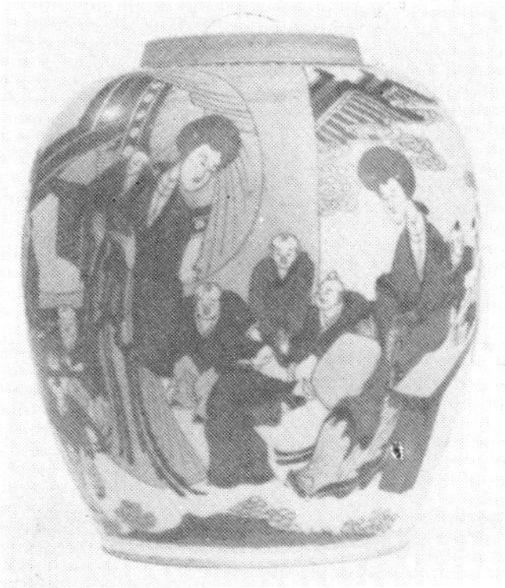

A blue and white jar, painted with elegant ladies watching over small boys at play before a pavilion on a terrace beside plantain, Kangxi, 9¼ in. high.
£300-400

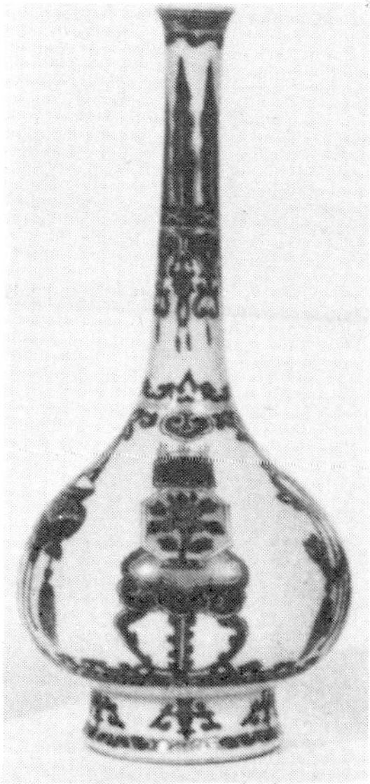

A blue and white sprinkler bottle, painted with dragon loop pendants, tripod bowls and tables of flowers, the tall neck with ruyi lappets and stiff leaves, 27 cm. high, c. 1680, flower mark. **£400-600**

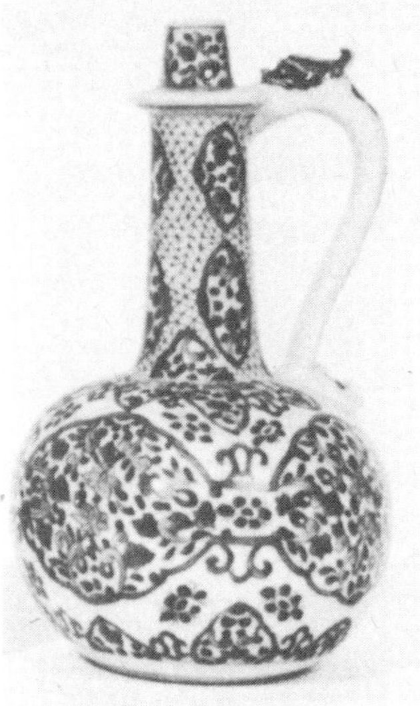

A fine and rare pair of blue and white bottles, painted with quatrefoil panels of lotus meander linked by flowerheads above a band of floral lappets, the decoration not quite identical, one handle with a slight chip, 24 cm. high, c. 1680. **£1,000-1,500**

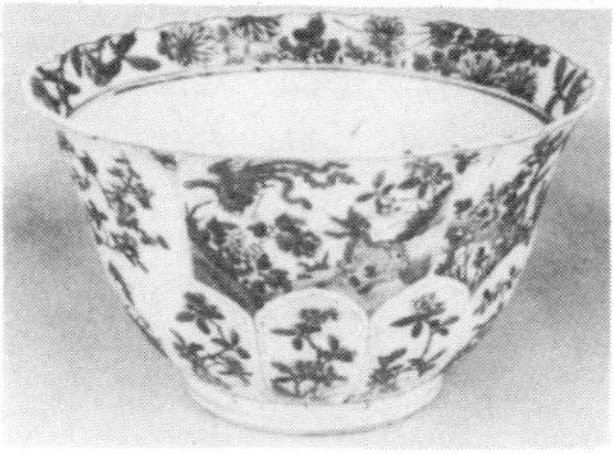

A large bowl, with lotus panels with flowering plants below panels with birds and animals in landscape, Kangxi, 34 cm. diam. **£600-900**

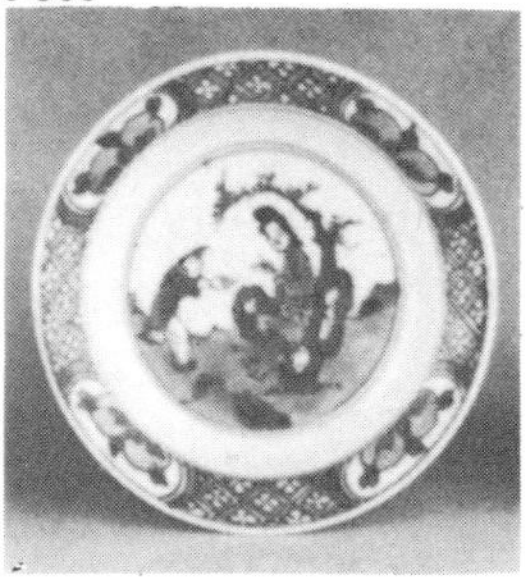

12 small plates, decorated with a lady and a boy near rocks and trees, 10.5 cm. diam., Kangxi. **£300-500**

The 'Jumping Boy' pattern also appears on Liverpool porcelain c. 1760.

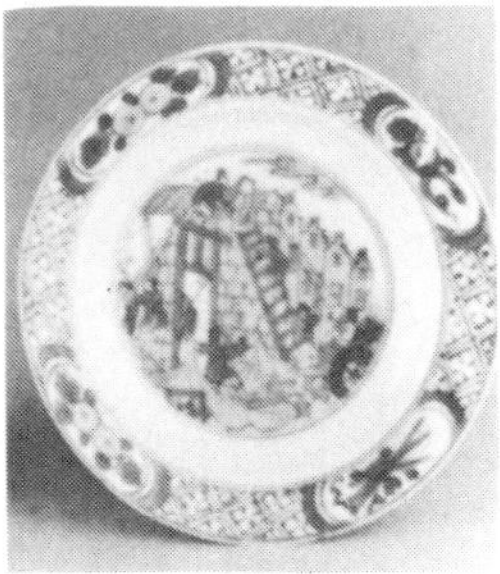

A set of four small plates decorated with the 'Costerman riots at Rotterdam' bearing incised Johannaeum Dresden inventory marks, c. 1690, 11 cm. diam. **£600-800**

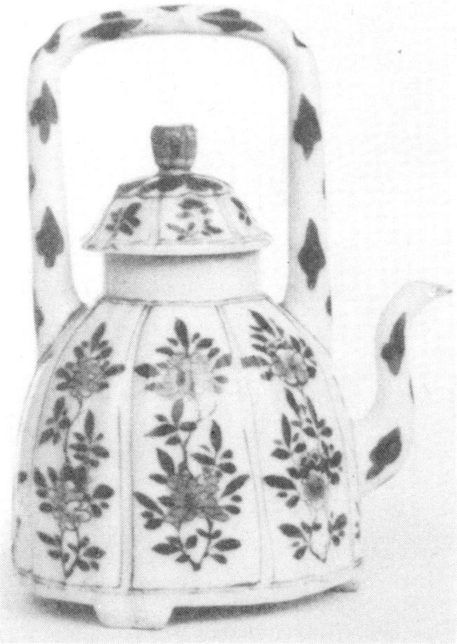

Right
A blue and white fluted beehive-shaped teapot and cover, painted with panels of peony and peach below clouds on the rectangular arch handle, chipped, Kangxi, 6½ in. high. **£250-£300**

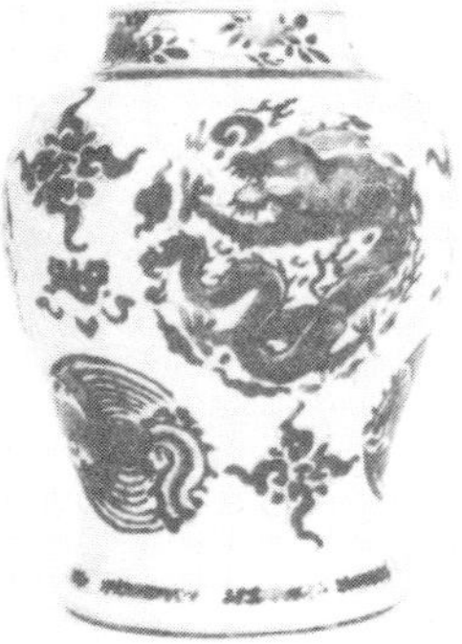

A blue and white baluster vase, painted with three roundels of dragons pursuing flaming pearls amongst clouds above smaller roundels of flying phoenix surmounted by precious emblems, Kangxi, 9¼ in. high. **£150-200**

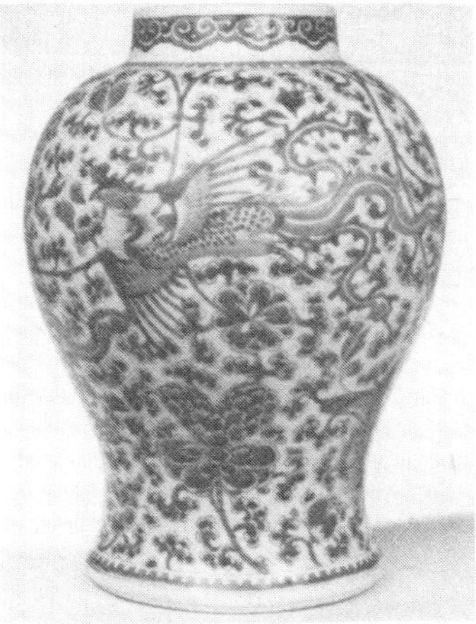

A blue and white baluster vase, painted with four phoenix in flight amongst scrolling peony below a band of ruyi heads, Kangxi, 13¾ in. high. **£350-450**
A very common form and decoration for this period. Note the castellated or cogged borders.

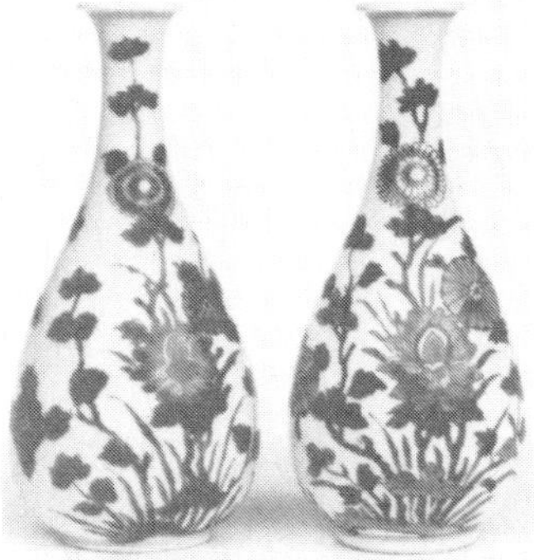

A pair of blue and white pear-shaped bottles, vividly painted on either side with peony, chrysanthemum and lotus issuing from rockwork, one chipped, Kangxi, 6¾ in. high. **£300-400**

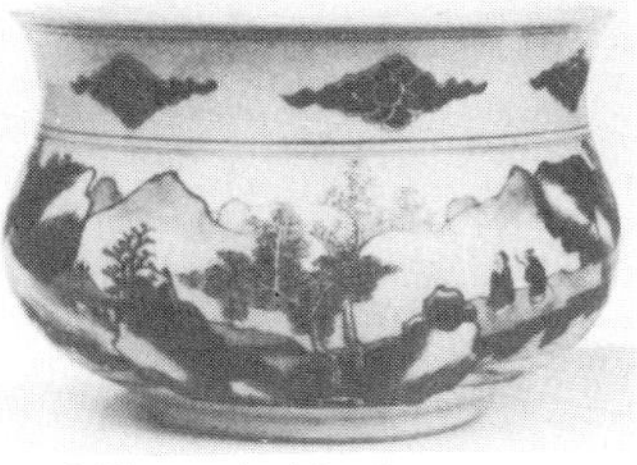

A blue and white deep censer, painted with two scholars walking along a rocky bank towards a retreat and a fisherman punting his boat across a wide river, Kangxi, 9 in. diam. **£300-400**

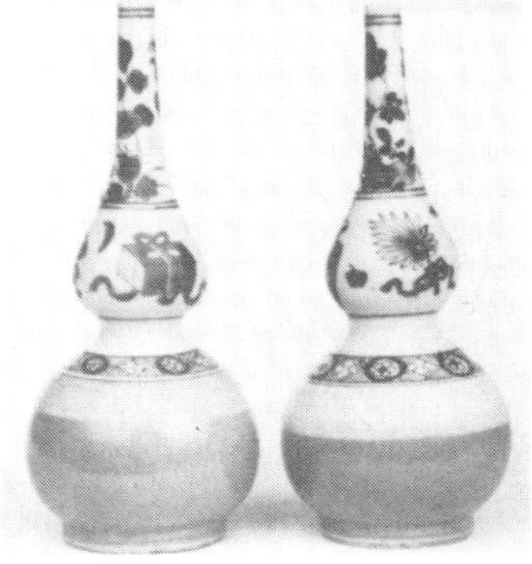

A pair of double-gourd sprinkler bottles, painted in underglaze blue with precious emblems below flowering branches on the slender cylindrical necks, the lower sections under pale café-au-lait glazes, one chipped with associated cracks, Kangxi, 7¼ in. high. **£250-350**

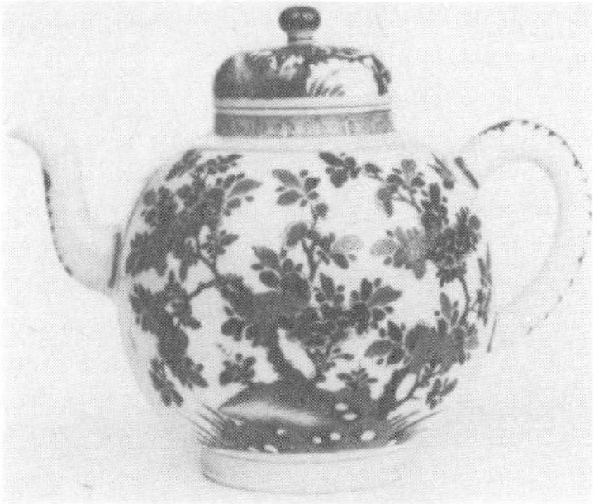

A large blue and white teapot and cover, painted with a bird in flight above tree peony issuing from rockwork, handle base cracked, Kangxi, 10 in. wide. **£400-500**

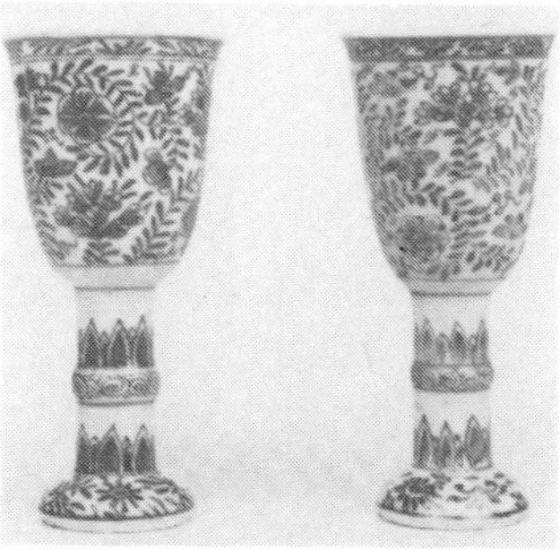

A pair of blue and white shallowly fluted deep stem bowls, modelled as European glasses and painted with scrolling foliage above bands of lotus petals, chipped, one cracked, Kangxi, 6 in. high. **£150-250**

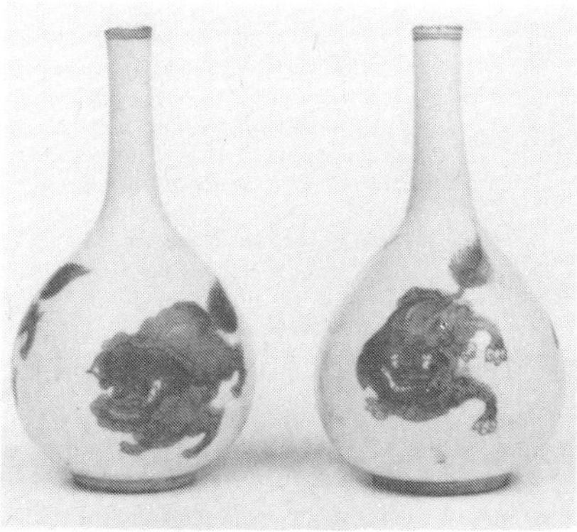

A pair of blue and white pear-shaped bottles, vividly painted with three Buddhist lions in playful postures, chipped, one neck interior slightly cracked, Kangxi, 5½ in. high. **£350-450**

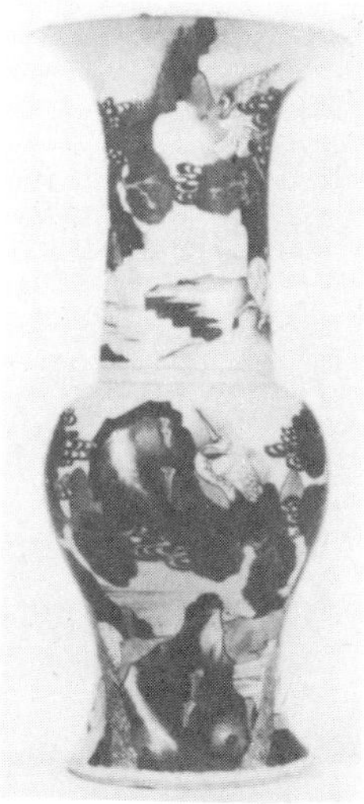

A blue and white Yanyan vase, painted with storks in flight and perched upon pine above deer in two bands of continuous mountainous landscape, chipped, Kangxi, 18 in. high. **£600-800**

This form (Yanyan) first appeared in blue and white during the reign of Kangxi. It was not popular after this reign until Kangxi wares were copied in the 19th century. The ceramic painters of this period were especially adept at using outline and wash techniques in underglaze blue, the present vase being a good example of this.

Make the most of Millers...

Remember that this book is a price *guide*, not a price *list*. Valuations given throughout apply to the specific prices shown and, though they may reasonably be taken as a guide to the values of other similar articles, other factors may also apply.

Condition of any article is of the utmost importance and must always be taken into account when negotiating the sale of any antique.

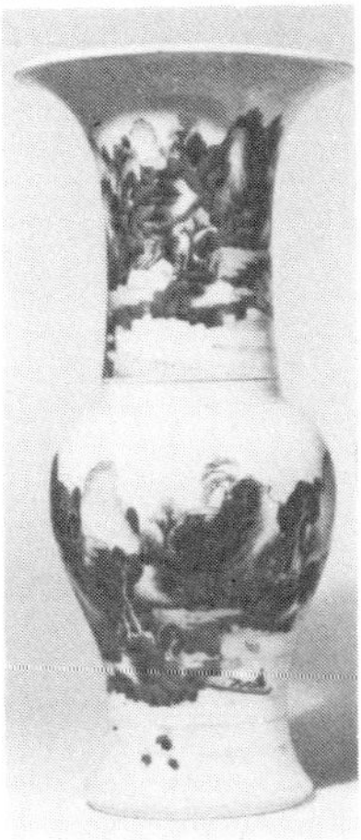

A blue and white Yanyan vase, painted with a fisherman in his boat and scholars in conversation near a retreat in a rocky river landscape, chipped and fritted, Kangxi, 18¼ in. high. **£500-600**

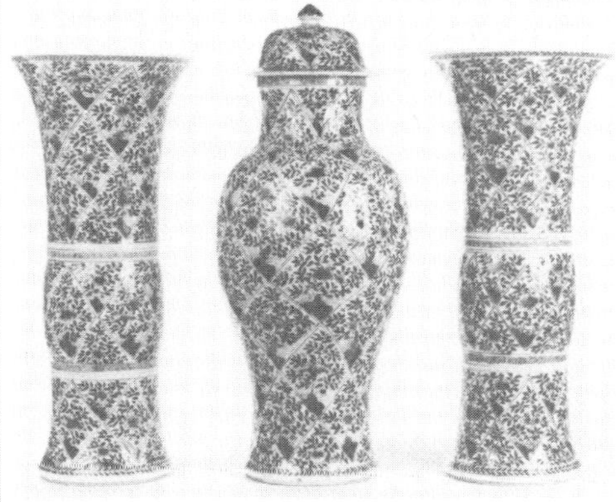

A garniture of three blue and white vases, each painted with panels of peony and camellia issuing from rockwork within borders of foliage, whorls, chevron and key pattern, comprising: a baluster vase and cover, side star crack, cover chipped, 19½ in. high, two beaker vases, one with minor chips, 17¼ in. high, all with encircled lingzhi marks, Kangxi. **£1,700-2,200**

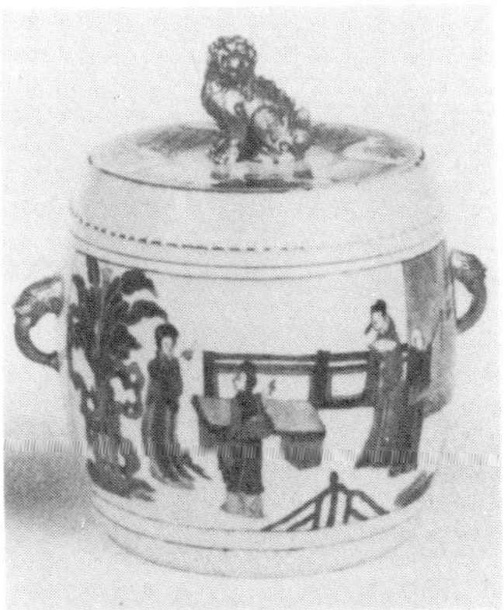

Two blue and white jars and covers, painted with panels of scholars and ladies, the finial lions both looking to the left, the covers with frit chips, Kangxi, both about 8¼ in. wide. **£600-£900**

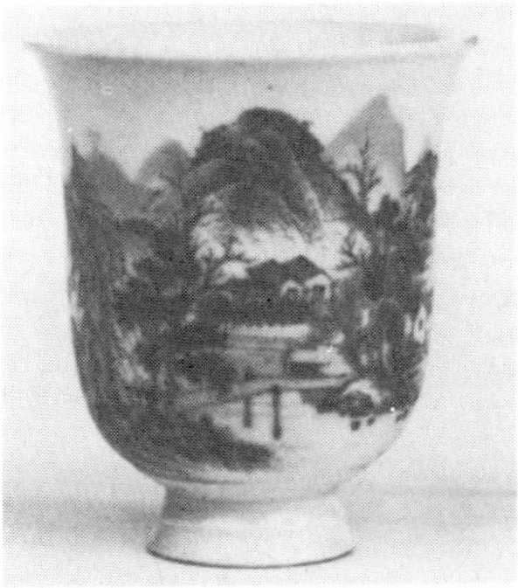

A blue and white soft-paste beaker, painted with two scholars seated watching a boat from a rocky bank in a mountainous river landscape, rim chips reduced, encircled Chenghua four-character mark, early 18th C., 4 in. high. **£200-£300**

'Hua shih' or soft paste porcelain is particularly receptive or sympathetic to the brush and a softer but more detailed effect can often be achieved.

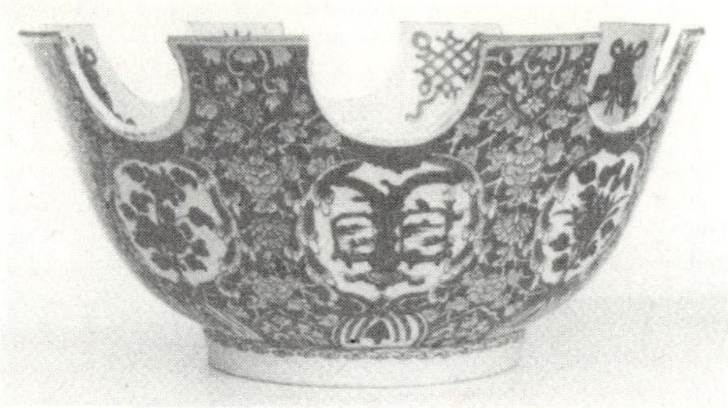

A blue and white monteith, painted with shaped panels of vessels and flower sprays on a ground of densely scrolling peony, the interior with archaistic vases within a foliate band below precious emblems, fritted, encircled flower mark, Kangxi, 12½ in. diam. **£1,000-£1,500**

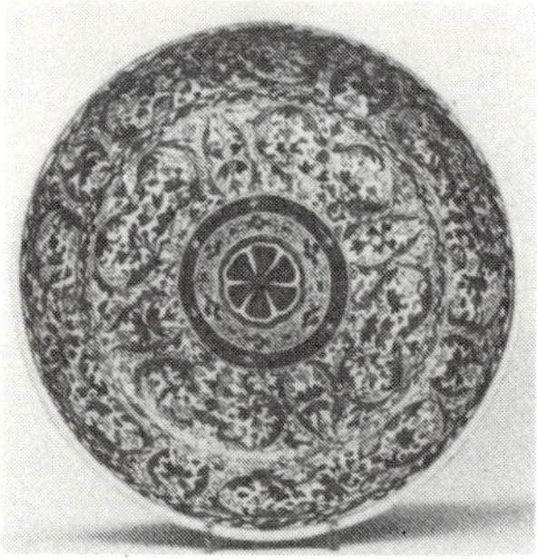

A famille verte deep dish, painted with formal scrolling foliage around a central flowerhead in the interior and four cruciform peach clusters on the exterior, slightly chipped, Kangxi, 13 in. diam. **£300-500**

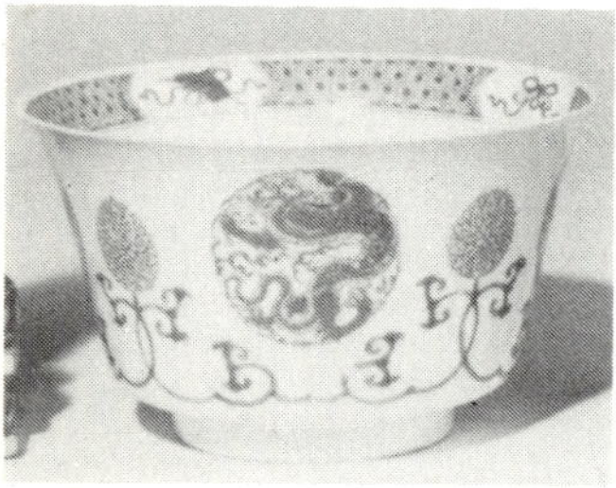

A pair of famille verte deep flaring bowls, painted in the interior with a central phoenix roundel below a band of cell-pattern at the rim, the exterior with alternate phoenix and dragon roundels, one restored, Kangxi, on wood stands, 7¼ in. diam. **£400-600**

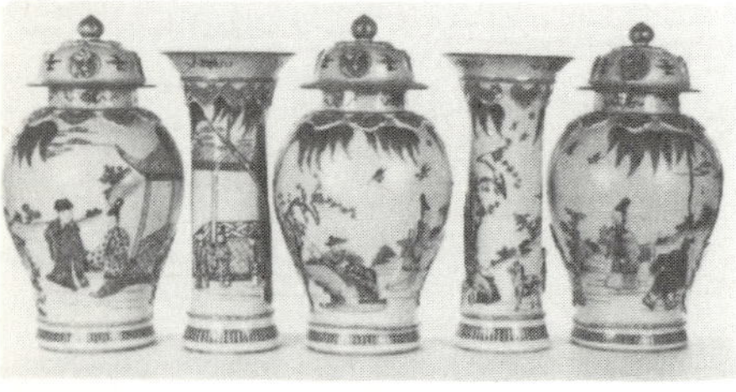

A garniture of five famille verte vases, comprising: two beaker vases, the necks repaired, 15¾ in. high, and three baluster vases, damaged, with covers, 17¾ in. high, Kangxi. **£4,400-£5,000**

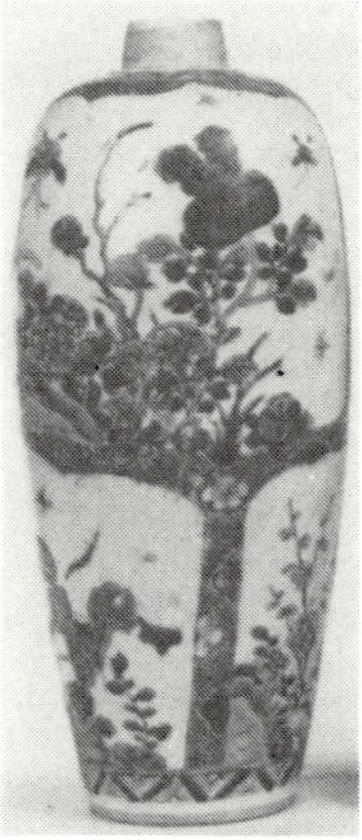

A famille verte vase, Kangxi, 11½ in. high. **£440-500**

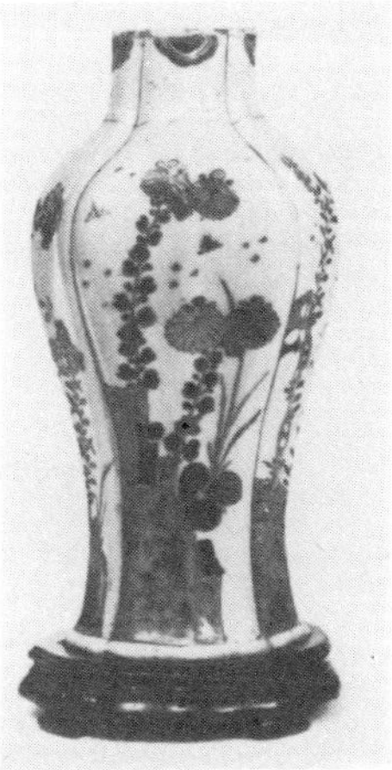

A famille verte baluster vase, of oval quatrefoil cross-section, painted with insects in flight above peony and chrysanthemum, chipped, the neck cracked, Kangxi, mounted as an electric lamp with wooden stand, 9½ in. high. **£120-180**

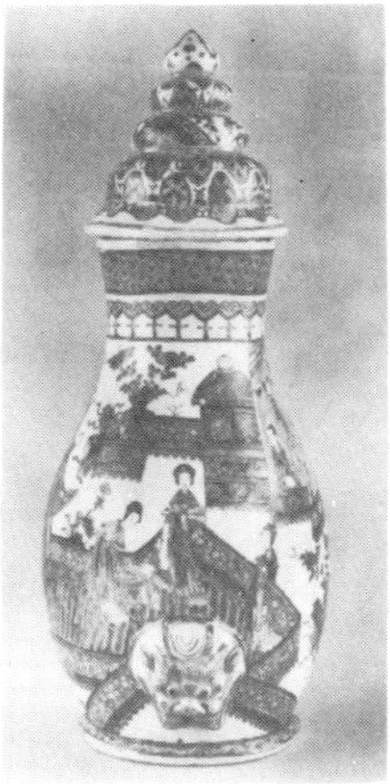

A baluster wall fountain and domed cover, a projecting dragon-head mask below pierced for a tap, painted in famille verte colours with ladies and a boy on a terrace, 55.5 cm. high, Kangxi. **£1,000-1,500**

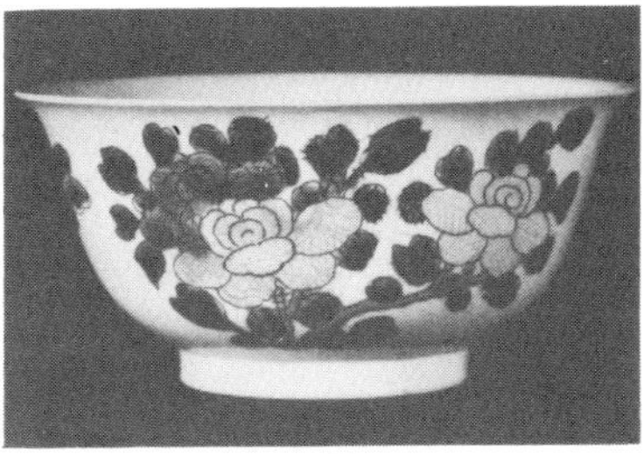

A fine famille verte Chinese taste bowl, the exterior incised with two dragons in mutual pursuit of flaming pearls and over-enamelled in yellow, aubergine and green with peony branches divided by butterflies, 15.5 cm. diam., Kangxi six-character mark and of the period. **£900-1,200**

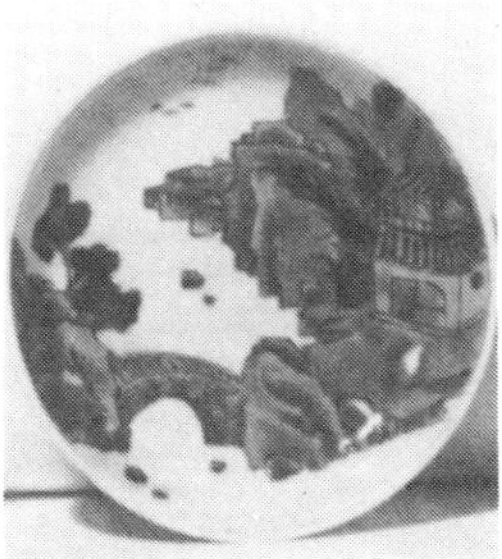

Two famille verte saucer dishes, painted with pavilions in mountainous river landscapes, one slightly fritted, the other with a short rim crack, encircled jue marks, Kangxi, 16 cm. diam. **£400-600**

A famille verte armorial barber's bowl, painted with the arms of Holland and a coronet, between butterflies and tree peony sprays, the border with five panels of cockerels, sheep and a buffalo on an underglaze blue ground, 10½ in. diam., late Kangxi. **£600-900**

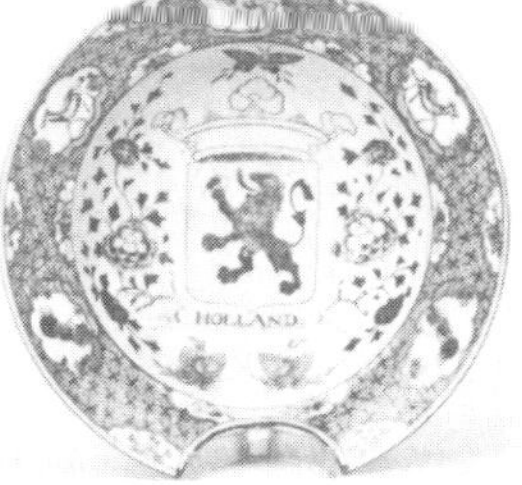

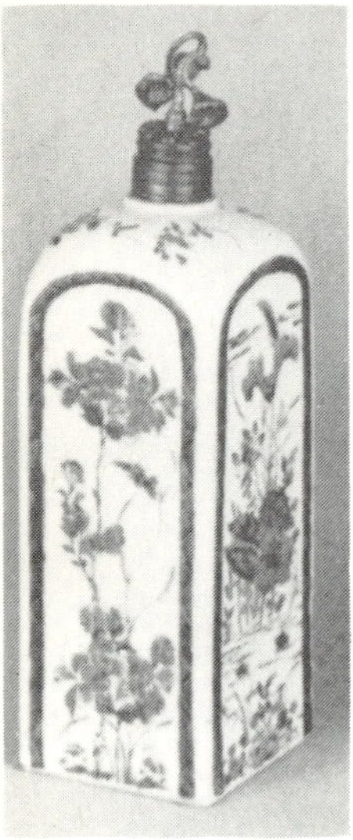

A square famille verte bottle, painted with lotus in a pond and tree peonies, 26 cm. high, Kangxi. **£600-900**

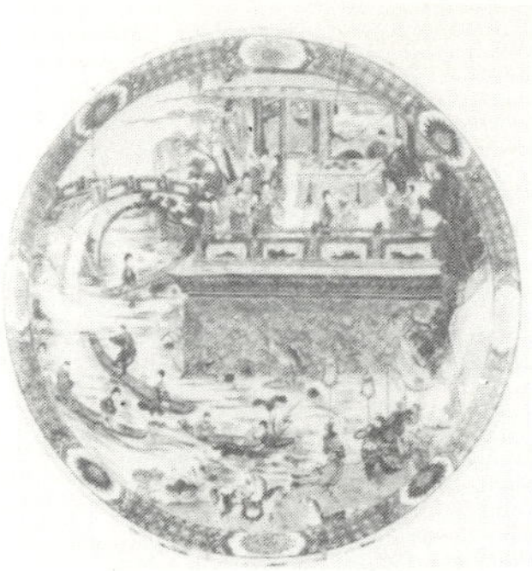

A large famille verte saucer dish, painted with ladies and gentlemen on a villa terrace standing in conversation above figures punting on a stream before soldiers with their mounts on the far bank, repaired, encircled Chenghua six-character mark, Kangxi, 25¼ in. diam. **£1,000-1,500**
The busy all-over decoration and cell diaper border are typical of late Kangxi or Yongzheng export ware.

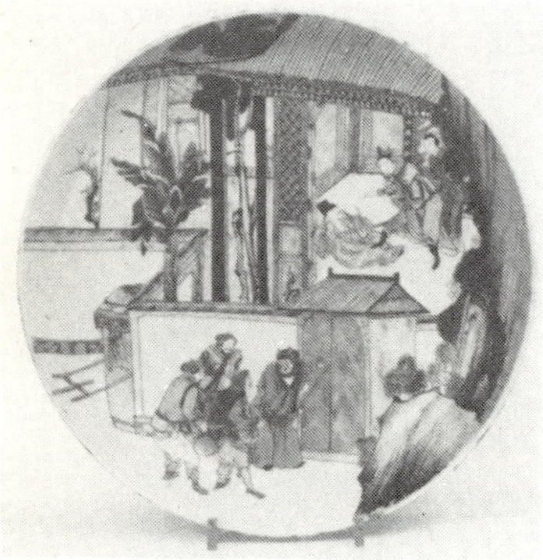

A famille verte saucer dish, painted with a scene from a novel, a dignitary, a horn blower, a drummer and a cymbal player at the gate of a pavilion below a lady watching a scholar standing with one leg over a fallen rival and pointing an accusing finger at him, chipped, encircled leaf mark Kangxi, 10¾ in. diam. **£800-1,000**

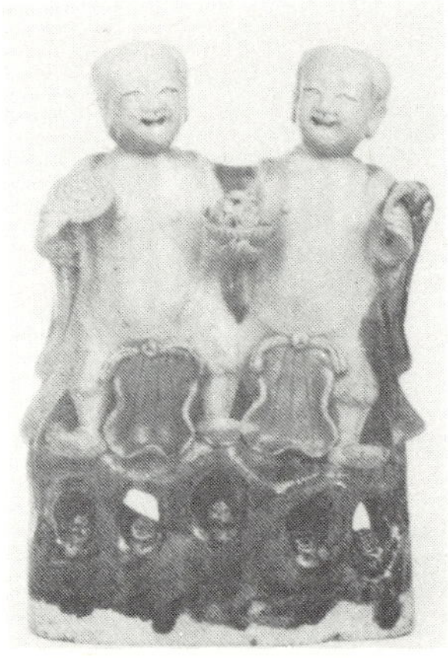

A famille verte biscuit group of the laughing twins, seated on pierced aubergine rockwork holding a whisk, a flower-head and a dish of cash emblems, in green and yellow, one neck repaired, Kangxi, 5½ in. high. **£200-300**

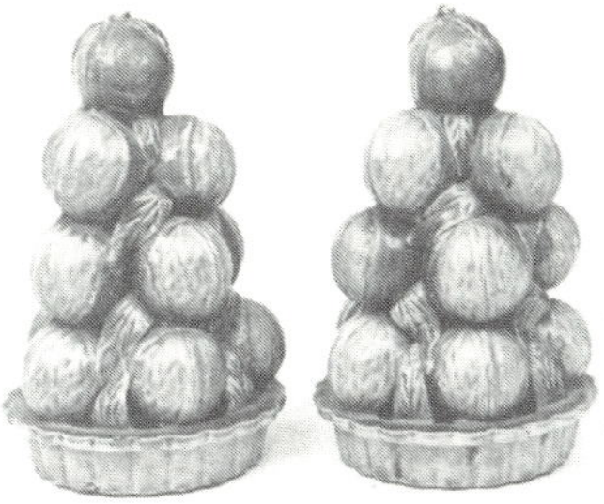

A pair of famille verte biscuit models of walnut piles, the nuts under mustard yellow glazes and the leaves green, 5½ in. high, 18th/19th C. **£200-350**

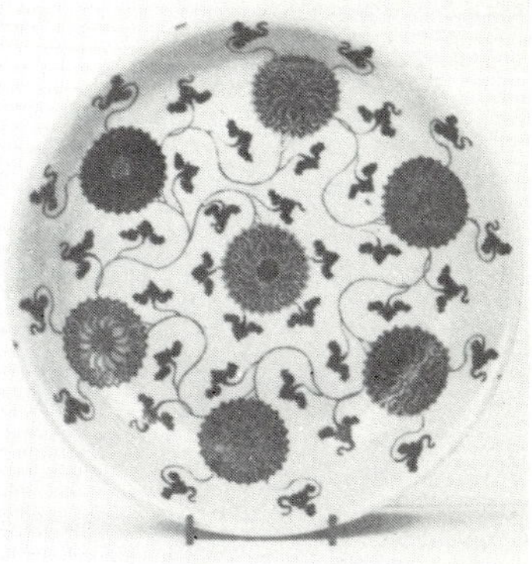

A famille verte saucer dish, painted with six large peony heads around a similar central flower, chipped, encircled leaf mark, Kangxi, 13¾ in. diam. **£350-450**
This is a popular design.

A famille verte saucer dish, painted with two ladies carrying fans and flowers standing beside a table below prunus on a terrace, iron-red and gilt 'pie-crust' rim, rim with minute crack and chips, Kangxi, 7¼ in. diam. **£550-700**

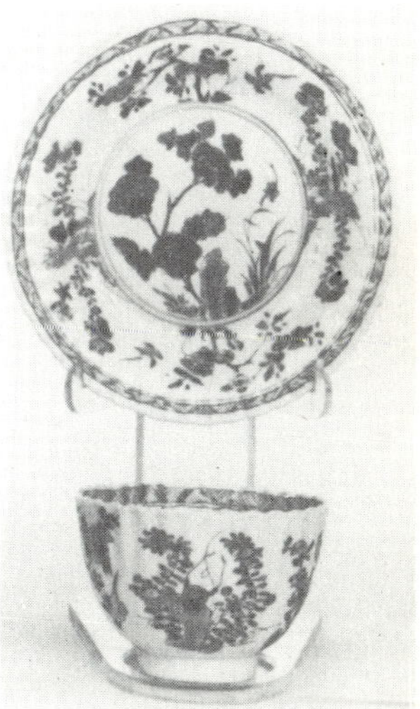

A famille verte teabowl and saucer, moulded with two bands of interlocking petals and painted with insects and birds amongst prunus, daisy and pinks, encircled flower mark, Kangxi. **£250-300**

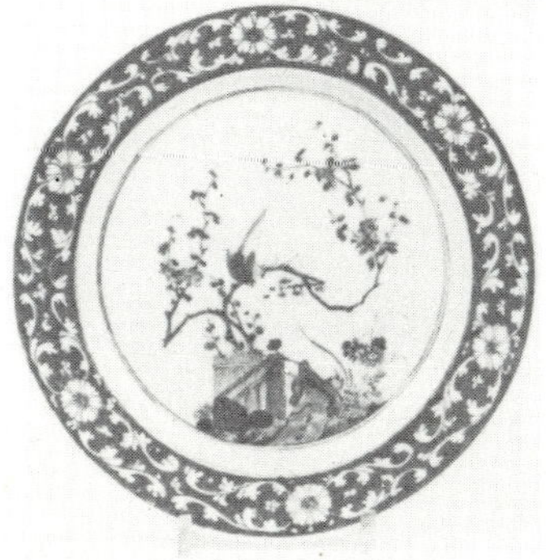

A famille verte plate, painted with a bird perched upon a tree beside a fence below scrolling camellia reserved on an iron-red ground at the rim, minutely chipped, encircled lingzhi mark, Kangxi, 8¾ in. diam. **£250-350**

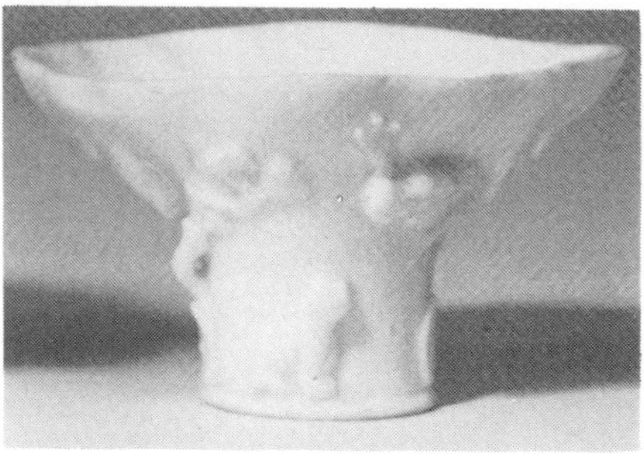

A pair of blanc-de-Chine oval libation cups, each moulded with a tiger and a deer at the slender base below a dragon and a crane, rims reduced in places, 18th C., 4¼ in. wide. **£150-200**

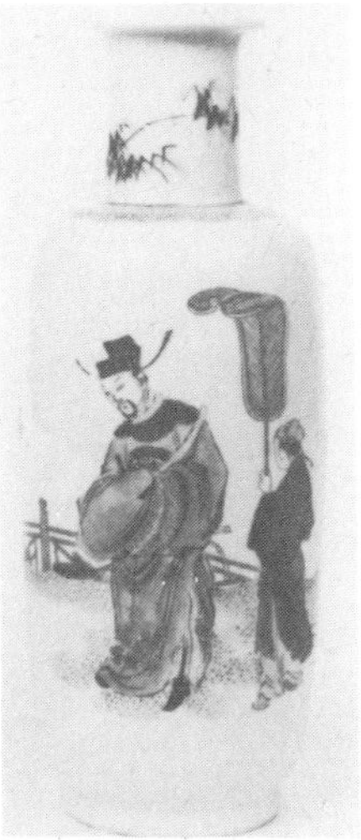

A famille verte rouleau vase, painted with a scholar holding a sceptre and wearing a green robe, standing with a fan-bearer and a servant holding a vase of persimmon and a ruyi sceptre below iron-red ruyi heads on the shoulder and black bamboo on the neck, minor foot crack, enamel fritting repainted, Kangxi, 10¼ in. high. **£800-£1,000**
A good example of late Kangxi brushwork, the bamboo on the neck is characteristic of this period.

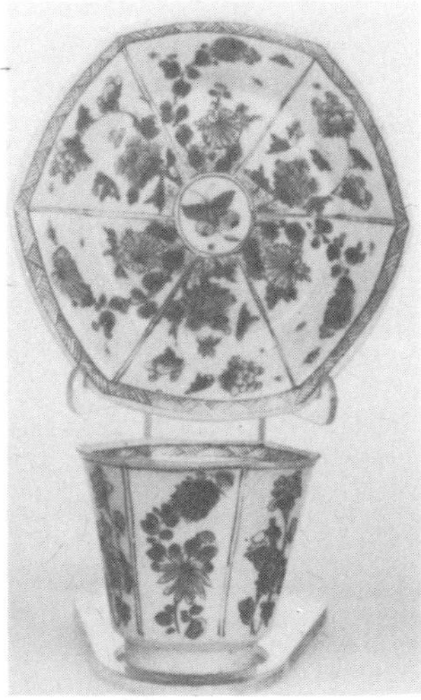

A set of three famille verte hexagonal beakers and saucers, each beaker painted on the biscuit with flower sprays and the glazed saucers each with flowers in panels radiating from a butterfly medallion at the centre, chipped, encircled flower marks, Kangxi. **£600-800**

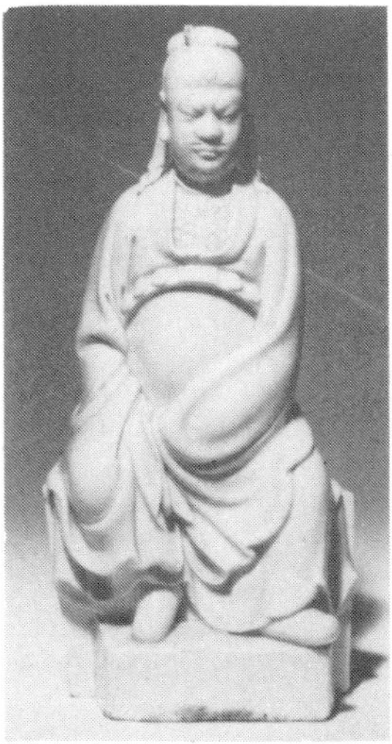

A blanc-de-Chine figure of Guandi, chipped, 17th C. **£1,000-1,500**
'Blanc-de-Chine' wares were exported during the late 17th and 18th centuries to Europe. Not only were the figures of Buddhist and Taoist deities popular but also figures representing Europeans appeared from time to time.

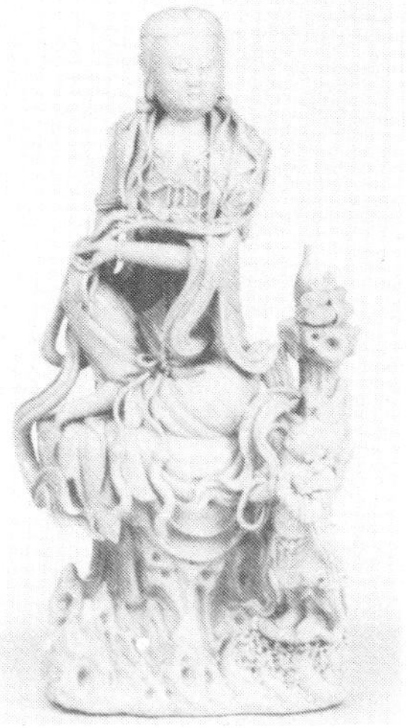

A blanc-de-Chine figure of Guanyin, wearing elaborate jewellery and holding a ruyi sceptre, her amphora beside a bundle of scrolls at her left side above a boy acolyte standing below her, minor extremity damage, Dehua mark in a double gourd and four-character mark, early/mid 19th C., 14¾ in. high. **£450-600**

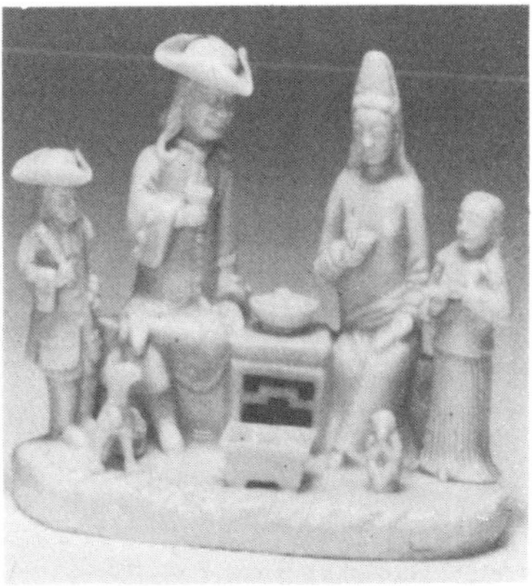

A rare European subject blanc-de-Chine group, modelled as four figures in European dress, the two males with tricorn hats, the ladies with simple robes, the front set with a small jardinière, a seated dog and monkey, small chips, an object missing from behind the table, 16 cm. wide, c. 1750. **£1,250-1,500**

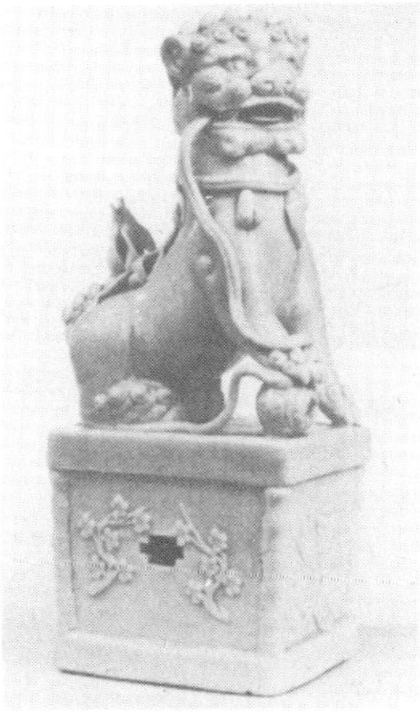

A blanc-de-Chine figure of a seated Buddhist lion, holding a brocaded ball under its forepaw, the base applied with prunus and peony sprays between bamboo stems, extremities chipped, 18th C., 11¾ in. high. **£250-350**

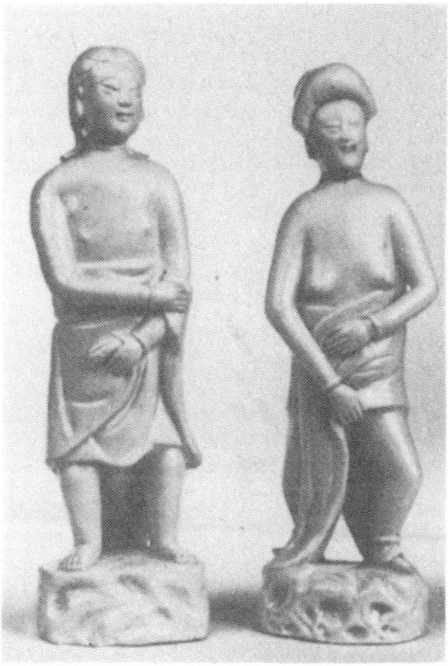

Two blanc-de-Chine figures of a man and woman, he with centrally parted hair and she with a high coiffure, one neck repaired, 18th C., 9 in. high. **£500-600**

The figures are traditionally thought to represent Adam and Eve. It has also been suggested that they may depict native minority peoples.

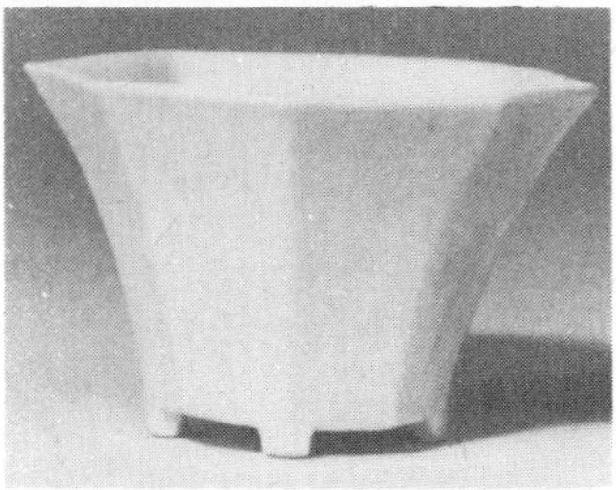

A pair of blanc-de-Chine octagonal libation cups, each incised on two of the flaring faces with a poem, under ivory glazes, 17th/early 18th C., 4½ in. wide. **£150-200**

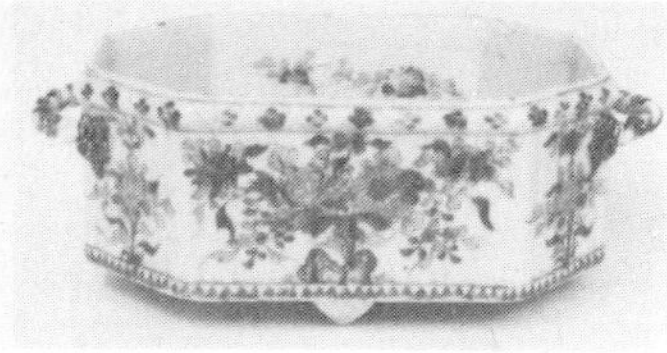

A Chinese Imari jardinère, with three short pyramidal feet, chipped, early 18th C., 11½ in. wide. **£350-450**
The Chinese adopted the Japanese Imari palette of underglaze blue, iron-red and gilding in order to combat the commercial initiative which they had lost when the Japanese started exporting during the late 17th and early 18th centuries.

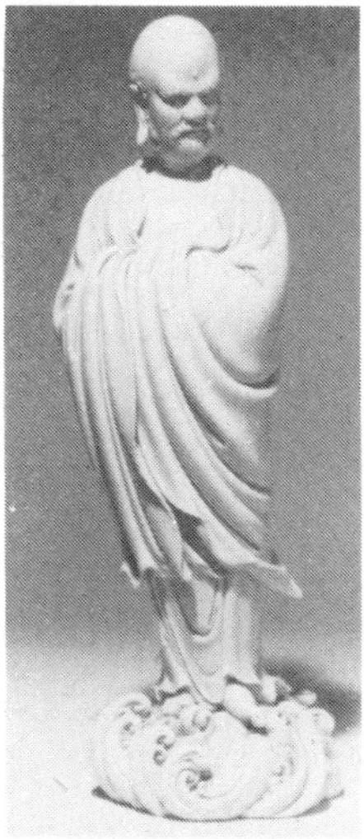

A blanc-de-Chine figure of Bodhidharma, finely modelled with curling eyebrows, moustache and beard, his eyes glaring to the left, some restoration at the neck, impressed square seal mark He Chaozong yin, 17th C., 17 in. high. **£3,000-4,000**

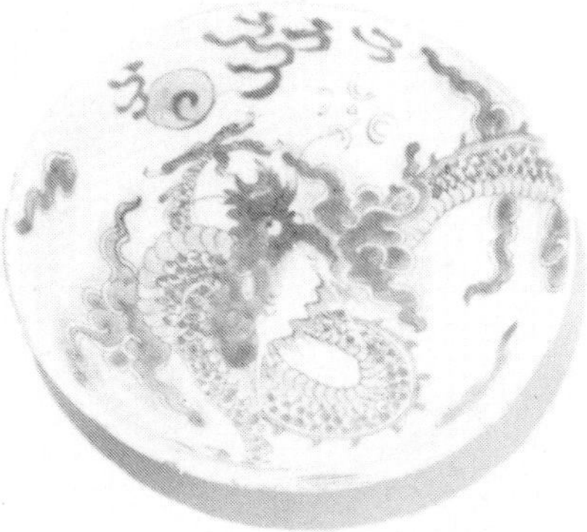

A blue and white dish, some chips, probably Fujian (Southern China), 18th C., 7¼ in. diam. **£20-25**

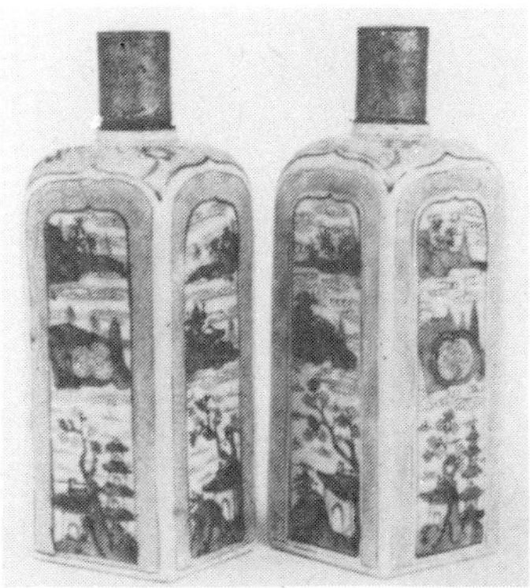

A pair of gilt-metal mounted Chinese Imari square jars, each painted in underglaze blue, iron red and gilt with landscape panels below flowersprays, early 18th C., the necks with gilt-metal collars and covers, 9 in. high. **£600-800**
Contemporary Japanese Imari wares also appeared in this form.

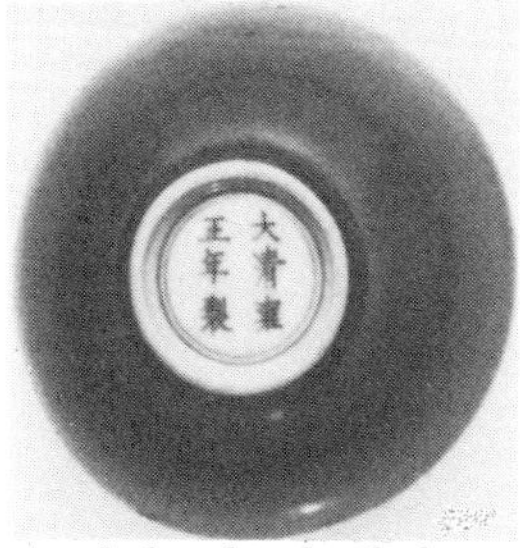

A red-glazed teabowl, the interior plain white and the exterior under a semi-translucent cherry-red glaze pooling and firing to a deep colour around short foot, encircled Yongzheng six-character mark and of the period, 2¾ in. diam. **£600-800**
A perfect specimen of the six-character mark of this period.

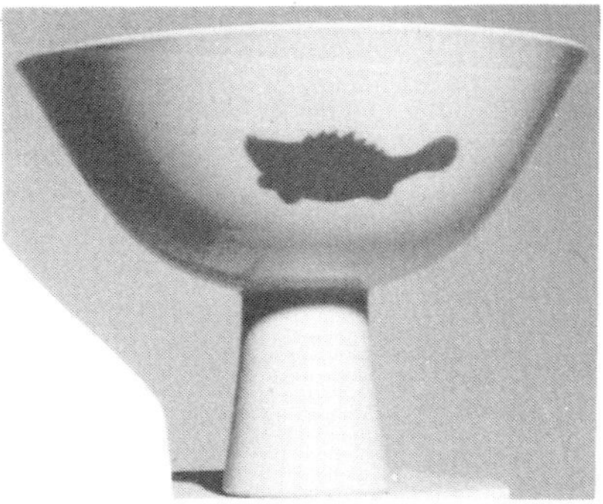

A stem-cup, painted in underglaze copper-red with three spine-backed fish on the exterior of the bowl, small exterior chip filled in, Yongzheng six-character mark and of the period, fitted box, 15.5 cm. diam. **£6,500-8,500**

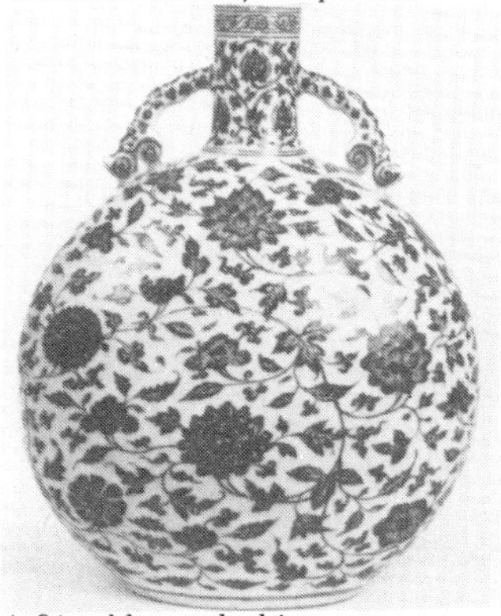

A Qing blue and white moon-flask, Yongzheng six-character seal mark, 14 in. high. **£1,000-£1,200**
Excellent copies of early Ming blue and white were manufactured during the Yongzheng and Qianlong reigns. This particular example is based on an early 15th century original dating from either the Yongle or Xuande periods (1401-36).

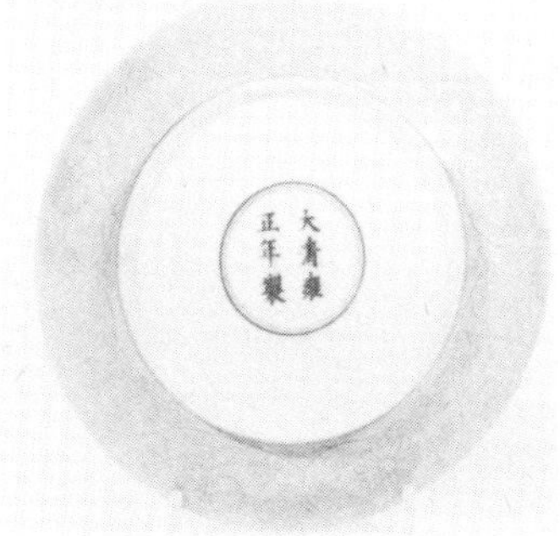

A pair of Imperial yellow saucer dishes, the saucers incised on the outsides with loose formal flowering foliage scrolls under a pale egg-yolk yellow glaze, 15 cm. diam., Yongzheng six-character marks within double circles and of the period. **£1,800-£2,200**

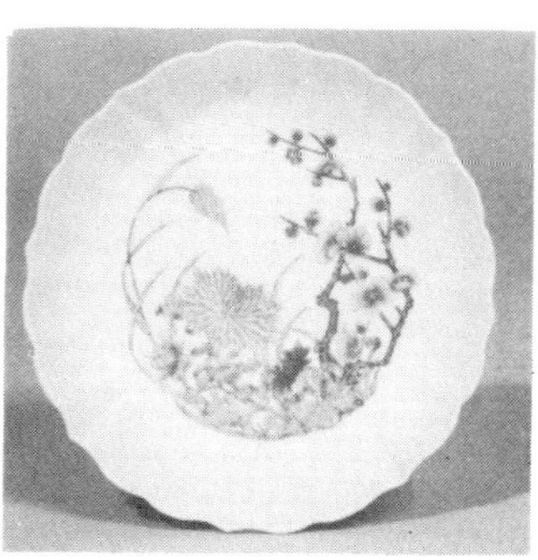

A Chinese taste famille rose saucer dish, enamelled in colours, 15 cm. diam., in a fitted box, Yongzheng six-character mark and of the period. **£3,000-£4,000**

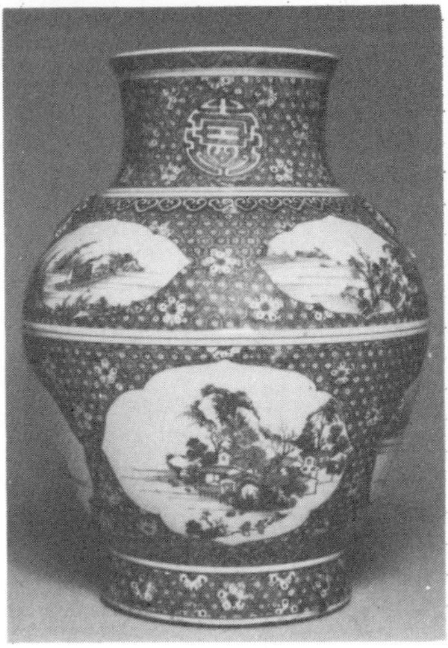

A very fine underglaze decorated vase, painted in underglaze copper red and cobalt blue with long quatrefoil panels of figures in river and mountain landscapes, with two flat relief butterfly handles, the waisted neck with shou medallions, all reserved on floral cell pattern grounds enriched with scattered flower heads, 48.5 cm. high, Yongzheng. **£8,000-10,000**

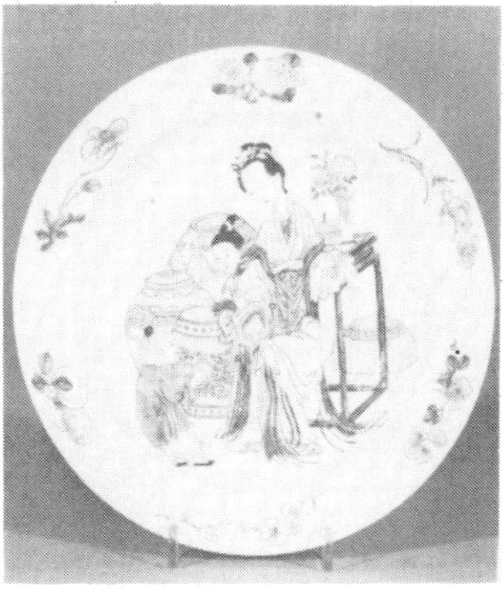

A famille rose rubyback eggshell deep plate, enamelled with an elegant lady leaning on a table beside two children, the border with fruit and flower sprays, the glaze with smoky inclusions, enamels slightly worn, 8¼ in. diam., Yongzheng. **£250-400**

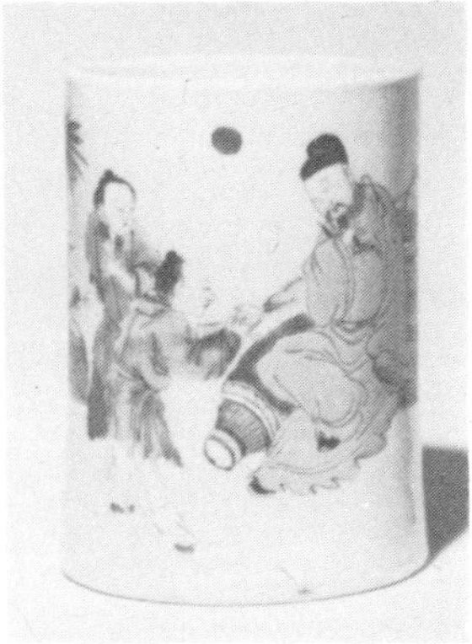

A famille rose brush-pot, painted with two boy servants in attendance on a pink-robed bearded scholar seated beside vats of wine, minor fritting, Yongzheng, 5 in. high. **£400-600**
This design could equally have appeared on famille verte wares of the late Kangxi and early Yongzheng.

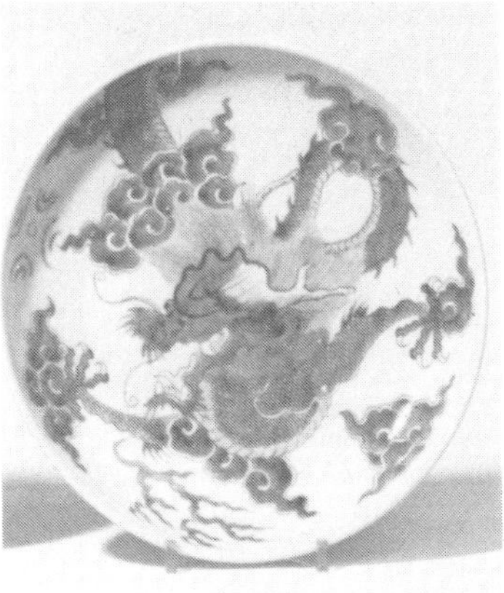

A pair of blue and white saucer dishes, each painted with a fierce four-clawed dragon writhing amongst cloud-scrolls below a moon, rims fritted, incised collector's mark san in each interior, encircled Yongzheng six-character marks and of the period, 10½ in. diam. **£500-700**
This design also occurs on Worcester and Liverpool porcelain of the 1760's.

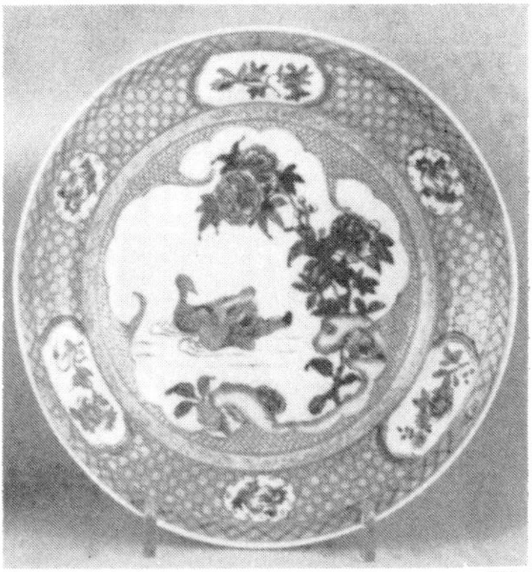

A rubyback style famille rose semi-eggshell porcelain plate, painted with ducks and peonies, 21.5 cm. diam., 19th C. **£150-200**

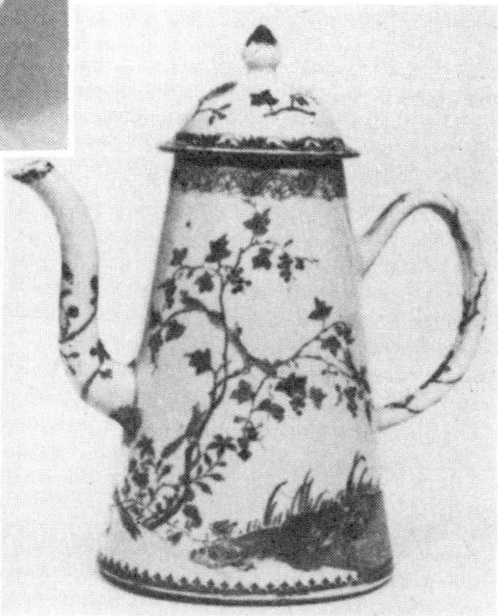

A famille rose chocolate pot and cover, painted with a peacock and a peahen below peony and ducks below squirrels amongst vine between camellia within bands of gilt scrolling foliage and spearheads, cracked and chipped, Yongzheng/early Qianlong, 8¾ in. high. **£140-200**

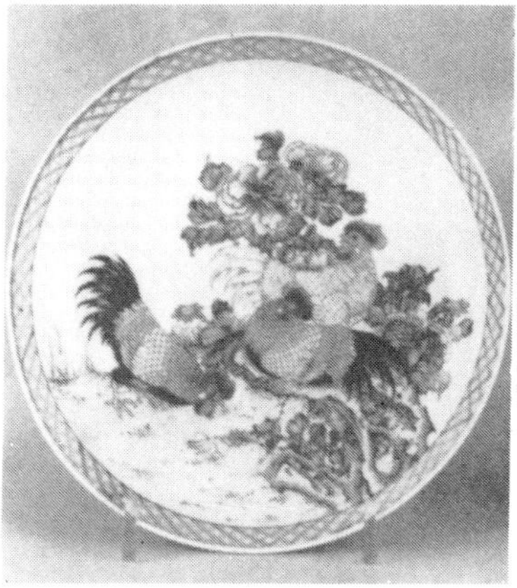

A pair of rubyback famille rose semi-eggshell porcelain dishes, painted with three cockerels, 19.5 cm. diam., Yongzheng/Qianlong. **£2,000-3,000**

A famille rose eggshell porcelain plate, painted with a lady and two boys within three borders painted 'en grisaille' and gold, 20.5 cm. diam., Yongzheng. **£500-800**

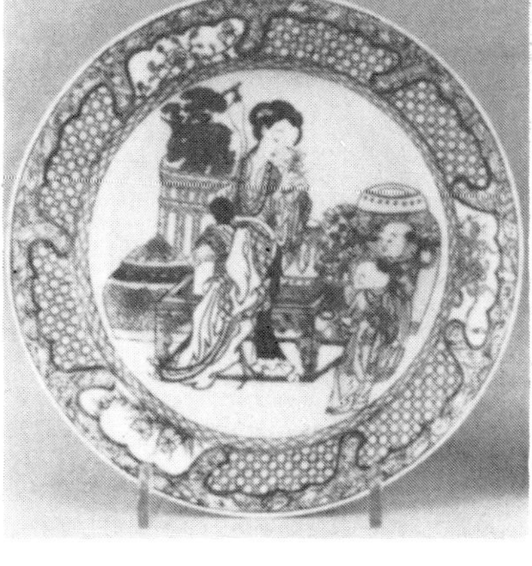

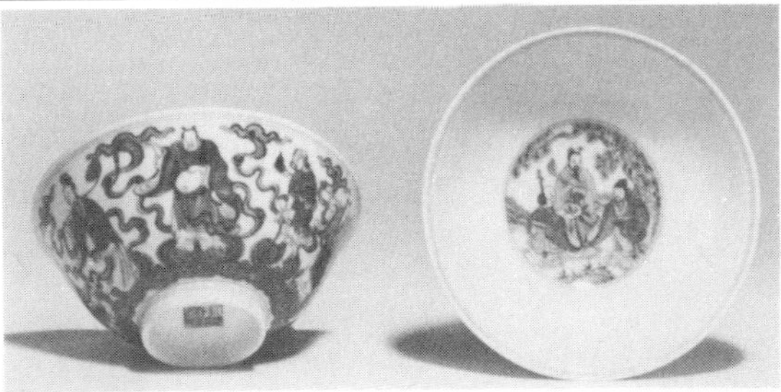

Two blue and white bowls, painted with the eight Daoist Immortals holding their attributes and standing amongst clouds, the interior with Shoulao holding a peach with two companions, one with frit chip, Qianlong six-character seal marks and of the period, 15 cm. diam. **£2,200-2,500**

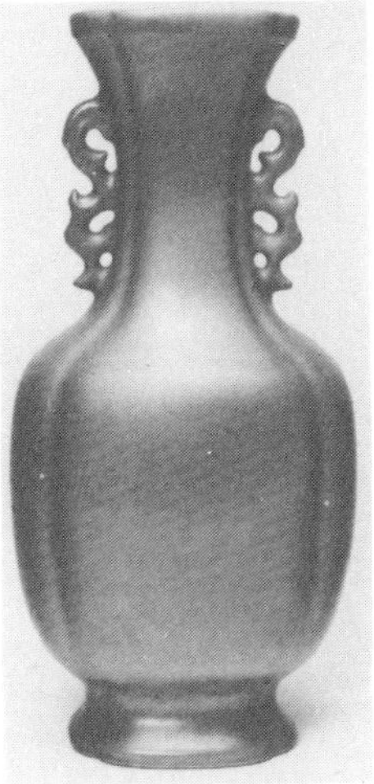

An olive tea-dust glazed vase, moulded with four lobes, set with two pierced dragon scroll handles, covered in an opaque very even olive green glaze, 18th C., 31 cm. high. **£600-1,000**

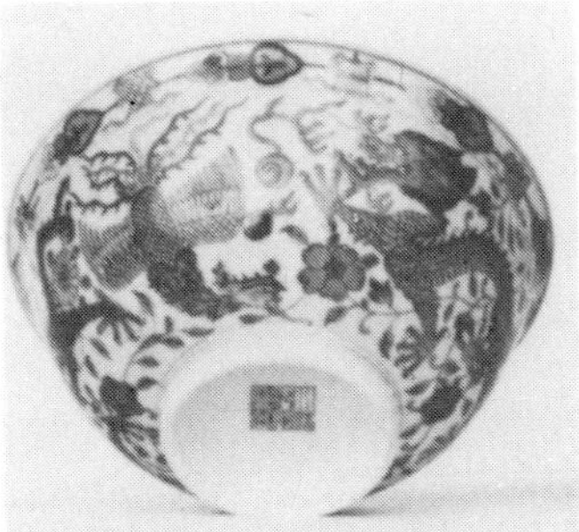

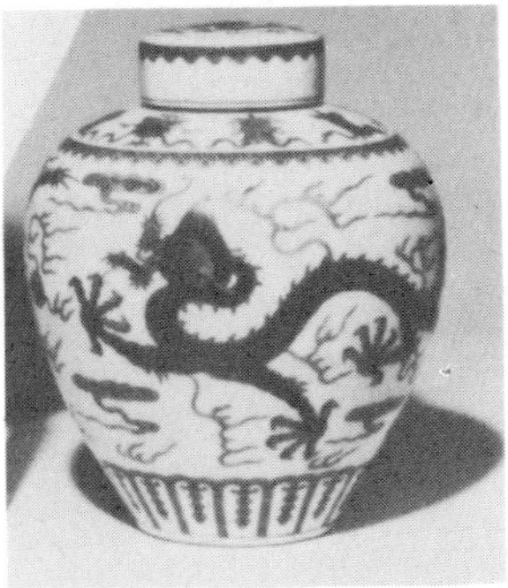

A 'Green Dragon' jar and cover, painted in green enamel outlined in underglaze-blue with two five-clawed dragons pursuing flaming pearls below a band of the eight Buddhist emblems, the neck restored, cover repaired, Qianlong six-character seal mark and of the period, 8¼ in. high. **£600-800**

A pair of polychrome bowls, each decorated with a five-clawed dragon pursuing a flaming pearl, at the centre of the interior, two similar dragons amongst chrysanthemums and peach divided by phoenix descending in flight below a band of the eight Buddhist emblems on the exterior, restored, Qianlong six-character seal marks and of the period, 5¾ in. diam. **£500-700**
If perfect £3,000-4,000.
Dragon and phoenix bowls have appeared in every reign from Kangxi through to Guangxu.

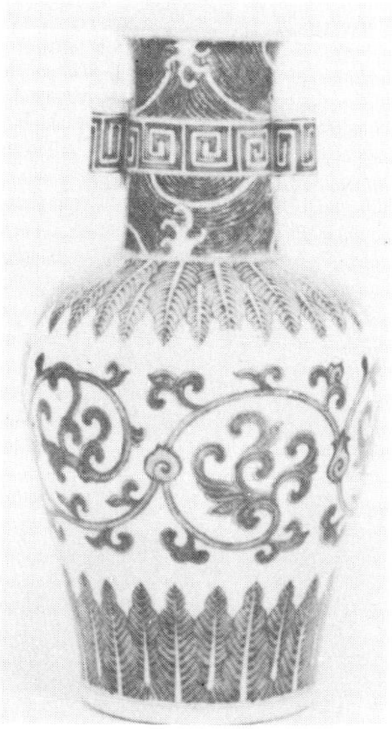

A Ming style blue and white arrow vase, painted in the mid 15th C. manner, with two vertical lug handles, everted rim, 19 cm. high, wood stand, fitted box, Qianlong seal mark and of the period. **£1,750-2,500**

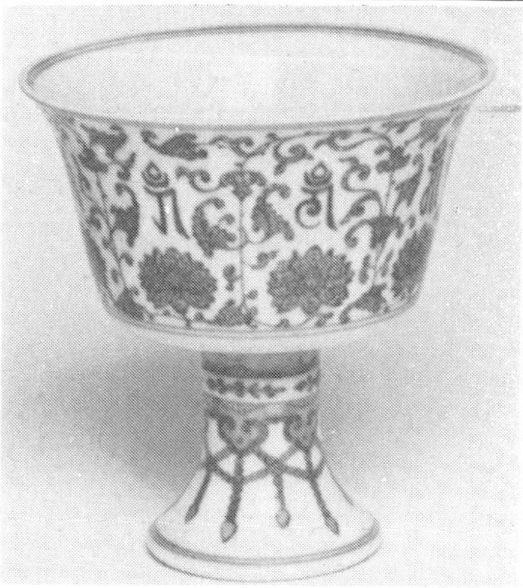

A blue and white stem cup, painted in the Tibetan taste with single characters within panels formed of leafy lotus head, rim slightly polished, 11 cm. high, Qianlong six-character mark and of the period. **£800-1,200**

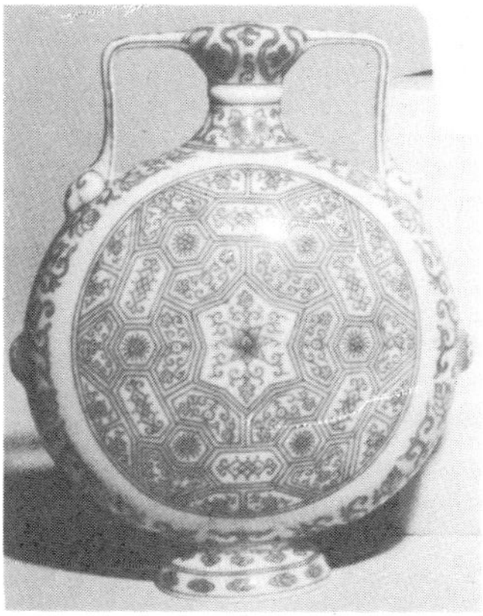

A red and white pilgrim bottle, painted in overglaze enamel after the early 15th C. style, the squared handles with ruyi lappets at their junctions with the shoulder, minor foot restoration, Qianlong six-character seal mark and of the period, in a fitted box, 17.5 cm. high. **£6,600-9,000**

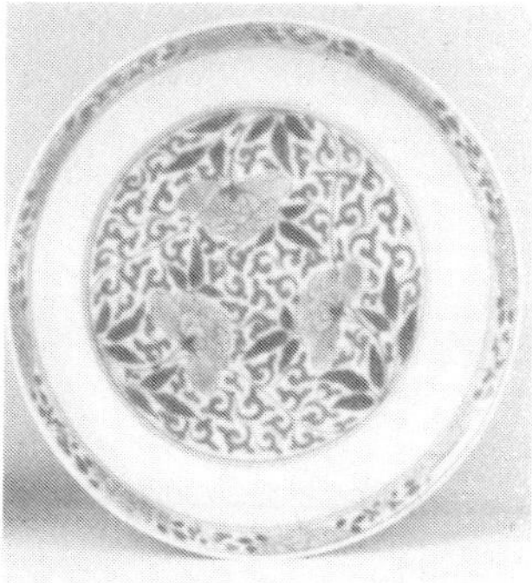

Two blue and white saucer dishes, each painted with three peony heads on a triangular meander amongst dense foliage within a plain white well and a border of narrower similar foliage at the rim of the interior, with four similar flowers on the exterior, one minutely fritted, Qianlong six-character seal marks and of the period, 5¼ in. diam. **£500-600**
An ancestral design repeated throughout the Qing dynasty.

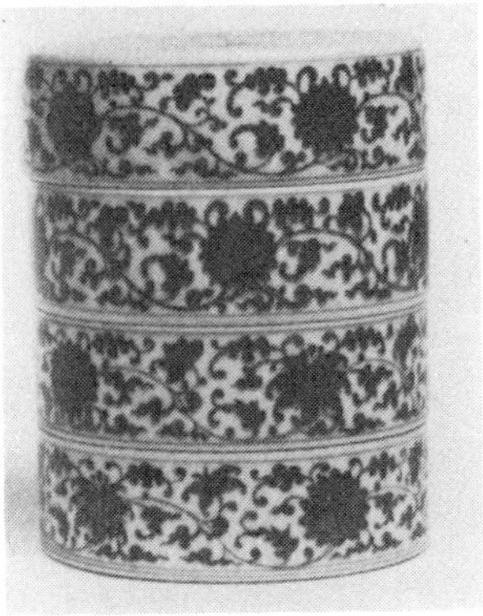

A blue and white three-tiered cylindrical box and cover, painted with peony, chrysanthemum and hibiscus on scrolling foliage, slightly chipped, encircled Xuande four-character mark, 18th C., 7 in. high. **£450-640**
Based upon, but slightly tighter than, the decoration on early 15th century porcelain.

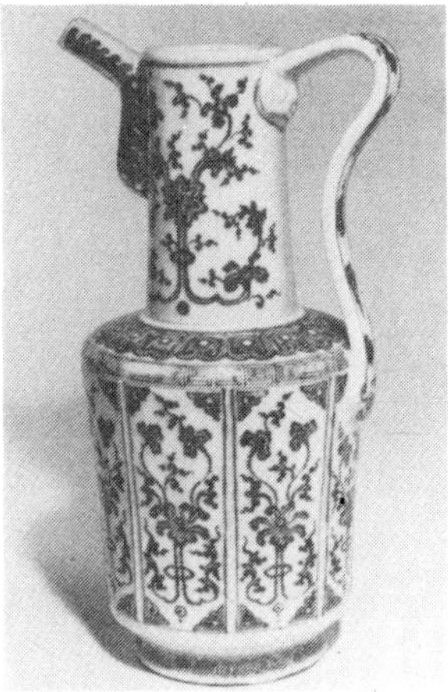

A blue and white tapering cylindrical ewer, with bowed loop strap handle, painted with formal foliage divided by bands of lappets and key-pattern, the spout made up, 18th C., 35 cm. **£800-1,000**
See Ming section (p. 13) for jug of similar Islamic form.

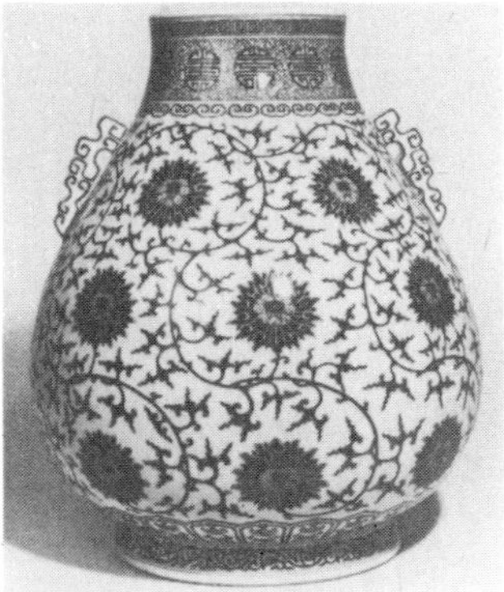

A large blue and white vase, with key-pattern bracket handles, painted with scrolling lotus, the flower-heads forming three horizontal rows above a band of floral lappets, the shoulder with interlocking ruyi lappets, and the neck with twelve shou medallions, Qianlong six-character seal mark and of the period, with wooden box and wooden stand, 45.5 cm. high. **£7,000-10,000**

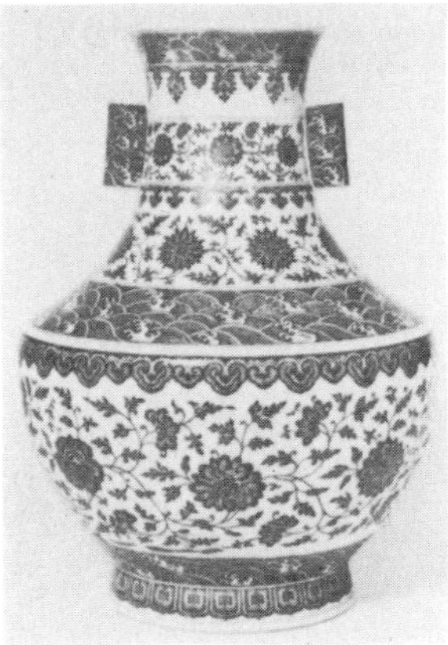

A Ming style blue and white bottle vase, decorated with bands of loose scrolling flowering peony between bands of lappets, breaking waves and flower scrolls, the tubular handles with waves, the neck restored, 20 in. high, Qianlong seal mark and of the period. **£1,250-2,000**

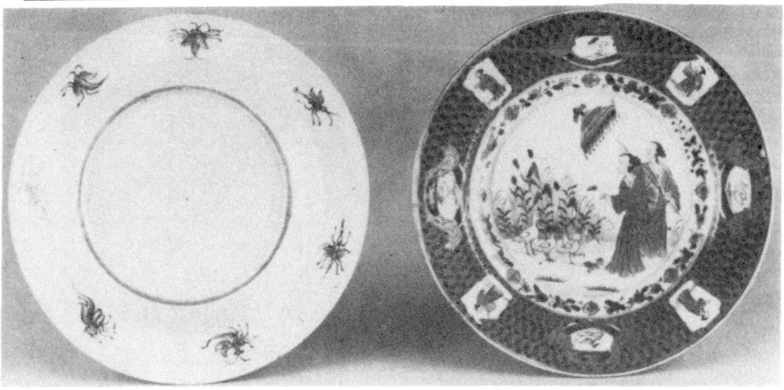

A pair of Chinese Imari Cornelis Pronck plates, 23.5 cm. diam., mid 18th C. **£800-1,200**

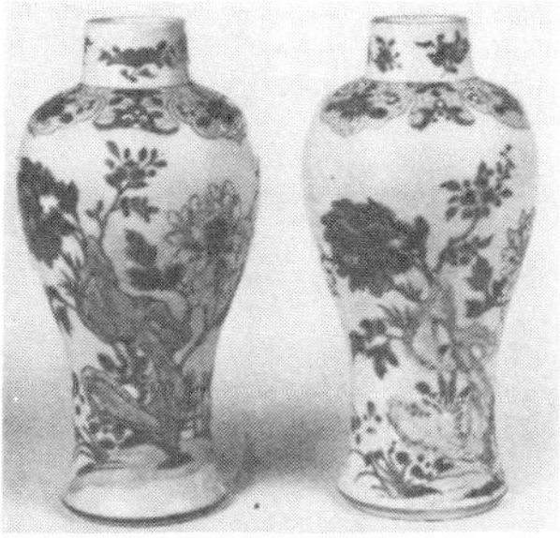

A pair of famille rose baluster vases, painted with peony and peach issuing from a rocky terrace below formal foliage in pale green lappets on the shoulders, one with minor base underside chips, Qianlong, 8¾ in. high. **£300-350**

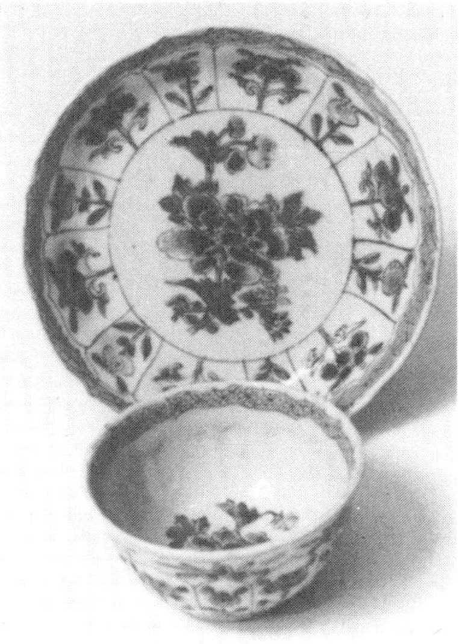

A famille rose teabowl and saucer, of average quality, c. 1765. **£60-68**

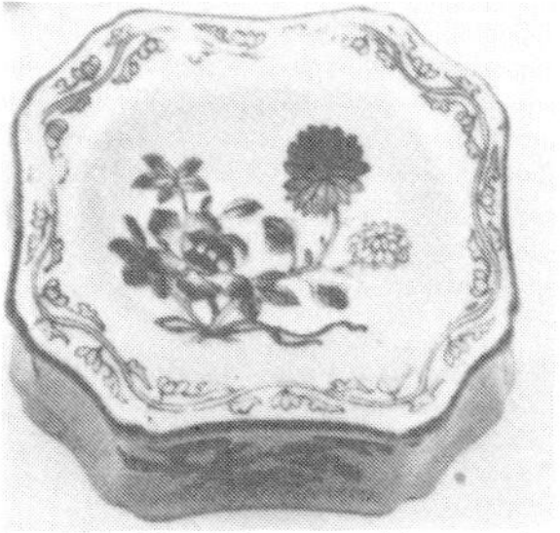

A pair of famille rose oblong octagonal salts, painted with peony and chrysanthemum sprays within bands of iron-red and gilt scrolling foliage, one chipped, Qianlong, 3 in. wide. **£150-250**

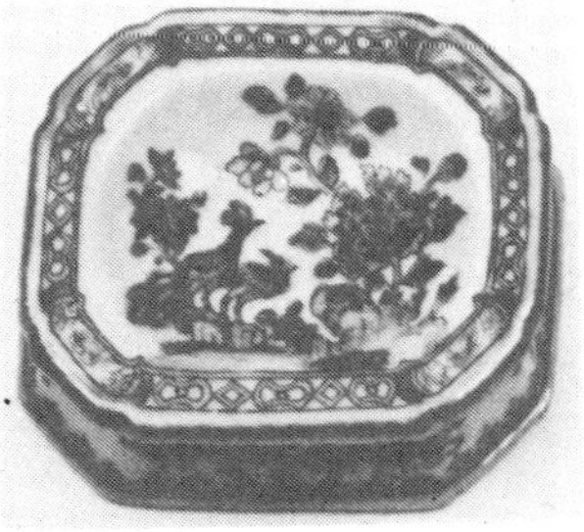

A pair of famille rose oblong octagonal salts, each painted with a pair of pheasants below peony issuing from rockwork within a band of iron-red and gilt chain-pattern, Qianlong, 3 in. wide. **£350-450**

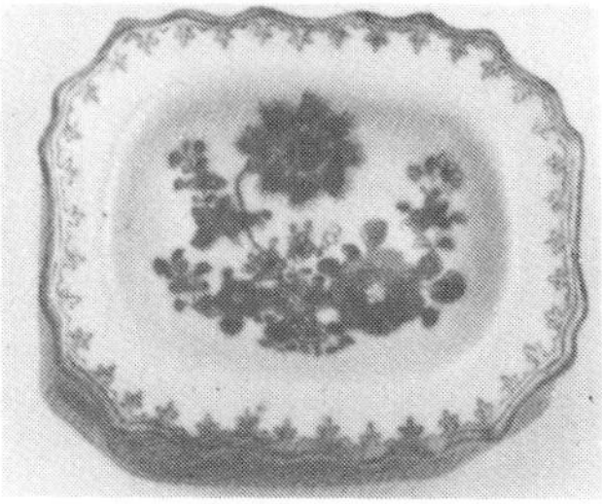

A pair of famille rose oblong octagonal salts, painted with a bouquet below spearheads at the foliate rim, one chipped, Qianlong, 3 in. wide. **£180-220**

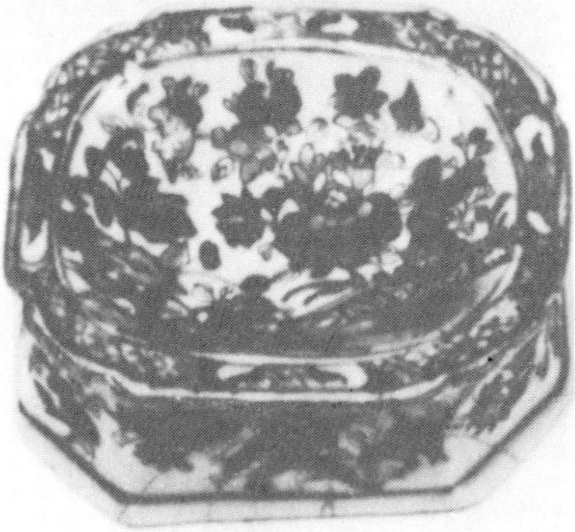

A pair of Chinese Imari oblong octagonal salts, painted with peony, pomegranate and daisy issuing from a rocky terrace, chipped, early 18th C., 3¼ in. wide. **£150-200**

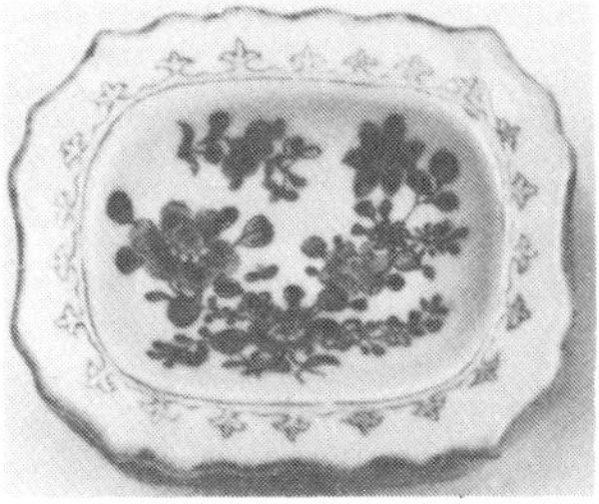

A pair of famille rose oblong octagonal salts, painted with flower sprays below spearheads at the foliate rim, Qianlong, 3¼ in. wide. **£250-350**

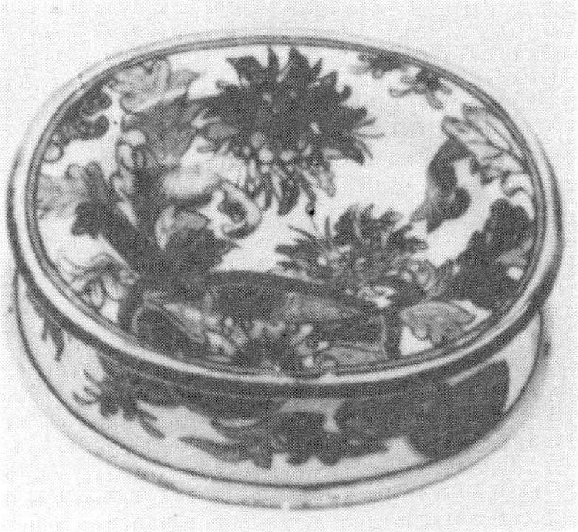

A pair of famille rose 'pseudo tobacco-leaf' oval salts, each painted with broad overlapping leaves and a mon, one chipped, Qianlong, 3 in. wide. **£300-400**

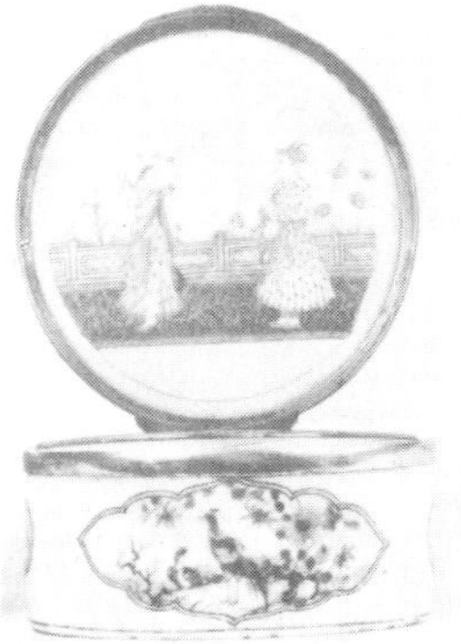

A famille rose snuff-box and cover, painted in the Mughal miniature style, the top of the cover with two noblemen, the interior of the cover with a female dancer performing before an elderly prince, the sides with alternate quatrefoil cartouches of birds and puce landscapes and the base with an openwork basket of flowers, fritted, Qianlong, mounted and hinged in silver metal, 3½ in. diam. **£900-1,200**

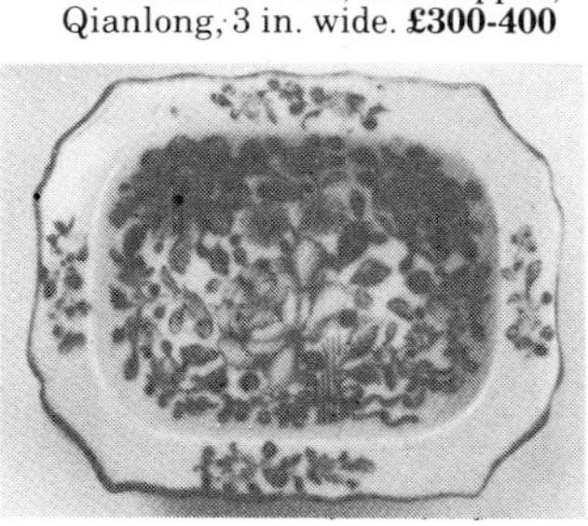

A pair of famille rose oblong octagonal salts, painted with rose sprays, the sides with floral cartouches, reserved puce cell and trellis-pattern, one chipped, Qianlong, 3¼ in. wide. **£200-250**

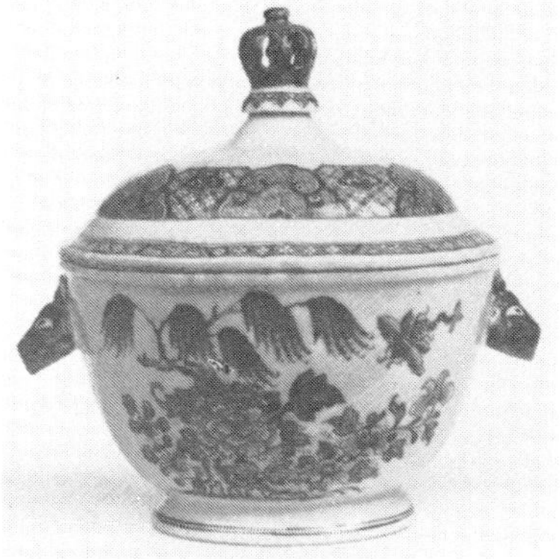

A blue and white shaped oval tureen and cover, with hare-head handles and coronet finial, painted with insects in flight beside willow and peony, the finial repaired, Qianlong, 13½ in. wide. **£250-350**

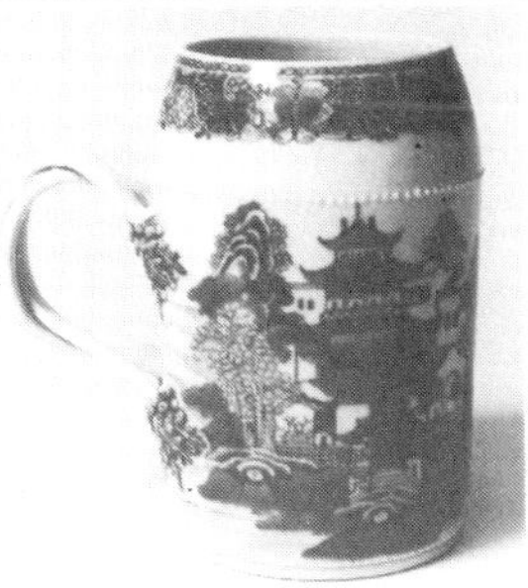

A Chinese Nankin blue and white tankard, of rare shape, c. 1785, 6½ in. high. **£130-150**
Note the complex multi-diaper border characteristic of the late Qianlong period. Very similar riverscapes also appeared on contemporary Caughley and Worcester porcelain.

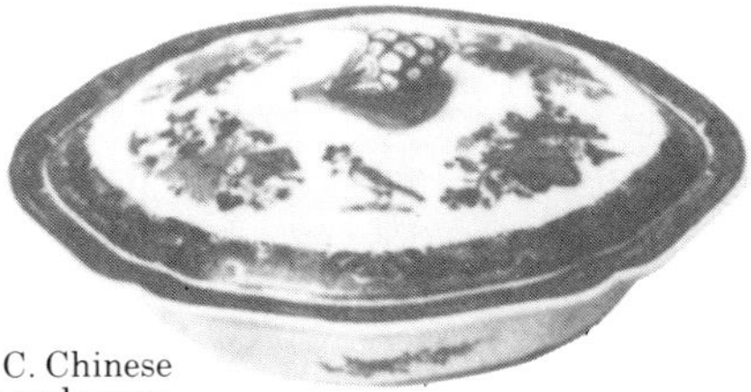

An early 19th C. Chinese vegetable dish and cover, decorated in underglaze blue, 11 in., c. 1800. **£200-250**
The design is a variation on one ordered by Thomas Fitzhugh, a Director of the East India Company in about 1780.

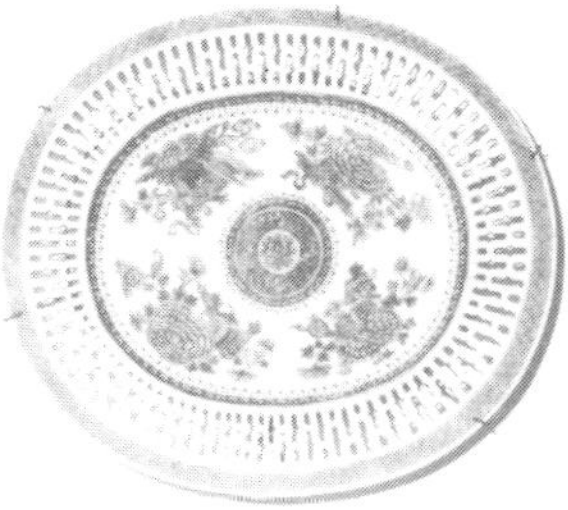

A Chinese export blue and white 'Fitzhugh' pattern basketwork plate, 9 in., c. 1790. **£38-48**

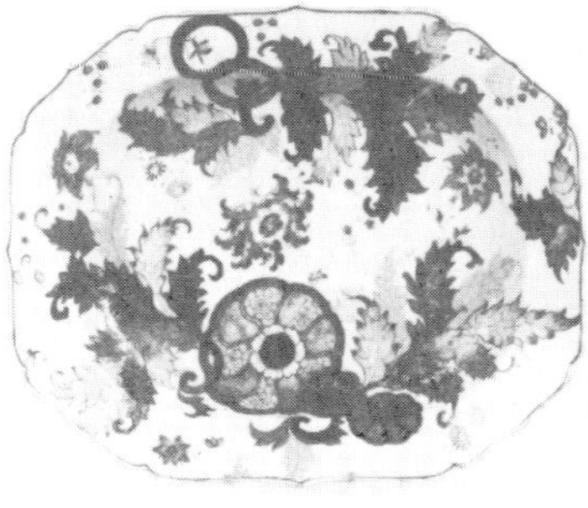

A famille rose 'pseudo tobacco-leaf' oblong octafoil tureen stand, painted with broad overlapping serrated leaves entwined with rings and mons, chipped, Qianlong, 14½ in. wide. **£700-£900**

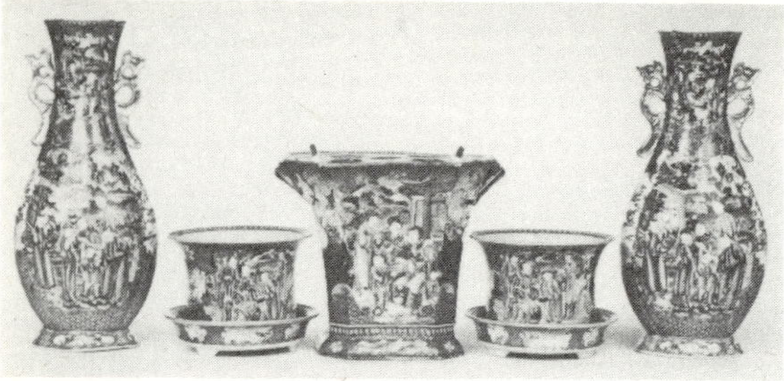

A famille rose garniture, painted with figures at leisure and with hawks and fighting cockerels, divided by bird vignettes within surrounds of iron-red grisaille and gilt Y-pattern, comprising a pair of pear-shaped vases with gilt dragon handles, 11½ in. high, a pair of jardinières and stands, 5½ in. diam., and a tulip vase and cover, 8½ in. wide, with some restoration, late Qianlong. **£600-900**

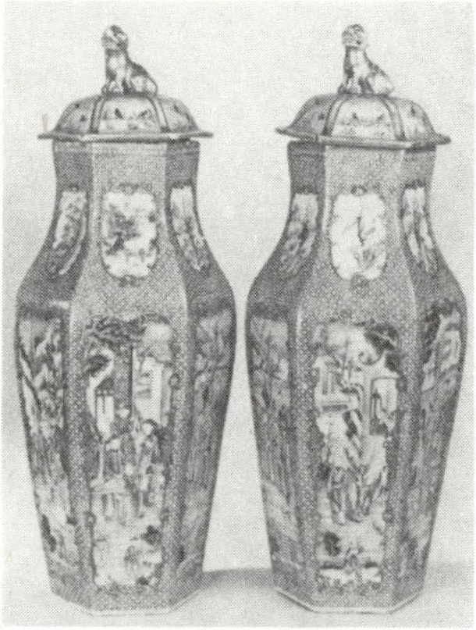

A pair of famille rose hexagonal vases and covers, with gilt seated Buddhist lion finials, painted with panels of figures at leisure, hawking, with cockerels, dogs and water-buffaloes, with surrounds of iron-red and grisaille floral cell-pattern, with some damage, 21½ in. high, Qianlong. **£500-800**

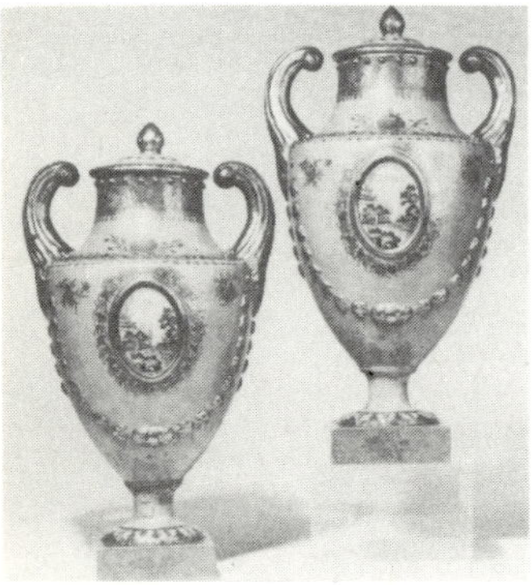

A pair of export urn-shaped vases and domed covers, each painted in iron-red, sepia and gilt, neck cracks, one with cover and foot restored, Jiaqing, c. 1800, 16¼ in. high. **£1,400-£1,800**

Though this shape is traditionally considered to be taken from a Marieburg original, it has been suggested the Chinese version was taken from a Wedgwood model.

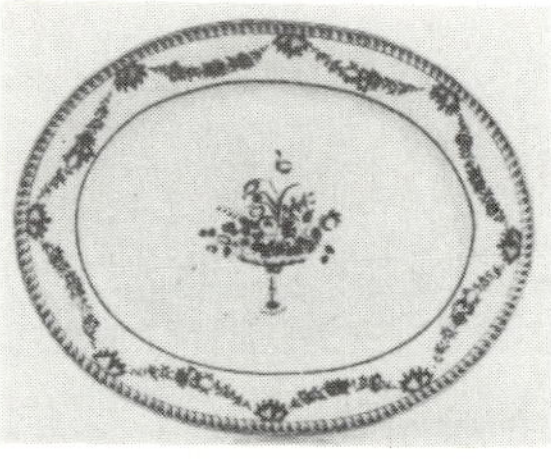

A pair of famille rose dishes, each painted with a central bouquet issuing from a grisaille tazza, with a puce rope-pattern at the rim, chipped, Qianlong, 14½ in. wide. **£500-600**

A typical neo-classical design imported from Europe.

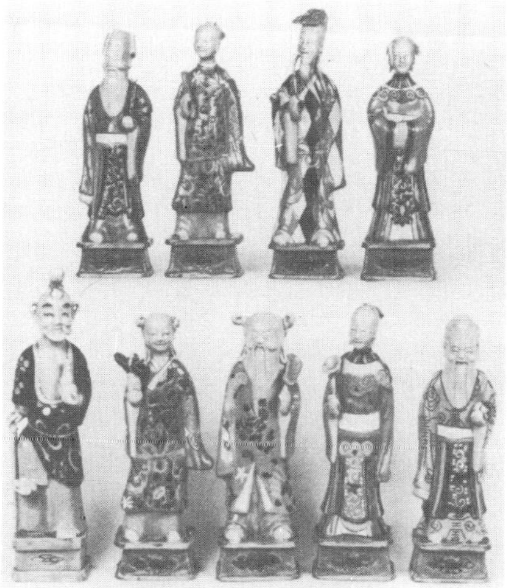

A set of nine famille rose figures of the eight Immortals and Shoulao, wearing harlequin robes, floral tunics, ceremonial aprons and striped skirts, each holding his attribute, three chipped, one repaired, four with some restoration, Qianlong, the tallest 9¼ in. high. **£2,500-£3,500**

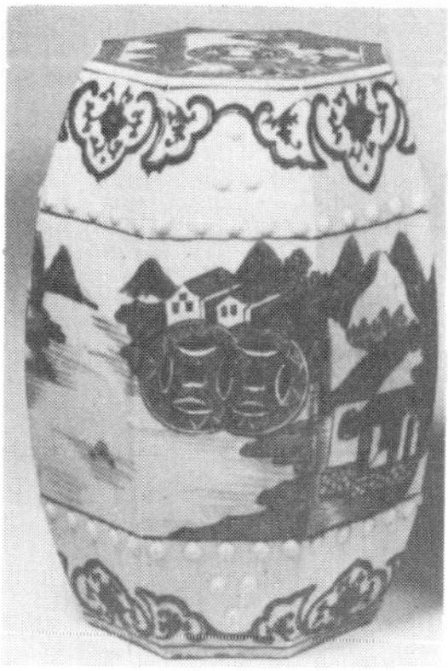

A pair of blue and white octagonal garden seats, one with minor damage, Qianlong, 19 in. high. **£1,500-1,700**

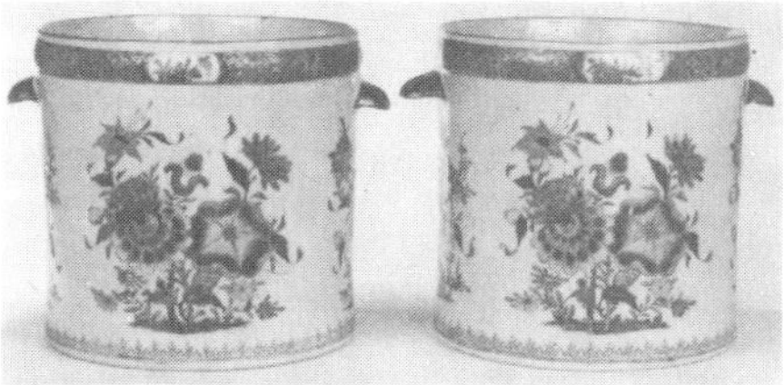

A pair of famille rose jardinières, chipped, one handle replaced, Yongzheng/early Qianlong, 10¼ in. wide. **£1,700-1,900**
Purely European form.

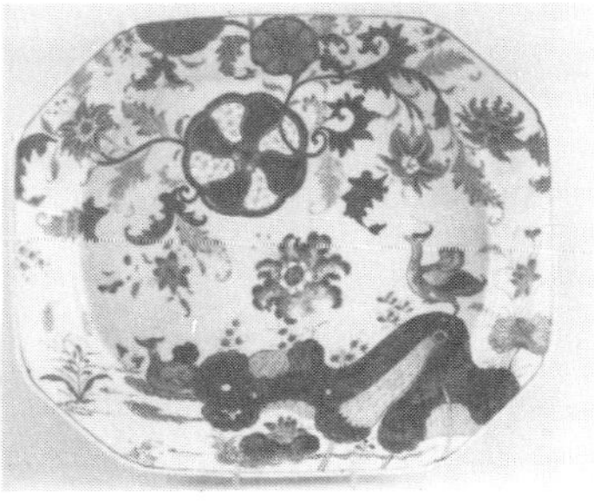

An oblong octagonal dish, painted with mandarin ducks and rosettes issuing flowering branches, Qianlong, 41 cm. long. **£300-500**

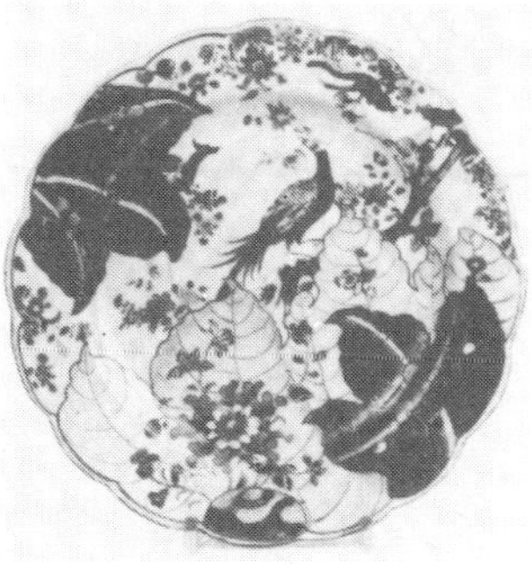

A pair of famille rose 'tobacco-leaf' foliate plates, each painted with a pair of pheasants below two squirrels amongst vine at the rim, fritted, one cracked, Qianlong, 9¼ in. diam. **£350-400**

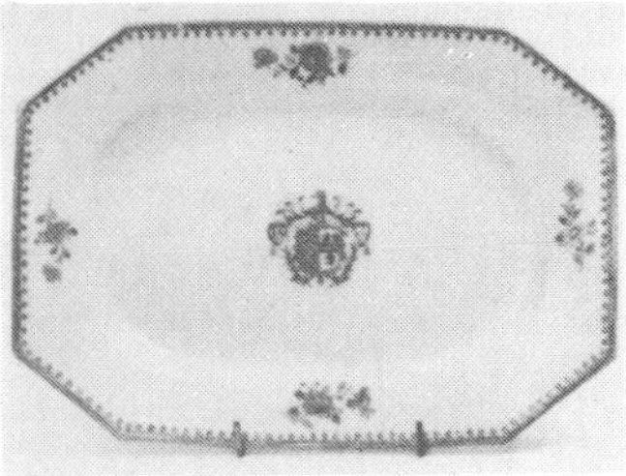

A pair of armorial dishes, painted in famille rose enamels with the Arms of Byam impaling Nichols, within a gilt border, Qianlong, 26 cm. wide. **£330-360**
The restrained decoration shows the influence of neo-classicism on exportware of the 1770's.

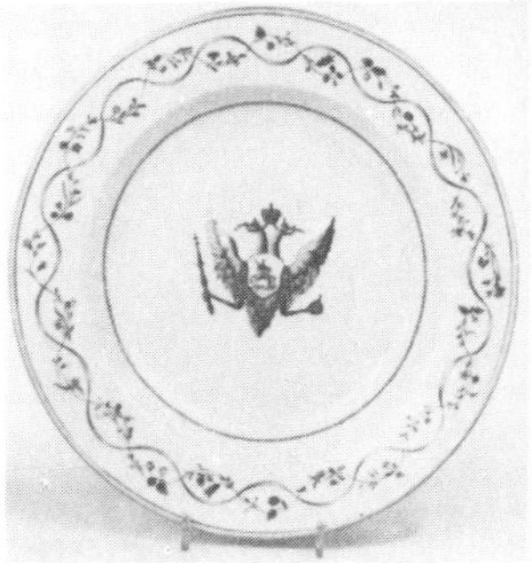

A pair of famille rose armorial soup-plates, each painted in sepia with a central coat-of-arms and crest below a band of rope pattern at the well and wavy ribbon intertwined with a floral garland at the border, 8¾ in. diam., c. 1785. **£450-600**
The arms are those of Russia. This is part of the second service made for Catherine II (The Great), which was probably ordered through the English East India Company.

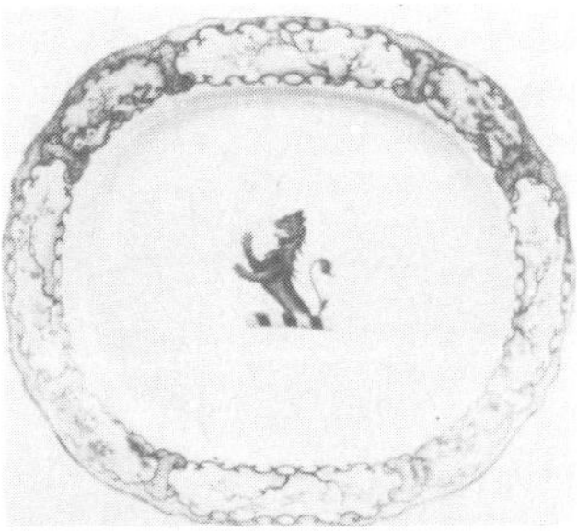

An armorial oblong octafoil dish, painted with a central crest below alternate cartouches of birds upon branches and sepia landscapes, reserved upon a gilt scrolling foliage ground, Qianlong, 16½ in. wide. **£400-£450**
The crest is that of Freeman.

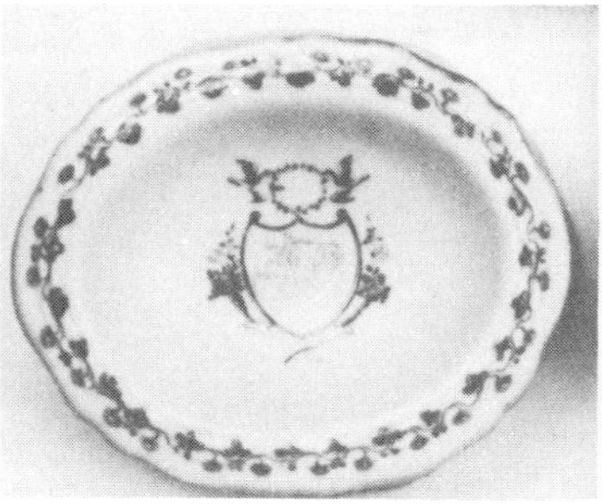

A pair of famille rose oval foliate salts, each painted with the initials 'JPL' on a shield supported by cornucopiae below birds carrying a garland within a floral wreath, one minutely fritted, Qianlong, 3½ in. wide. **£240-300**

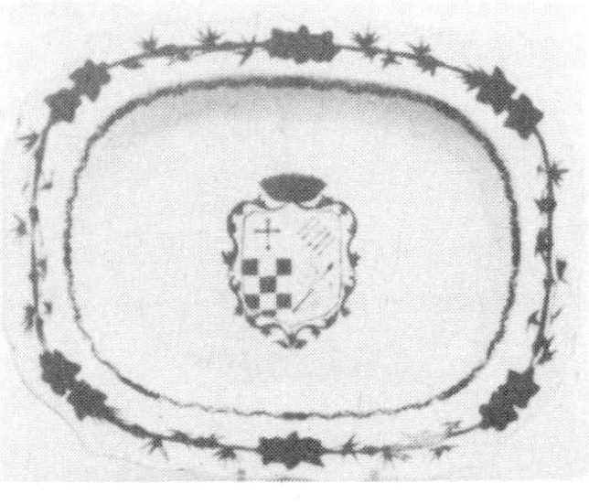

An armorial oblong octagonal tureen stand, painted in green enamel with a central coat-of-arms and coronet, chipped, Qianlong, 13½ in. wide. **£600-£700**
The arms are those of João Luiz de Mello.

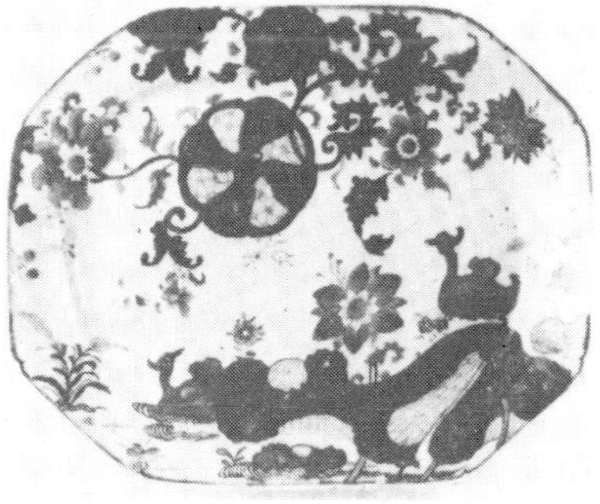

A famille rose 'tobacco-leaf' oblong octagonal dish, painted with two ducks beside lotus above rippling water below interlocking flower-heads and exotic foliage, minor frit chips, Qianlong, 14¾ in. wide. **£500-£600**

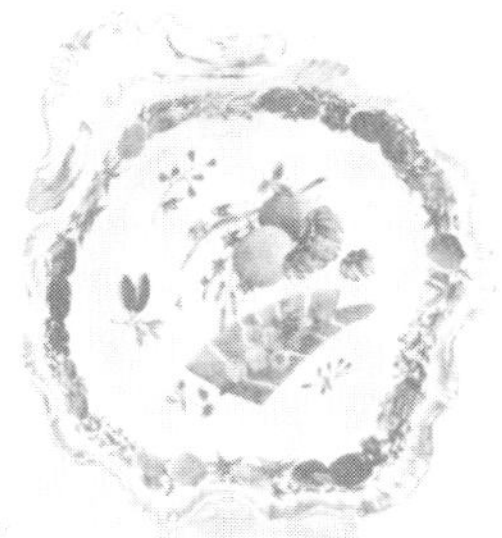

A pair of famille rose tripod shell-shaped dishes, painted with insects, peach, berries and pods within borders of similar fruit and foliage below gilt rims and pierced floral handles, minor fritting, Jiaqing, 9 in. wide. **£600-700**

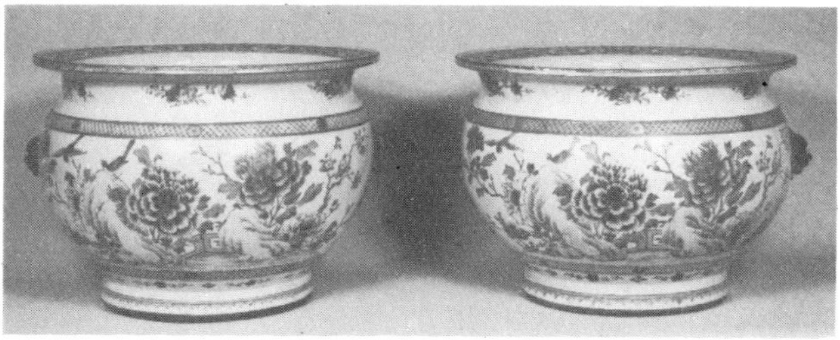

A pair of famille rose fish bowls, enamelled with large clumps of peony on a terrace and birds around outcrops of rock, with lion mask handles, the interior with five swimming carp amongst aquatic plants, handle surfaces worn, one small rim crack, Yongzheng/early Qianlong, 59 cm. diam., on high five legged pierced hardwood stands, overall height 95.5 cm. **£10,000-15,000**

Make the most of Millers...

Remember that this book is a price *guide,* not a price *list.* Valuations given throughout apply to the specific prices shown and, though they may reasonably be taken as a guide to the values of other similar articles, other factors may also apply.
Condition of any article is of the utmost importance and must always be taken into account when negotiating the sale of any antique.

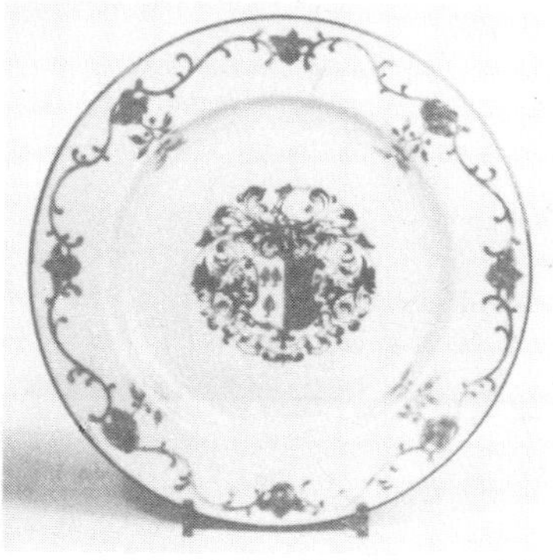

A set of six famille rose armorial plates, each painted with a large central coat-of-arms and crest below gilt berries descending from formal leaves supported by scrolling stems, four chipped, one cracked, Qianlong, c. 1750, 9 in. diam. The arms are those of Foulis impaling Jones. **£1,000-£1,200**
The uncluttered aspect with the attenuated almost cursive foliage is typical of earlier Qianlong.

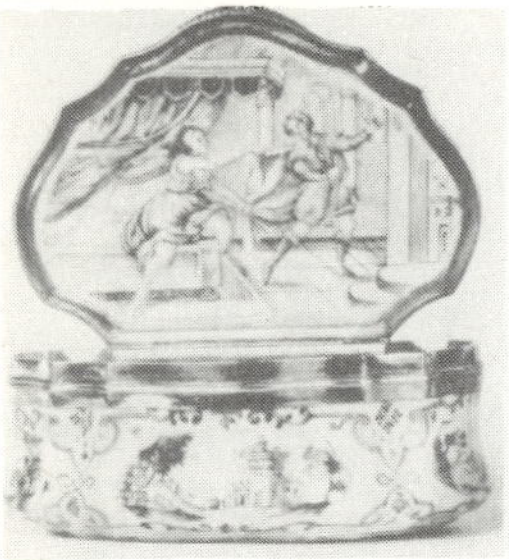

A famille rose shaped snuff-box and cover, painted after a Nuremberg enamel original with Biblical scenes, Qianlong, mounted and hinged in gilt-metal, 4 in. wide. **£2,500-3,000**

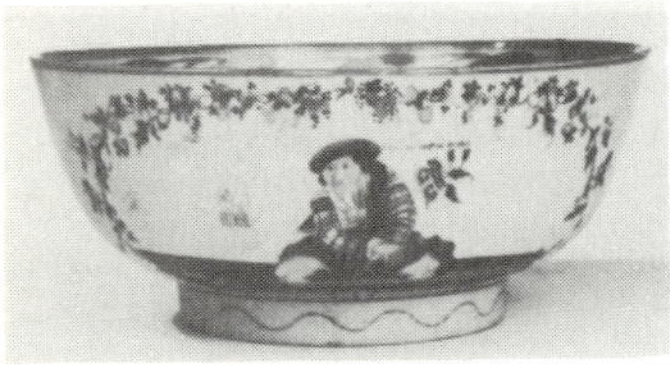

A famille rose punch bowl, painted with a kilted Scotsman seated on a commode below an inscription, a poster at his rear, with a long inscription on the exterior, restored, Qianlong, 11½ in. diam. **£500-600**
The first inscription reads 'Nemo me impune lacesit'. The poster reads 'O sawn oy why leaven thou thy nany to moan'. The long inscription reads 'Sauneys mistake dividing When first to the South sly Sauney came forth. He was sheun to a place quite unknown in the North; and That he is mistaken, you soon will explore, Yet he sold thes and S—s as no man did before. London, Published by Jn. Smith, No. 35 Cheapsate Robt. Sayer & Jn. Bennett No. 53 Fleet Street, as the Act directs 11 Sepr 1730' (sic).
This bowl satirizes the Scotsmen who drifted to London in the wake of the Jacobite Rebellion of 1745. They are represented by the character 'Sly Sauney' who, in his ignorance, is seated upon a double commode with one leg in each bowl.

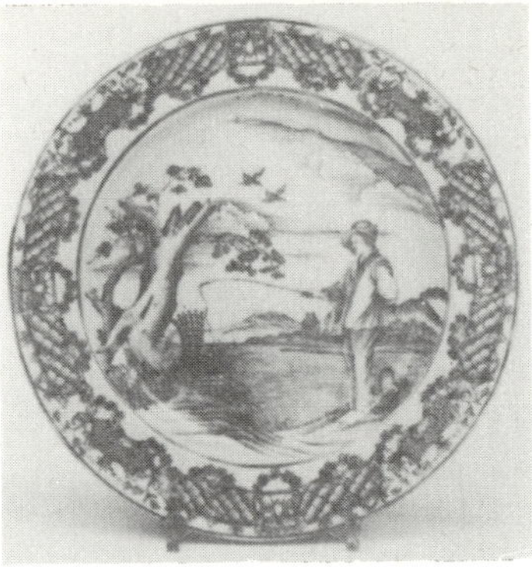

A famille rose plate, painted en camaieu after 'Le Pecheur', a drawing by Abraham Bloemaert, depicting a bare-footed boy, a basket at his feet, on a river bank holding a fishing rod, the border with four peacocks at the compass points, the rim slightly reduced, Qianlong, c. 1750, 9 in. diam. **£400-600**

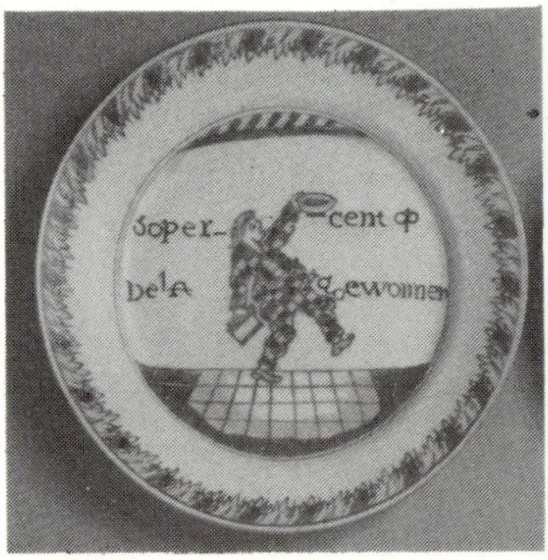

A Doucai Commedia dell'Arte plate, for the Dutch market, painted with harlequin dancing on a tiled stage between the inscription '50 percent op Delft gewonnen' minutely chipped, Kangxi/Yongzheng, c. 1722, 8¼ in. diam. **£1,800-2,200**
The inscription may be translated as 'Fifty per cent profit on Delft'. This plate belongs to a series of six, four more of which follow, that was known as 'Het Grote Tafereel de Dusaasheid' (The Great Scene of Folly). It utilised the satirical medium of the Commedia dell'Arte to warn the Dutch public about the dangers of speculation in John Law's 'Company of the Indies' and in the London South Sea Company.

An armorial plate, painted in famille rose enamels and gilding, decorated with the arms of Mordaunt, Qianlong, 23 cm. diam. **£200-250**

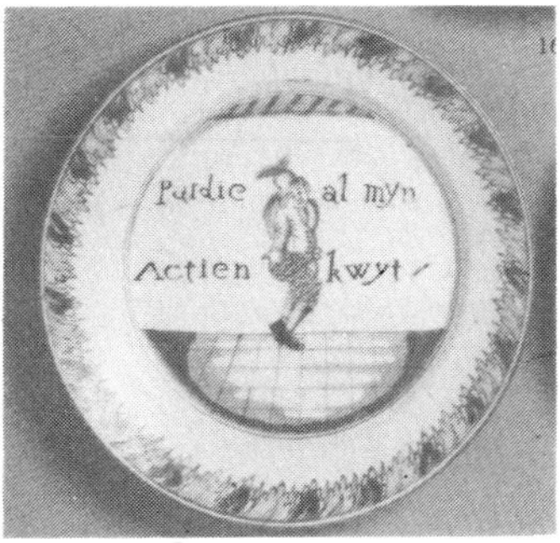

A Doucai Commedia dell'Arte plate, painted with a hunch-backed figure standing on a tiled stage, holding his right hand out in despair, between the inscription 'Pardie al myn Actien kwyt', Kangxi/Yongzheng, c. 1722, 8¼ in. diam. **£2,000-£2,400**
The inscription may be translated as 'By God, lost all my shares'.

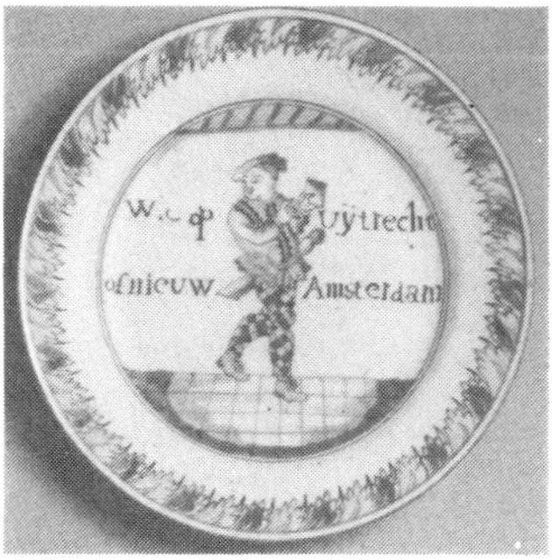

A Doucai Commedia dell'Arte plate, for the Dutch market, painted with a figure standing on a tiled stage, between the inscription 'Wie op Uytrecht of nieuw Amsterdam', minutely chipped, Kangxi/Yongzheng, c. 1722, 8¼ in. diam. **£2,200-£2,500**
The inscription may be translated as 'Who wants to speculate on Utrecht or New Amsterdam'.

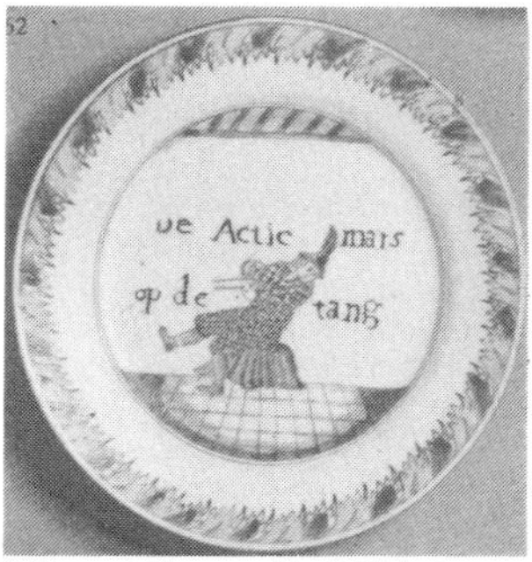

A Doucai Commedia dell'Arte plate for the Dutch market, painted with a figure wearing a chequered jerkin and breeches and feathered cap, between the inscription 'De Actiemars op de tang' (sic) Kangxi/Yongzheng, c. 1722, 8¼ in. diam. **£2,200-£2,600**
The inscription may be translated as 'The march of the share values played on the tuning fork'.

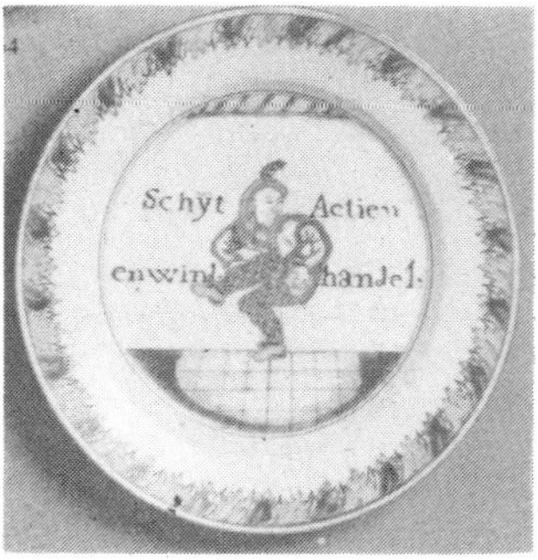

A Doucai Commedia dell'Arte plate, painted with a figure dancing on a tiled stage, between the inscription 'Schyt Actien en windhandel', rim restored, Kangxi/Yongzheng, c. 1722, 8¼ in. diam. **£1,000-1,400**
The inscription may be translated as 'Shares and Swindle'.

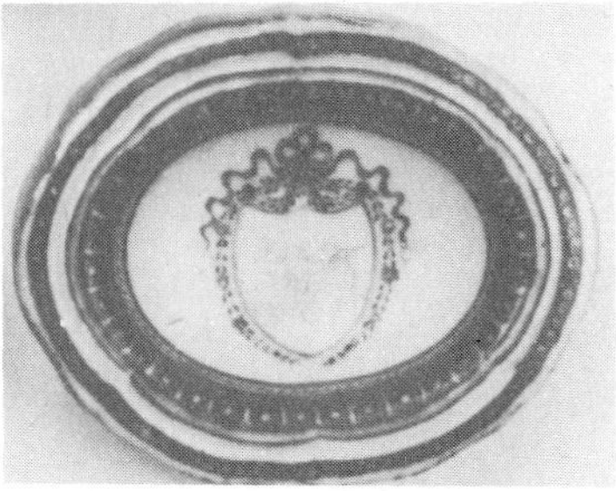

A famille rose armorial oval salt, painted with a coat-of-arms and crest below the motto 'Fit via vi' within underglaze-blue chain-pattern, restored, 3¼ in. wide, an oval foliate salt with the initials 'ALJ' on a floral shield, fritted, both Qianlong, 3½ in. wide. **£300-350**
The arms are those of Campbell of Inverneill.

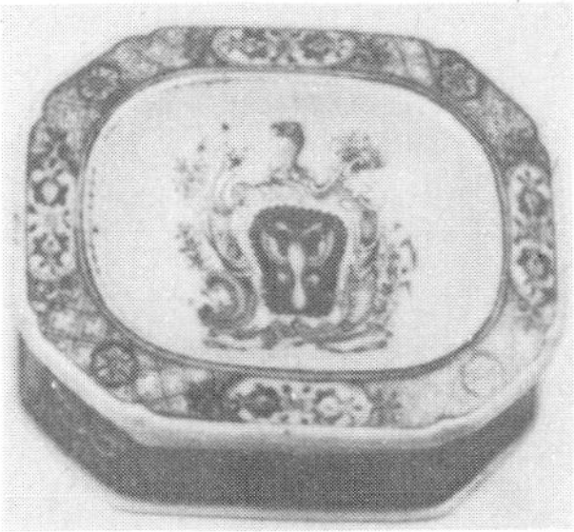

A pair of famille rose armorial oblong octagonal salts, each painted with a coat-of-arms and crest, within a band of underglaze-blue flowers reserved on trellis-pattern above FitzHugh pattern on the foot, fritted, one chipped, Qianlong, 3½ in. wide. **£400-500**
The arms are those of Hoare.

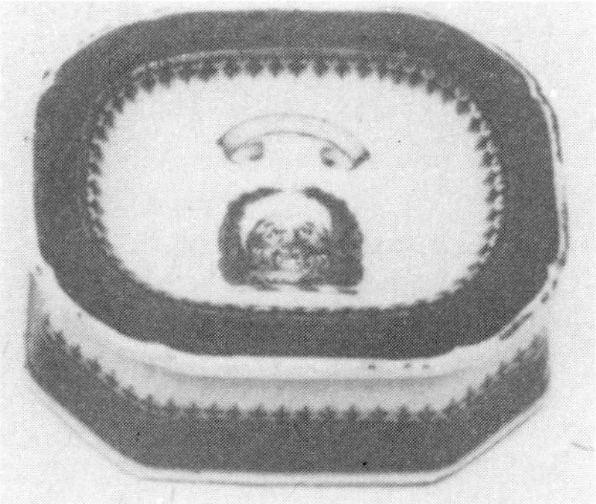

A pair of famille rose armorial oblong octagonal salts, each painted with a crest below the motto 'Essayez' below underglaze-blue trellis-pattern, fritted, Qianlong, 3½ in. wide. **£300-400**
The crest is that of Dundas.

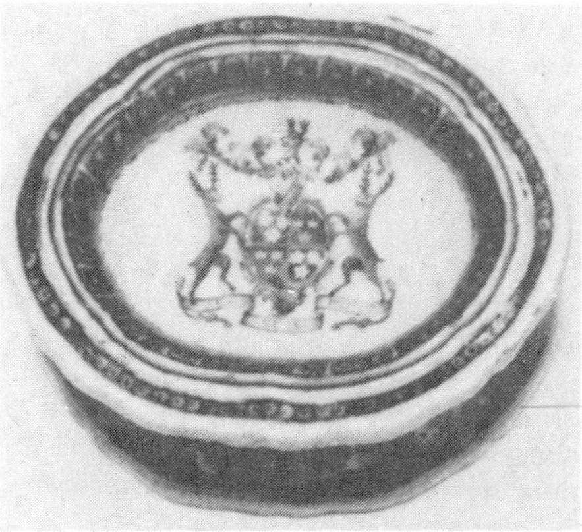

Right
A pair of famille rose armorial oval foliate salts, each painted with a coat-of-arms, helmet, crest, supporters and motto 'Je Suis Prest' within a band of underglaze-blue cell-pattern above FitzHugh-pattern on the foot, fritted, Qianlong, c. 1785, 3½ in. wide. **£400-500**
The arms are those of Fraser.

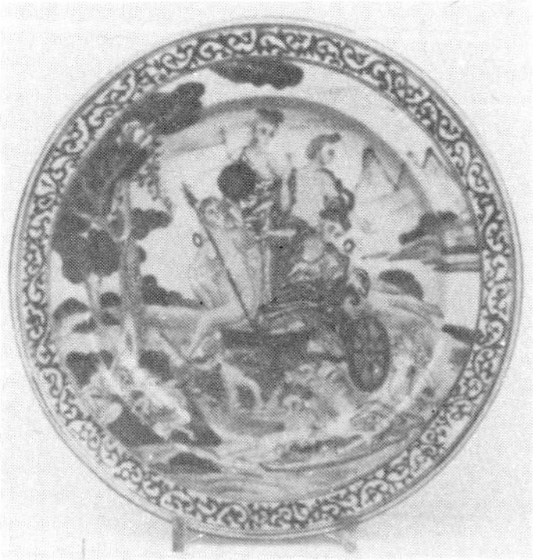

A famille rose shallow soup plate, painted after an allegorical scene by Francesco Albani, depicting four Goddesses reclining on a chariot beside putti, below blue scrolling foliage at the rim, minute frit, Qianlong, c. 1745, 9 in. diam. **£1,000-1,200**
This scene represents 'Earth', one of a series of four engravings symbolising the Four Elements.

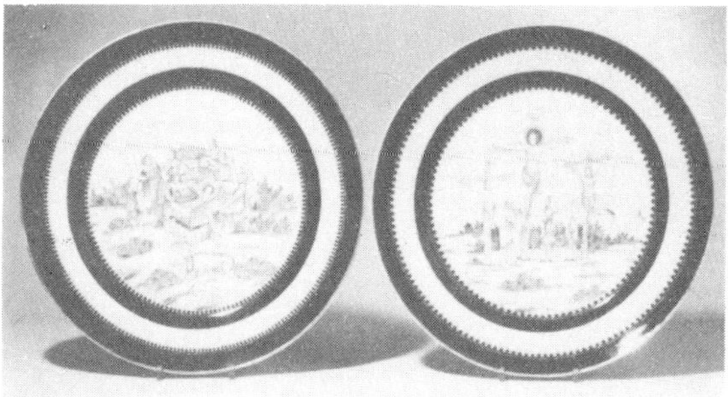

Two blue and white and blue enamel circular dishes, one with a Nativity scene at the centre, the other with the Crucifixion, the haloes enriched in gilt, one cracked and slightly chipped, the porcelain and underglaze-blue Qianlong, the enamelling European and later, 37.5 cm. diam. **£2,500-3,500**

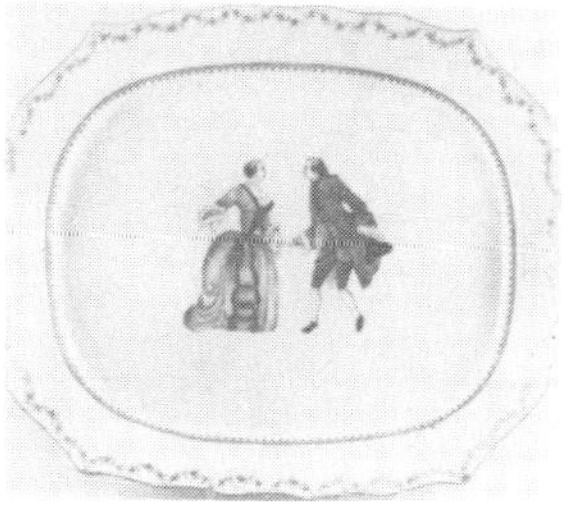

A shaped oblong dish, painted with a European gentleman and a lady, Qianlong, c. 1780, 41 cm. long. **£400-600**

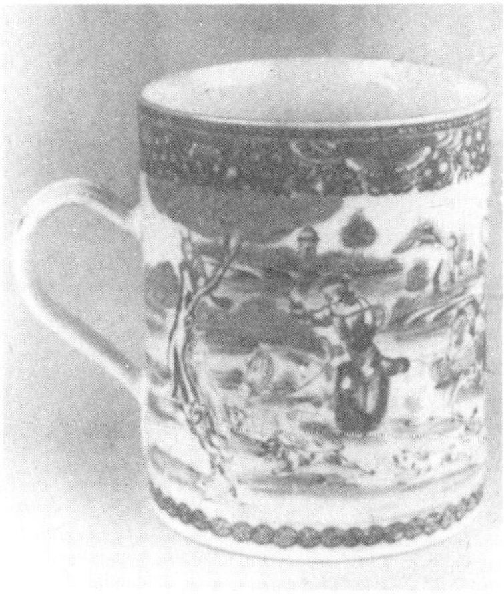

A cylindrical famille rose mug, painted with a fox-hunt, Qianlong, c. 1770, 14.5 cm. high. **£300-400**

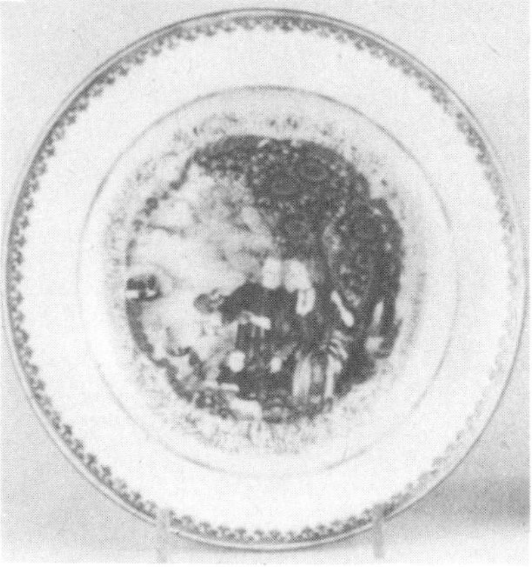

A dish, decorated en grisaille with European figures, mid 18th C., 23 cm. diam. **£400-600**

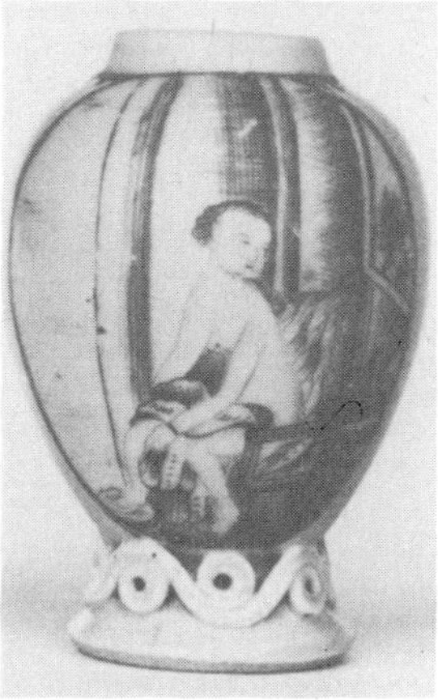

An oviform tea-caddy, painted en grisaille and in sepia with panels of a lady undressing and a scholar looking on, foot cracked, 18th C., 4 in. high. **£100-120**

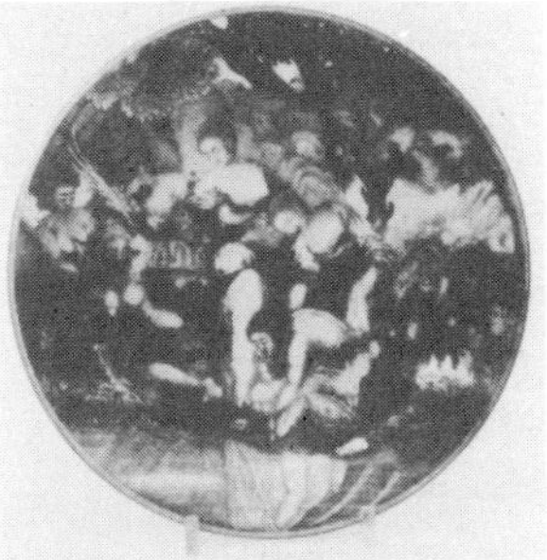

A rare plate, painted en grisaille with Thetis dipping Achilles in the Styx, watched by four other ladies and a servant holding a pan of burning coals below trees on a rocky river-bank, within a plain gilt rim, minutely chipped, Qianlong, c. 1740, 9 in. diam. **£1,800-2,200**

Painted after an engraving by Le Sueur, this design appears on armorial plates made for the French family of Thornidykes and Frenchlands in Berwickshire.

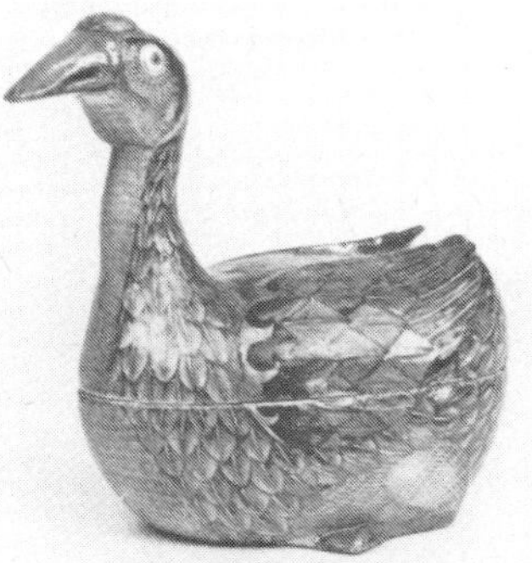

A famille rose sauce tureen, modelled as a duck, vividly painted with multi-coloured feathers and pink underparts, the cover and one foot restored, 7 in. long, Qianlong. **£300-500**

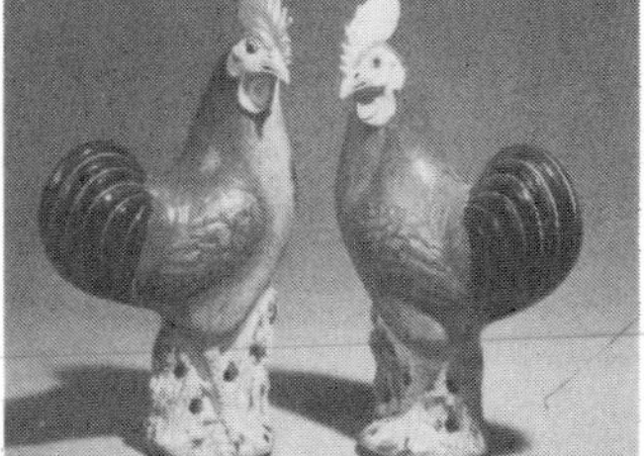

A pair of famille rose figures of cockerels, standing on pierced mottled blue, green and pink rockwork bases, the bodies painted in iron-red and gilt with naturalistic feathers, their tails black, beaks and claws yellow, eyes and ears green, one face and crest reserved in the biscuit, the other under a white glaze, crests chipped, Qianlong, 14 in. high. **£4,000-5,000**

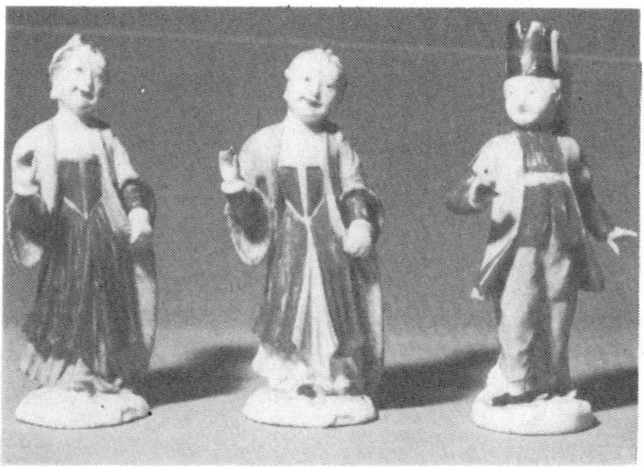

Three famille rose figures of two girls and a boy, after Meissen originals, each girl turned to the left and raising her right hand, palm outwards, the boy turned to the right with his right arm hooked and his left pushed to the rear, painted in green, turquoise, blue, yellow, puce and iron-red, minor restoration, extremities chipped, Qianlong, c. 1760-70. **£2,500-3,000**
These figures in the Turkish dress were inspired by the models of J. J. Kändler and Peter Reinicke of about 1745.

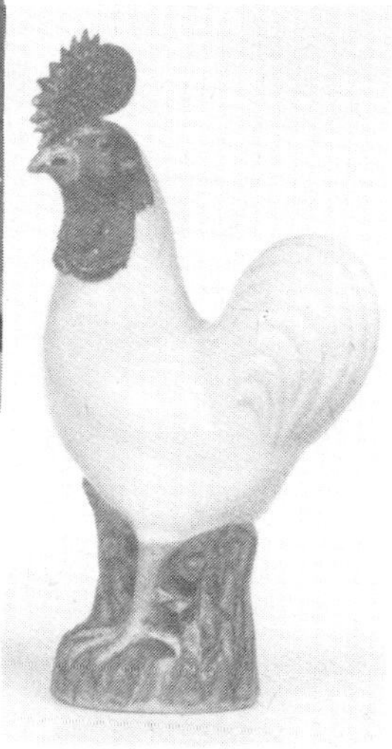

A pair of figures of cockerels, in white, red, yellow and ochre, one chipped, 15 in. high. **£700-770**

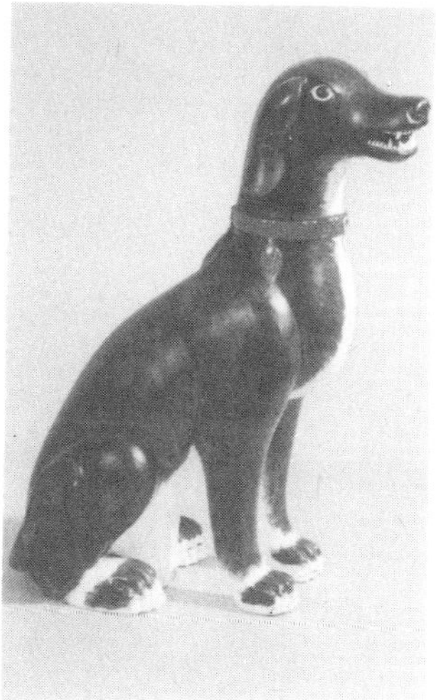

A large export figure of a seated hound, with a gilt-spotted iron-red collar around its neck, its underparts white, and its body hair in chocolate brown and iron-brown, the extremities slightly damaged, 21¼ in. high, Qianlong. **£3,000-5,000**

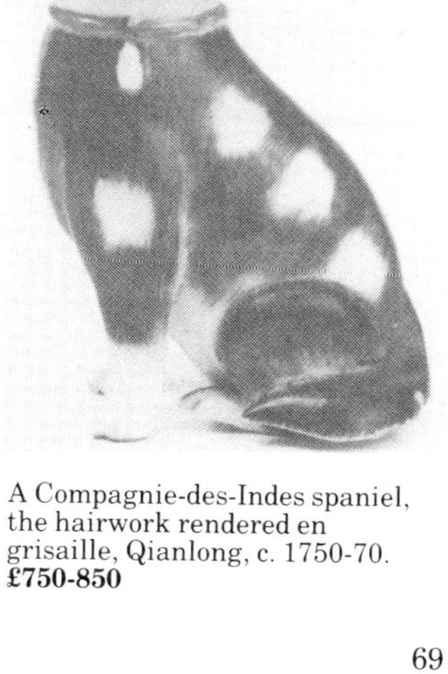

A Compagnie-des-Indes spaniel, the hairwork rendered en grisaille, Qianlong, c. 1750-70. **£750-850**

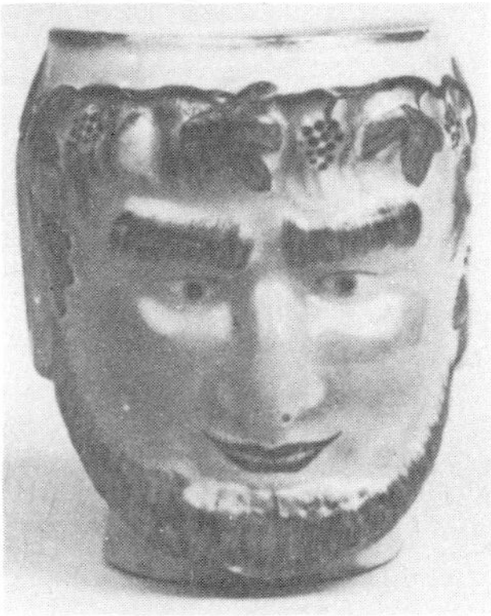

An export mug, modelled as the head of Bacchus, after a European original, with simple loop handle, restored, 4¼ in. high, Qianlong. **£250-400**

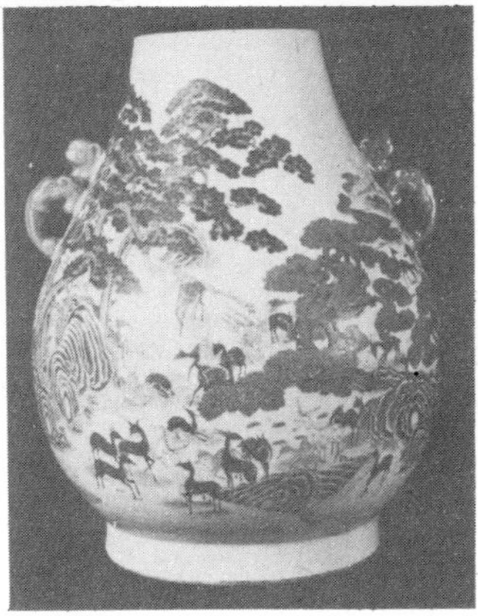

A large famille rose 'Hundred Deer' vase, modelled with iron-red lingxi loop handles enriched with gilding, the body enamelled with the classical scene of the hundred deer amongst pine and peach groves, the lip of the neck restored, 44 cm. high, Qianlong seal mark in underglaze blue and of the period. **£5,000-7,000**
Other Qianlong marked vases of this pattern are illustrated by Marquet de Vasselot and Ballot, 'The Louvre Museum: Chinese Ceramics,' pl. 43.

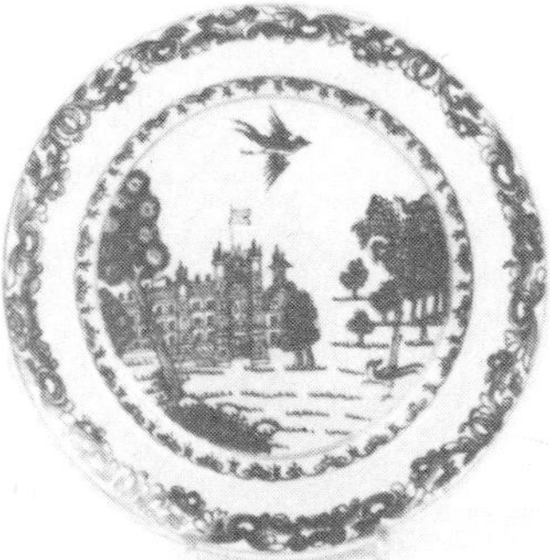

A pair of blue and white plates, each painted with a view of Burleigh House, near Stamford, with a bird in flight above a flag flown over the entrance, one cracked, one chipped, Qianlong, c. 1745, 9 in. diam. **£400-600**
The central scene is probably taken from an English print or drawing, though some intermediate source may have been used.

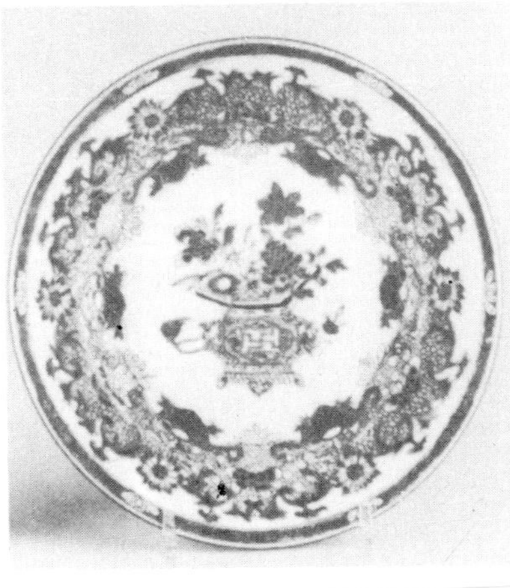

A set of five famille rose plates, painted with a jardinière within a border of ruyi and flowers, Qianlong, 23 cm. diam. **£500-800**

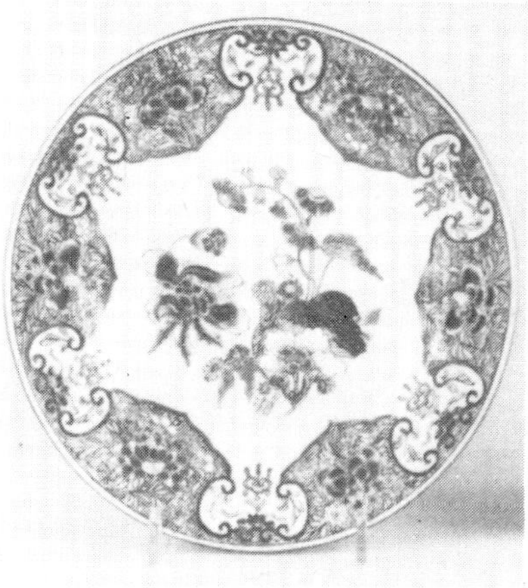

A famille rose plate, painted with a bunch of flowers including white lotus and begonia, within lambrequin border, 23 cm. diam., Qianlong. **£100-150**

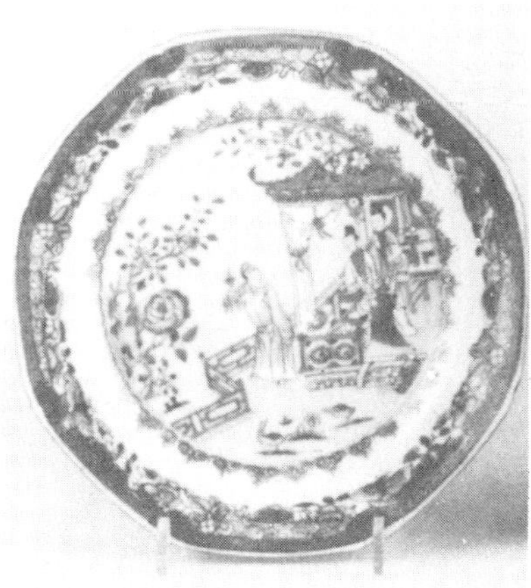

A set of five octagonal plates, decorated with 'famille princesse' pattern within blue and gilt borders, 23 cm. diam., Qianlong, damaged. **£300-500**

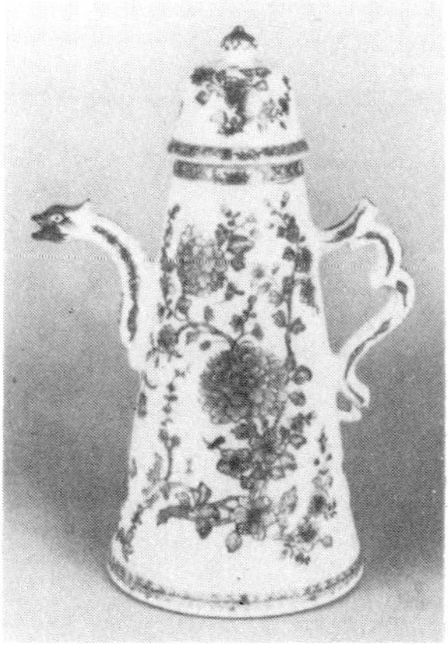

A conical export porcelain coffee urn and cover, with phoenix-headed spout, painted with flowering branches, damaged, Qianlong, 27 cm. high. **£200-300**

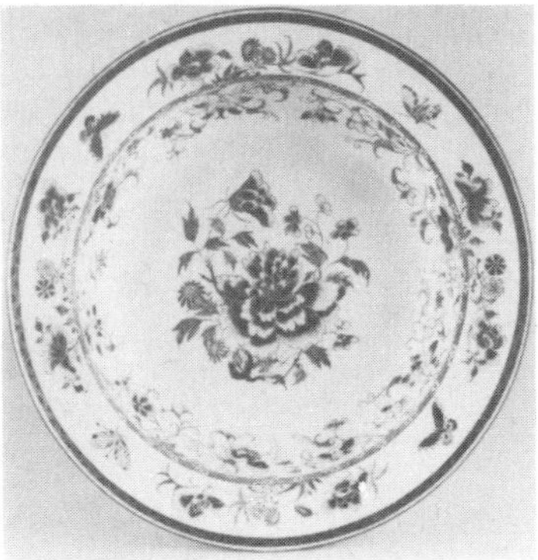

A famille rose deep dish, painted with peonies and many flowers issuing from a border with prunus on wave pattern, 40.5 cm. diam., Qianlong. **£300-£400**

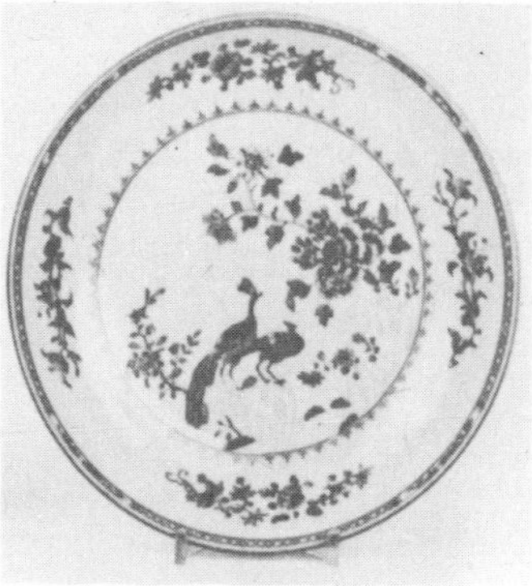

A pair of famille rose saucer dishes, each painted with a peacock and peahen perched upon rockwork below peony, within a band of spearheads and four flower sprays, Qianlong, 10 in. diam. **£500-650**

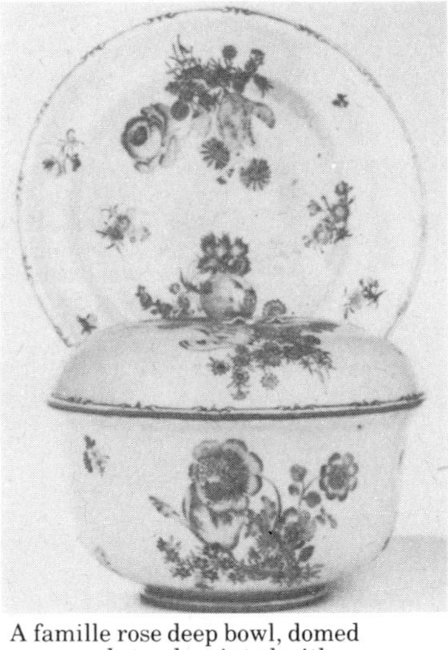

A famille rose deep bowl, domed cover and stand, painted with scattered sprays of roses, orchids, daisies, and chrysanthemum below iron-red and gilt formal scroll-work, bowl and cover restored, Qianlong, the stand $15\frac{1}{4}$ in. diam. **£700-900**
This style of flower painting was derived from Meissen.

Miller's is a price GUIDE Not a price LIST.
The price ranges given reflect the average price a purchaser should pay for similar items. Condition, rarity of design or pattern, size, colour, pedigree, restoration and many other factors must be taken into account when assessing values.

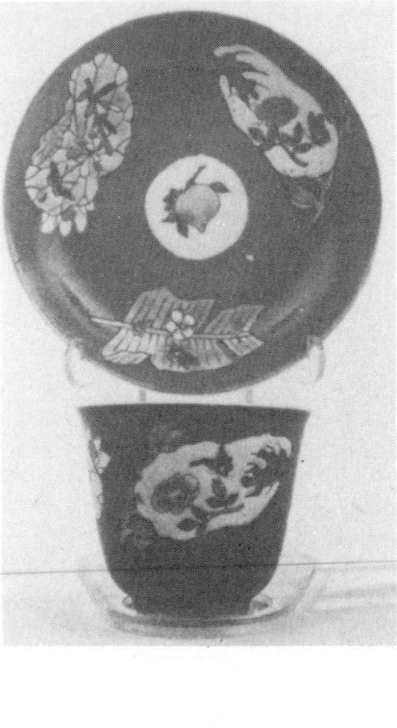

A pair of famille rose ruby-ground beakers and saucers, each painted with a finger citrus, a plantain and a lotus leaf, the saucers with a central panel of peach, one beaker chipped, Qianlong. **£450-550**

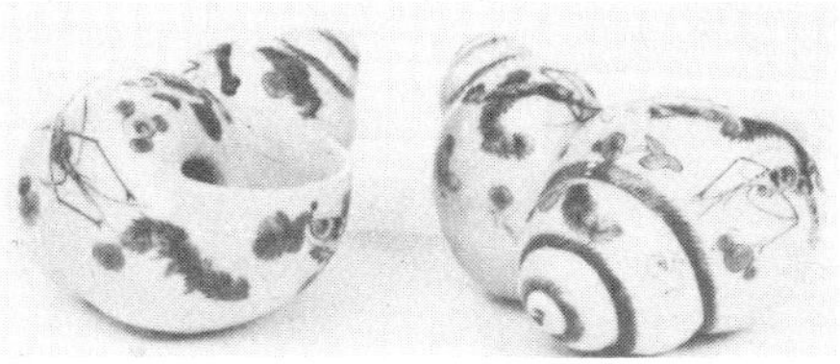

A pair of famille rose water-droppers, each modelled as two adjacent spiralling shells, the larger opening into a hemispherical bowl, painted with fish and crustacea amongst water-weed, Qianlong, 4 in. wide. **£1,200-1,500**

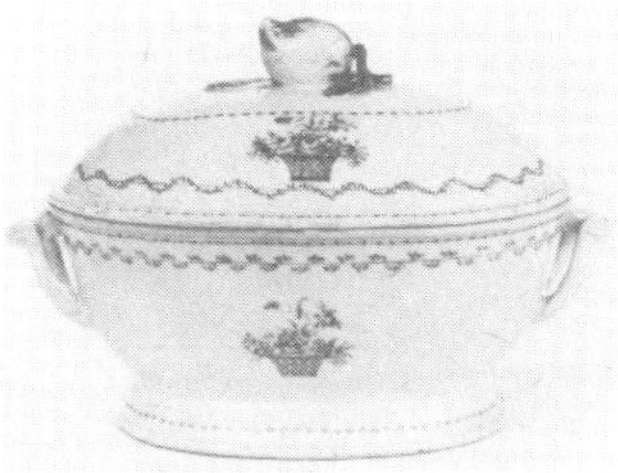

A famille rose oblong hexafoil tureen and domed cover, with moulded leaf-scroll bracket handles, painted with baskets of flowers between bands of blue enamel and gilt chain and dart-pattern, cover fritted, Qianlong, 12 in. diam. **£800-1,000**

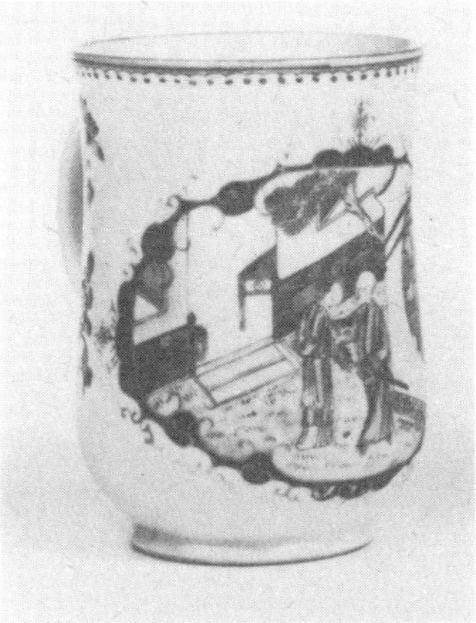

A famille rose bell-shaped mug, painted with a scene from a novel, a bearded man looking through a window at a hero and his lady in an oval panel, with a Meissen-style border between peony and chrysanthemum sprays, Qianlong, 5¾ in. high. **£250-400**

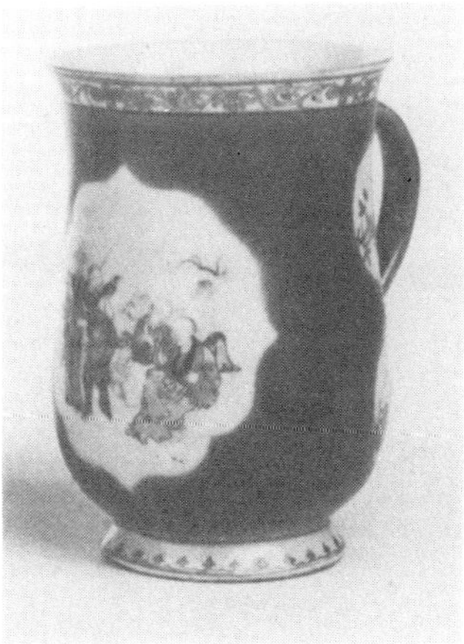

A famille rose blue ground bell-shaped mug, painted with four figures in a rocky landscape, Qianlong, 6 in. high. **£180-250**

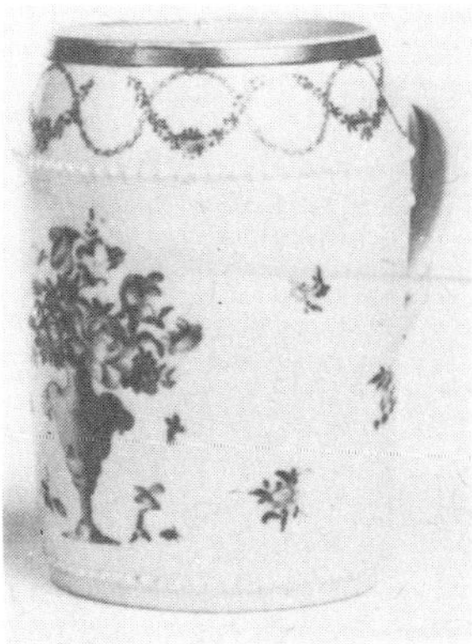

A famille rose mug, painted with a vase of peony and exotic flowers between insects and scattered floral sprays, Qianlong, 6¼ in. long. **£200-300**

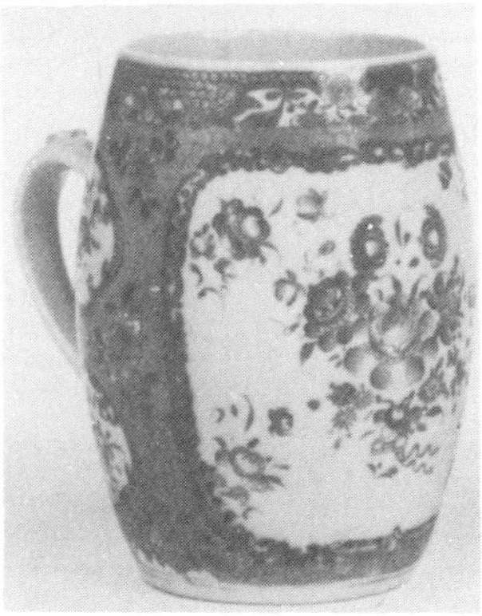

A famille rose barrel-shaped mug, painted with panels of peony and exotic flowers on an iron-red and gilt Y-pattern ground, Qianlong, 5¾ in. high. **£180-250**

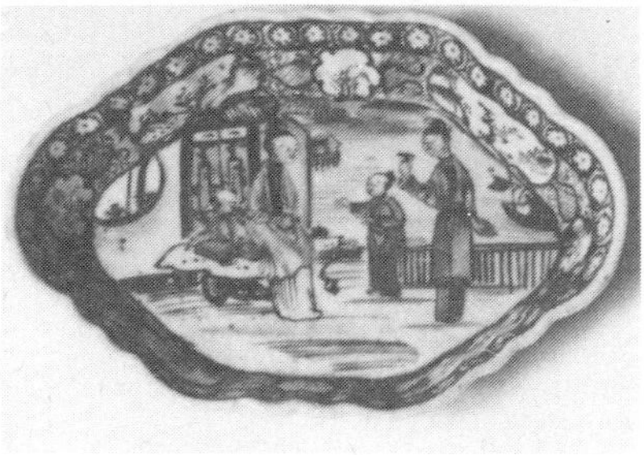

A Chinese famille rose exportware (Compagnie-des-Indes) spoon tray, decorated with mandarin figures—a favourite theme on late Qianlong wares, c. 1780, 5 in. wide. **£50-60**

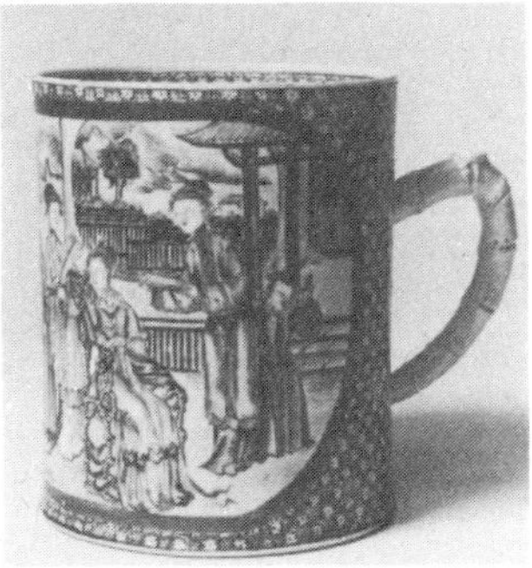

A good Chinese Mandarin period mug, with 'Mandarin pattern', c. 1780, 5¾ in. high. **£200-230**

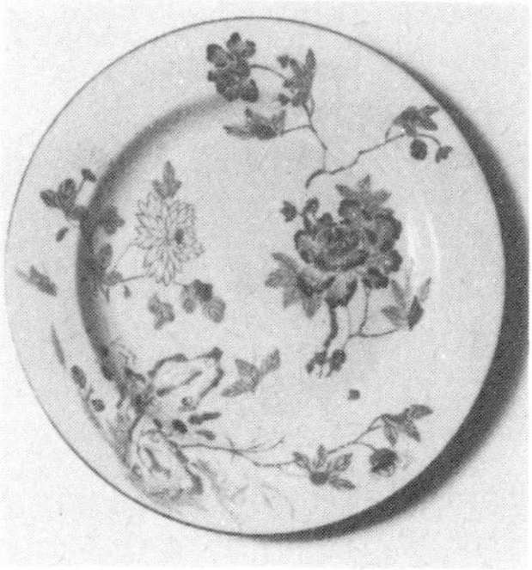

A famille rose plate, decorated with flowers, c. 1765, 9 in. diam. **£80-90**

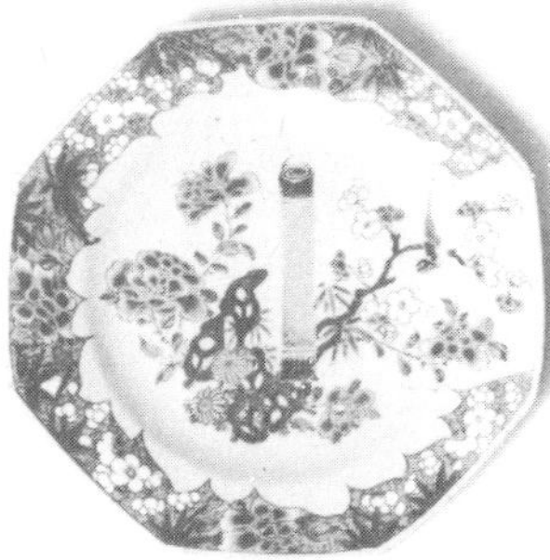

A pair of famille rose plates, decorated with an unusual design, 9 in. diam., c. 1760. **£330-£380**

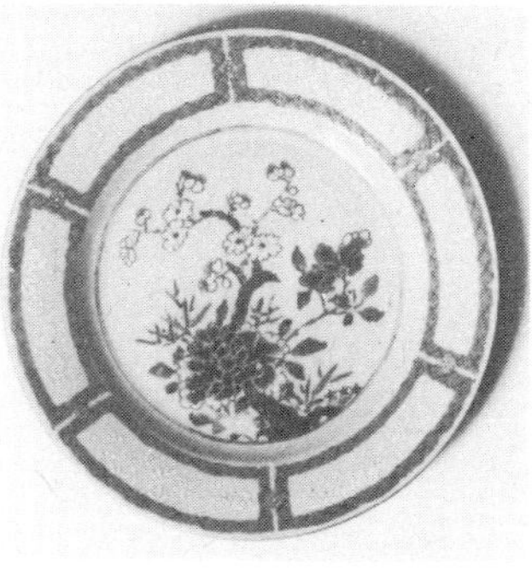

A famille rose plate, of good quality, decorated with a rare pattern, 9 in. diam., c. 1760. **£160-180**

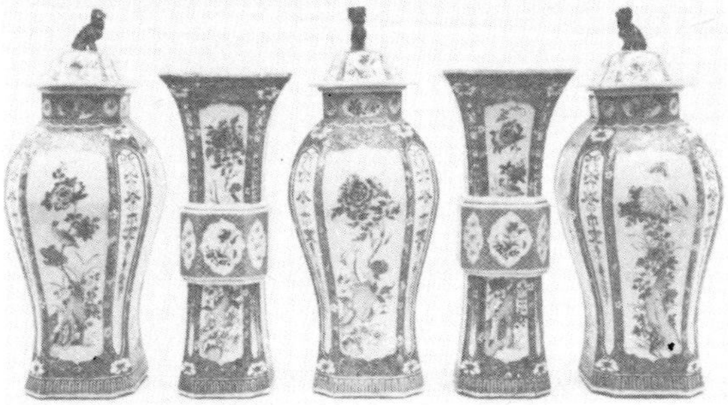

A Chinese famille rose garniture, comprising three vases and covers and two beakers, all of octagonal section, Qianlong, 21 in. and 17¾ in. **£5,000-6,000**

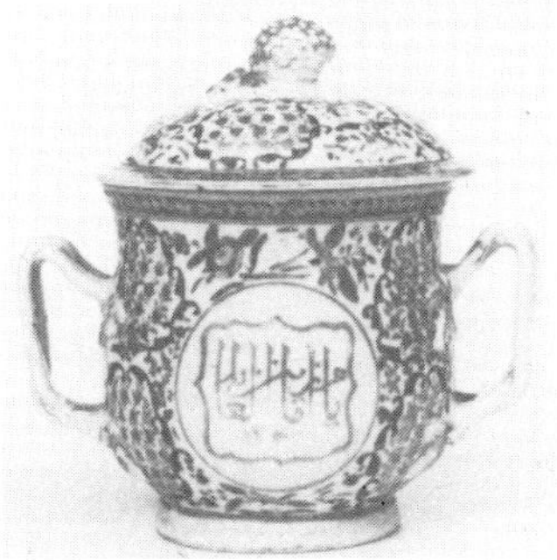

A famille rose two-handled bowl and cover, with entwined berried strap handles and strawberry finial, gilt on each side with roundels of Arabic calligraphy amongst dense foliage, dated 1240 A.H. (1825 A.D.) and of the period, 5½ in. wide. **£160-200**
Wares bearing this type of decoration are common in India and the Middle East.

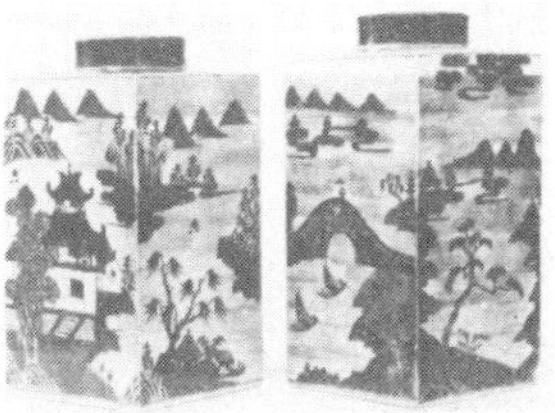

Two blue and white square tea jars, painted with figures, boats and pavilions in mountainous river landscapes, with some damage, one riveted, the necks mounted in copper, 13¼ in. and 12½ in. high, 1820-30. **£150-250**

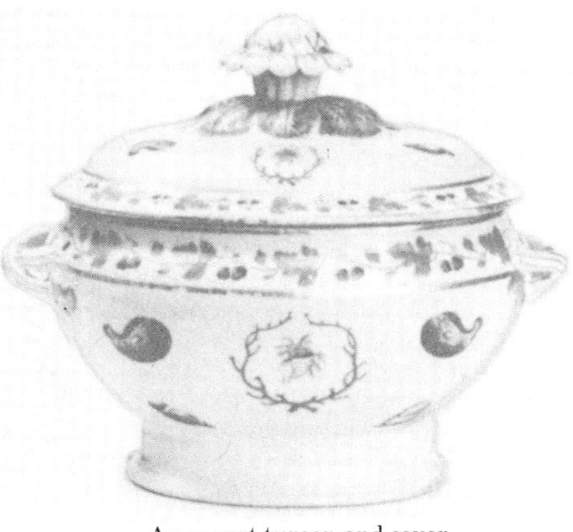

An export tureen and cover, Jiaqing, 35 cm. wide, c. 1810. **£570-650**

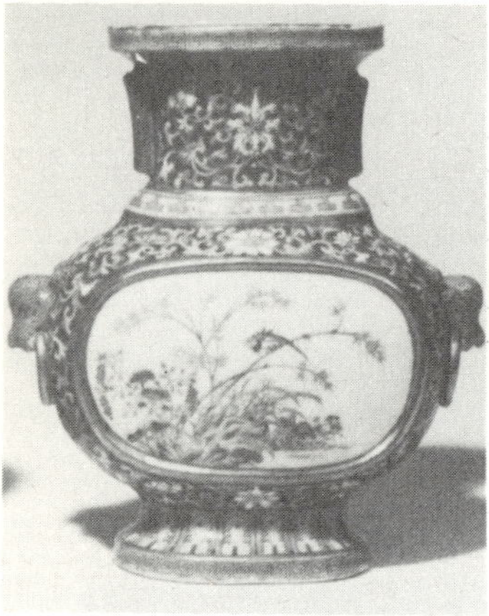

A famille rose ruby-ground baluster vase, painted with panels of a pheasant on bamboo and birds above magnolia, with blue and gilt animal-mask handles amongst formal scrolling foliage, iron-red Daoguang six-character seal mark, 6¼ in. high. **£500-700**

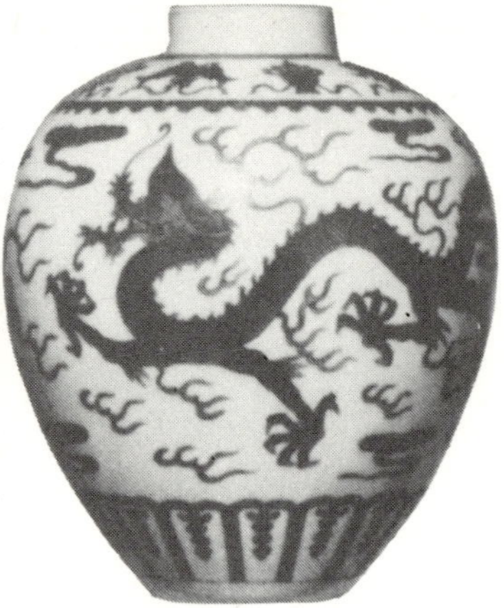

A 'Green Dragon' oviform jar, painted in green enamel outlined in underglaze-blue with two five-clawed dragons pursuing flaming pearls, the shoulder with the eight Buddhist emblems between bands of whorls and ruyi heads, Daoguang six-character seal mark and of the period, 8 in. high. **£800-1,200**

Vases of this form and decoration appear throughout the Qing dynasty from Kangxi onwards.

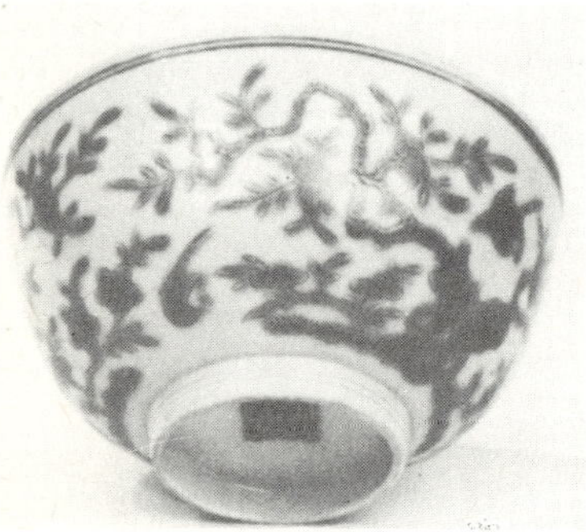

A green and yellow bowl, incised and painted in green on a yellow ground, cracked, Daoguang six-character seal mark and of the period, 4¾ in. diam. **£100-150**

A pair of famille rose lemon-yellow-ground bowls, painted with the Eight Buddhist emblems amongst formal hibiscus, above a band of pink key-pattern, iron-red four-character marks Daoguang yuzhi, Imperially commissioned during the Daoguang period and probably of the period, 5½ in. diam. **£500-600**

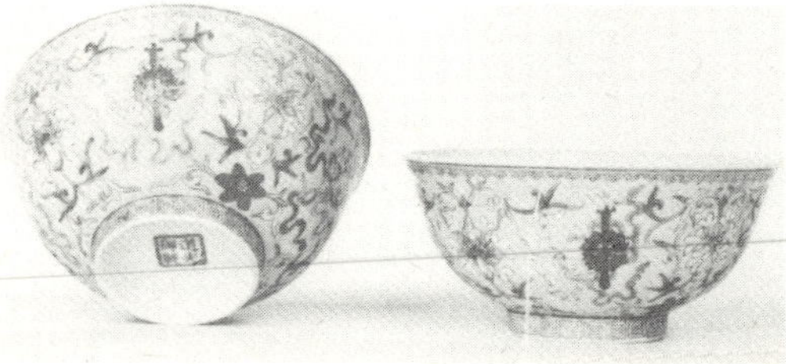

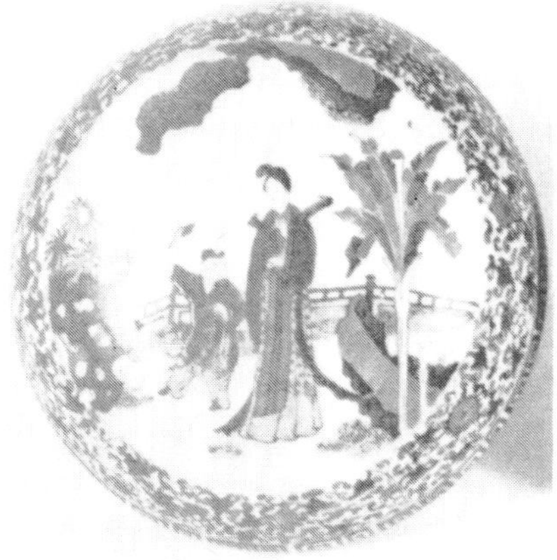

A Wucai bowl and cover, well painted with figures in a garden, 22.5 cm., mark of Wanli, period of Jiaqing. **£200-400**

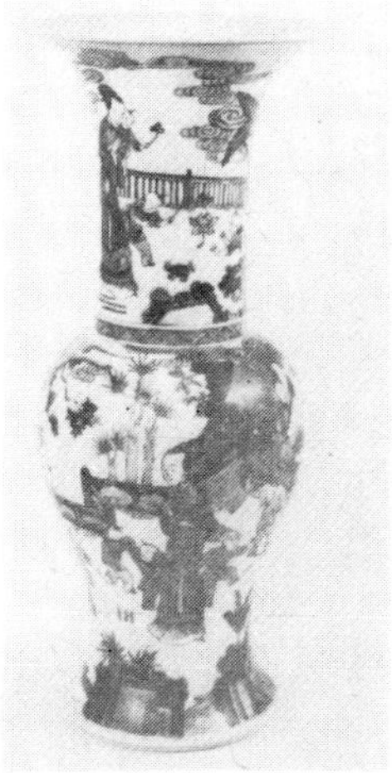

An underglaze-blue and enamel vase, decorated with women and children playing in a garden, 46 cm., Daoguang. **£200-300**
An example of a 19th century copy of a Kangxi Yanyan vase.

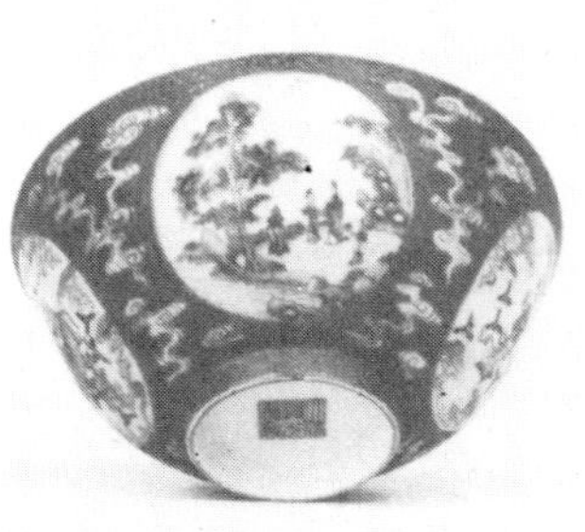

A famille rose graviata blue-ground bowl, painted with roundels of Immortals on the exterior and in underglaze-blue with similar Immortals with birds and clouds in the interior, minutely fritted, Daoguang six-character seal mark and of the period, 5¾ in. diam. **£450-550**
These solid ground bowls with roundels are of a style found in every reign of the 19th C.

Make the most of Millers...

Remember that this book is a price *guide,* not a price *list.* Valuations given throughout apply to the specific prices shown and, though they may reasonably be taken as a guide to the values of other similar articles, other factors may also apply.
Condition of any article is of the utmost importance and must always be taken into account when negotiating the sale of any antique.

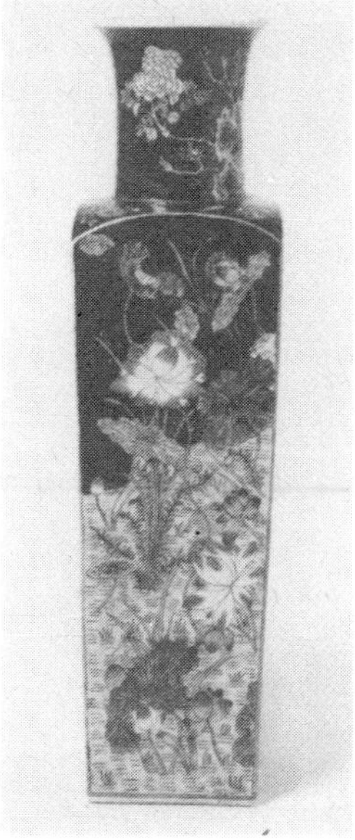

A famille noire vase, painted with flowers, foliage and rocks, 49.5 cm., underglaze-blue scroll and leaf mark, Daoguang. **£400-£500**

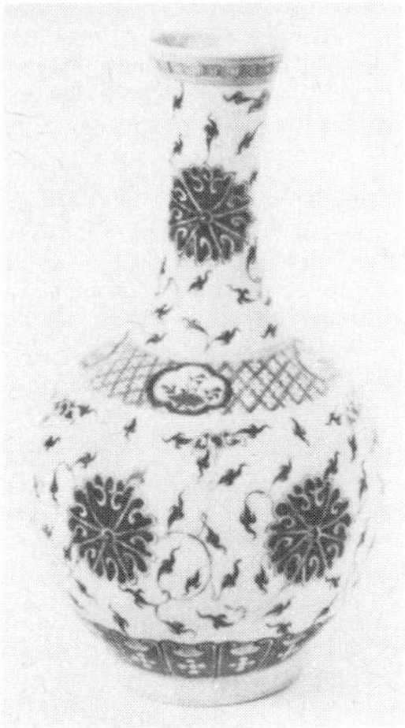

A blue and white vase, with a globular body and flared neck, painted with flowerheads and scrolling foliage, 32 cm., mark of Kangxi, period of Daoguang. **£200- 300**

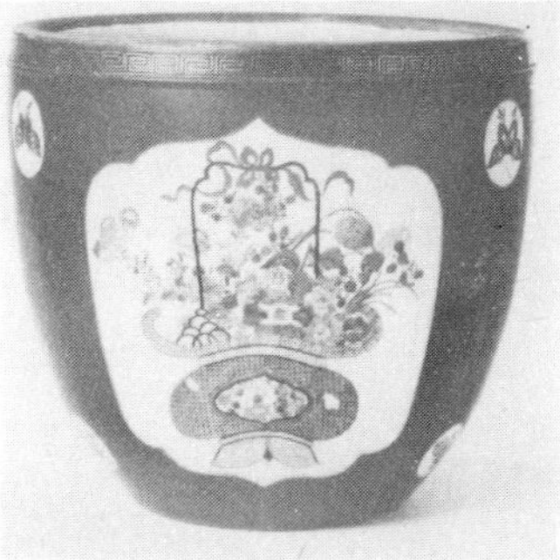

A famille verte jardinière, painted with three panels of flower arrangements, on a powder-blue ground, 32 cm., Daoguang. **£300-500**

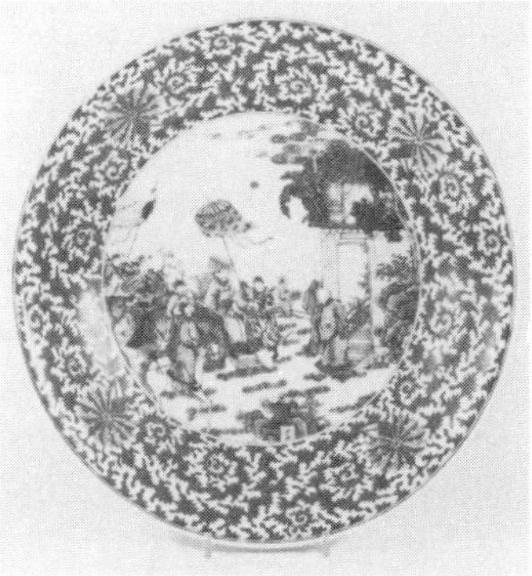

A good famille verte dish, painted with courtiers and warriors outside a building, 40 cm., painted leaf mark, Daoguang. **£500-700**

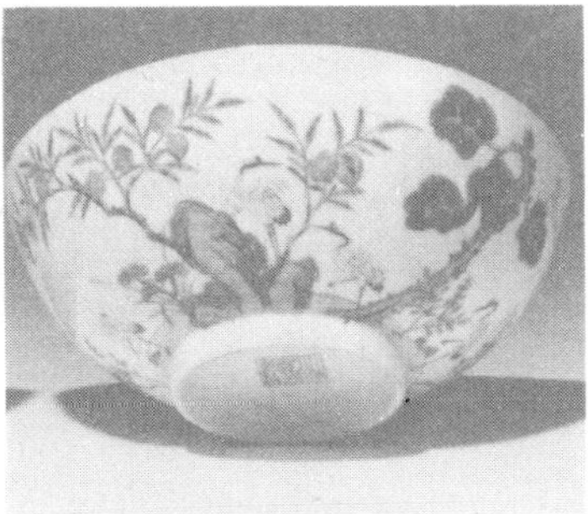

A famille rose shallow bowl, painted with eight cranes, one holding a musical stone suspended from its beak above others amongst pine, lingzhi and a peach tree, iron-red Daoguang six-character seal mark and of the period, 6¾ in. diam. **£300-£500**

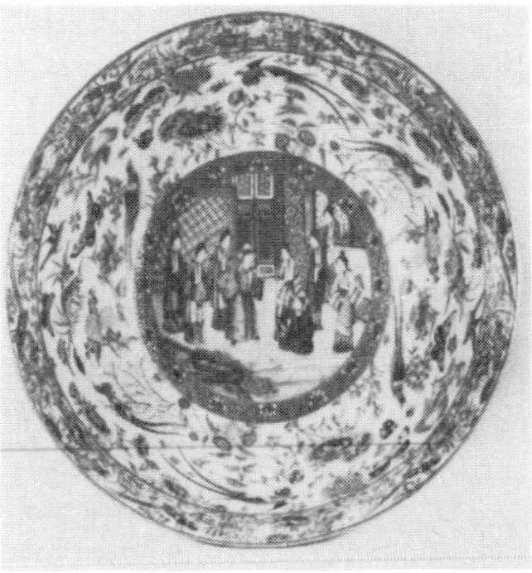

A Canton bowl, painted with figures in a room, the border and exterior painted with exotic birds and butterflies amongst flowers, 37 cm., Daoguang. **£500-£600**

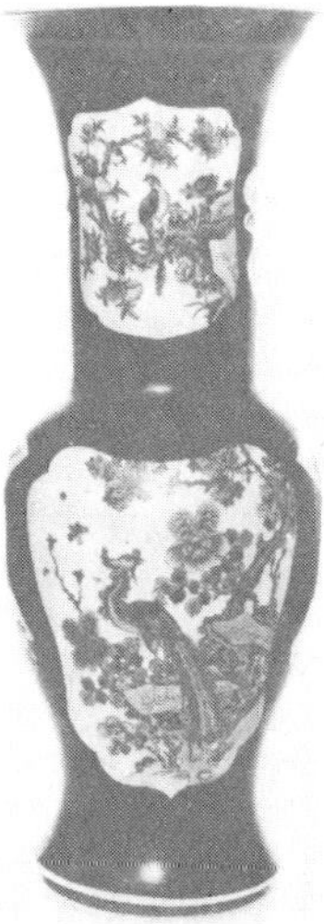

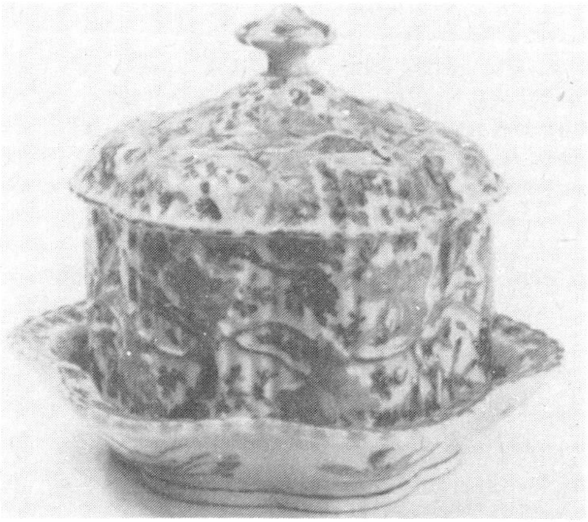

A Canton tureen, cover and stand, moulded bat and cash mark, 15.5 cm. overall, c. 1820-40. **£240-280**

A famille verte vase, with powder-blue ground, 85 cm., mark and period of Daoguang, with wooden stand. **£900-1,050**
An example of a 19th century copy of an earlier piece. The shape is fairly accurate but the painting is perhaps too fussy.

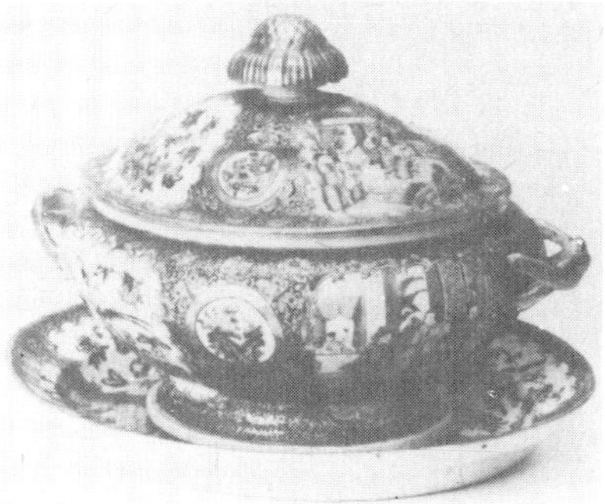

A Canton export porcelain tureen, cover and stand, decorated in famille rose enamels, c. 1830. **£520-600**
This piece is based on a European silver shape.

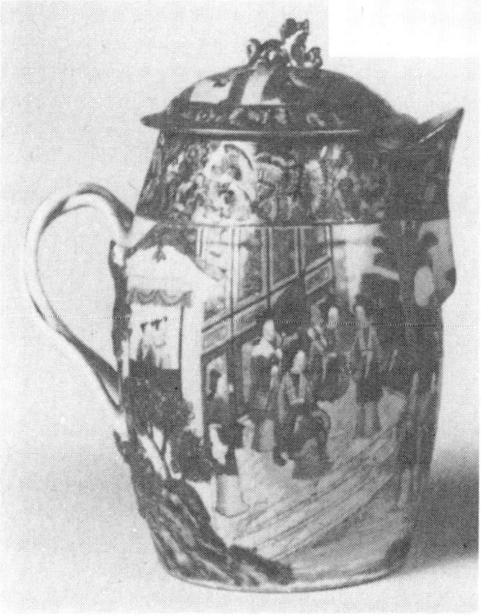

Left
A pair of Canton famille rose barrel-shaped cider-jugs and covers, with gilt entwined strap handles and seated lion finials, painted with scholars and ladies, with gilt borders, chipped, one handle cracked, the other spout cracked, Jiaqing/Daoguang, 10¼ in. high. **£500-700**

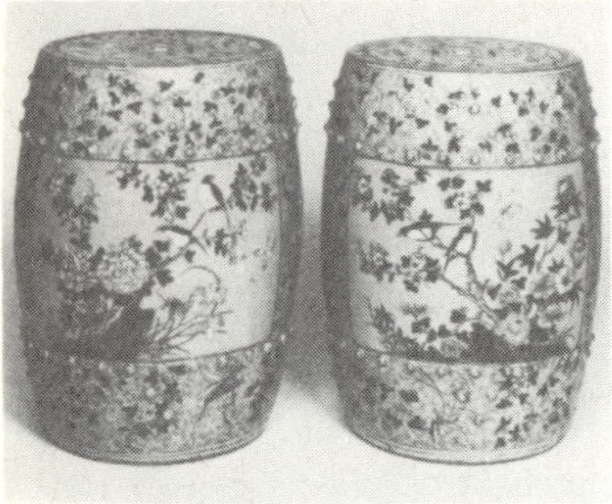

A pair of famille rose celadon-ground barrel-shaped garden seats, each painted with two panels of birds amongst hibiscus, between bands of studs and densely scrolling foliage, 18¼ in. high. **£1,500-2,000**

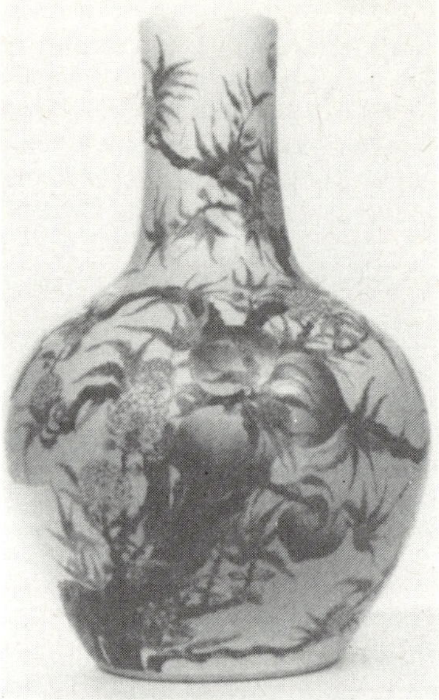

A large famille rose bottle vase, fritted, 20½ in. high, Qianlong six-character seal mark, late Qing dynasty, mid 19th C. **£1,600-1,800**

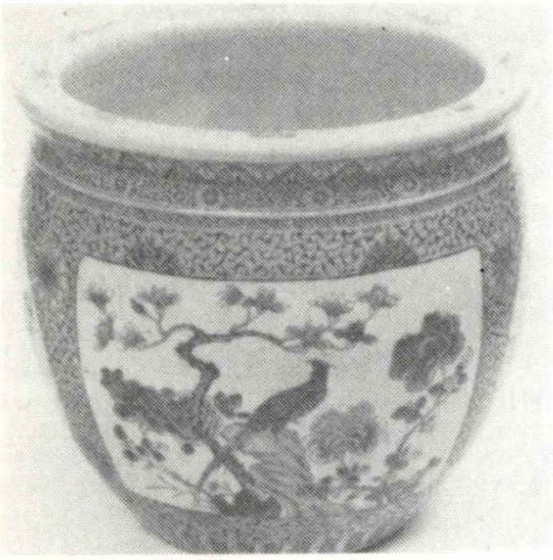

A large Chinese exportware jardinière, painted on a pink ground, 40 cm., mid 19th C. **£460-520**

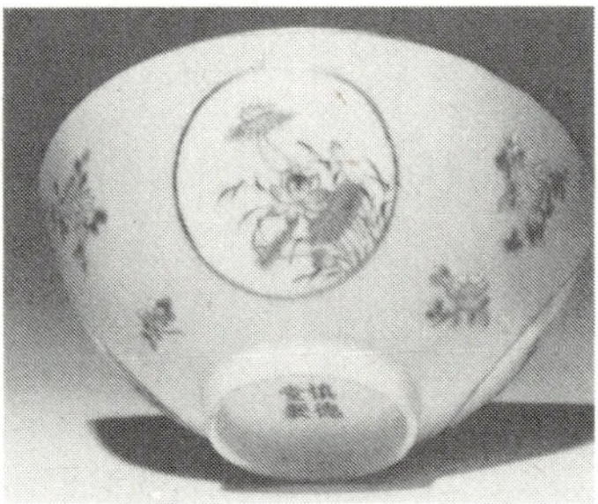

A famille rose yellow-ground bowl, painted with roundels of prunus, peach and lotus divided by sprays of peony, chrysanthemum and iris on a vivid lemon yellow sgraffiato ground, below a gilt rim, iron-red mark Zhende tang zhi (made for the Zhende Hall), early/mid 19th C., 6½ in. diam. **£300-400**

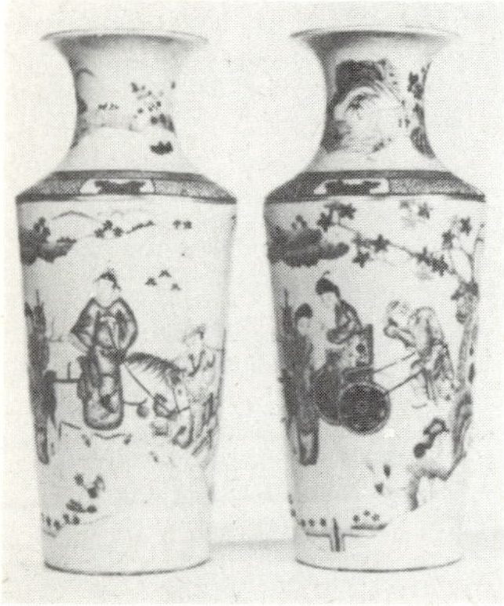

A pair of famille rose vases, each painted with an attendant leading a gentleman mounted upon a horse followed by a maid beside a lady seated in a carriage, 17¼ in. high, possibly Qianlong. **£1,000-1,300**

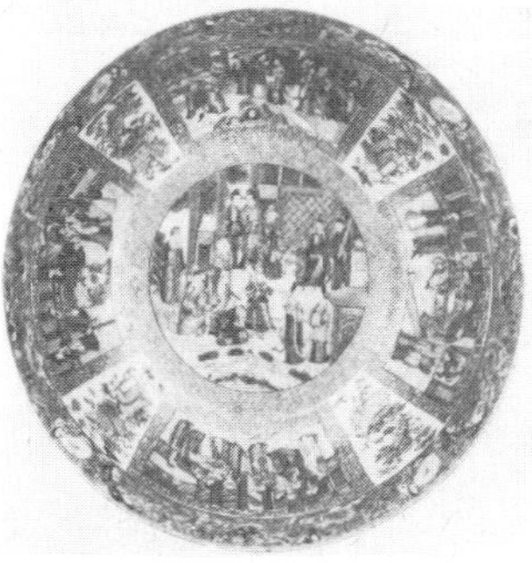

A Canton bowl, 47 cm., Daoguang, mid 19th C. **£1,200-£1,400**

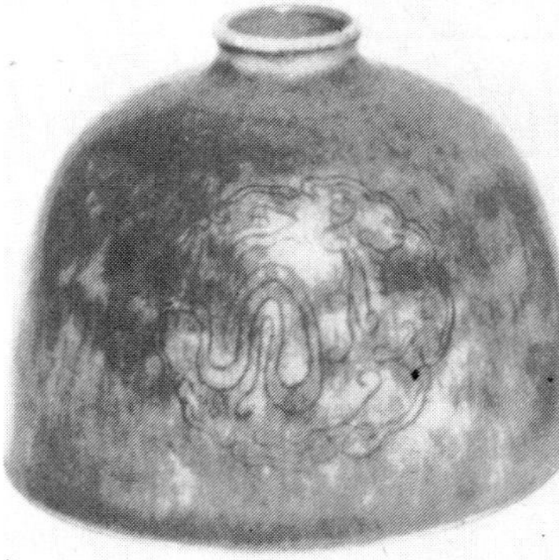

A beehive waterpot engraved with three medallions, the glaze of aubergine flecked with green, rim slightly ground, 9 cm., painted six-character mark of Kangxi, 19th C. **£100-£150**

An example of a copy. From the illustration it can be seen that the shape appears clumsy and the incised decoration lacks finesse.

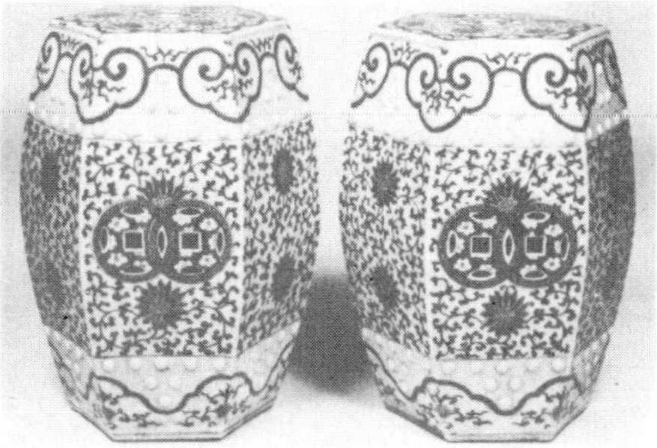

A pair of blue and white hexagonal garden seats, one repaired, 19½ in. high, mid 19th C. **£650-800**

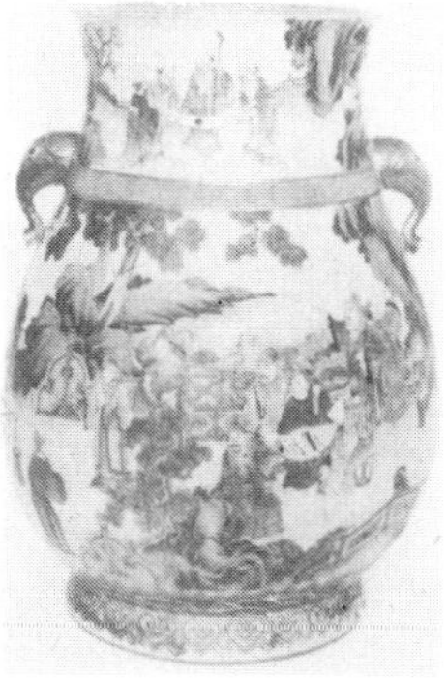

A Canton vase, the body enamelled with courtiers and their attendants seated in a garden, gilt mask and tongue handles, 51 cm., Tongzhi. **£1,000-1,500**

It is extremely difficult to ascribe any wares to a certain period unless they can be paralleled to marked specimens. Not only was this a very short reign but the kilns had been severely disrupted by rebellion at this time, thus production was limited.

Right
A famille verte vase, fitted for electricity, painted mark of Yongzheng, Tonghzi period, 45.5 cm. **£200-£250**

The somewhat clumsy or heavy form of this vase confirms its 19th C. origin.

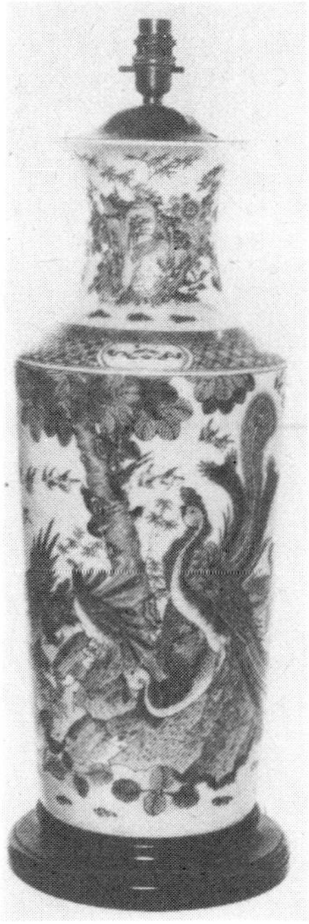

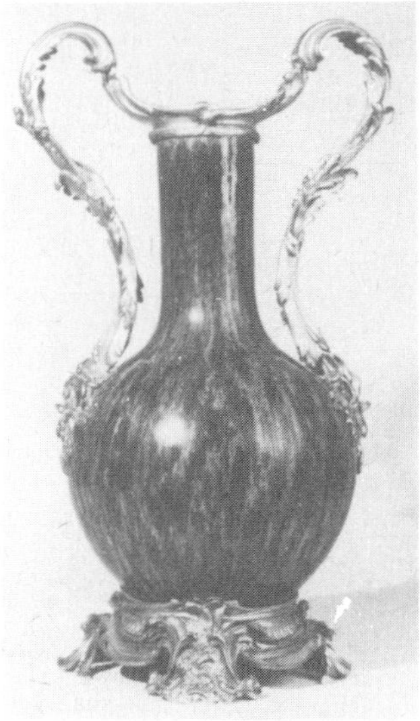

An ormolu-mounted Chinese porcelain vase, decorated with a flambé red and purple glaze, mid 19th C., 21¾ in. high. **£700-800**

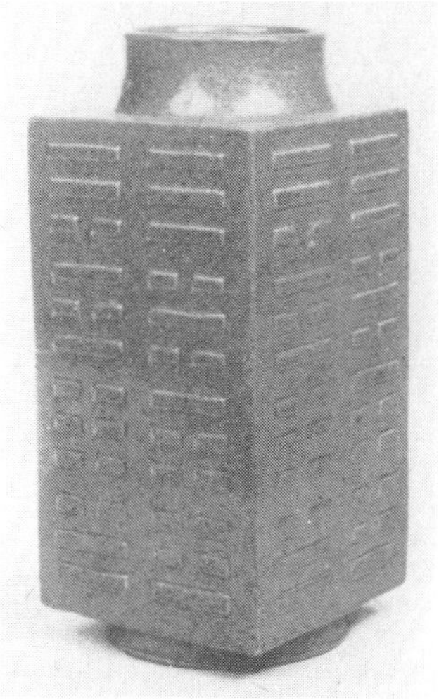

A robins-egg blue-glazed vase, impressed Qianlong six-character seal mark, with wooden stand, 9¾ in. high. **£320-£400**

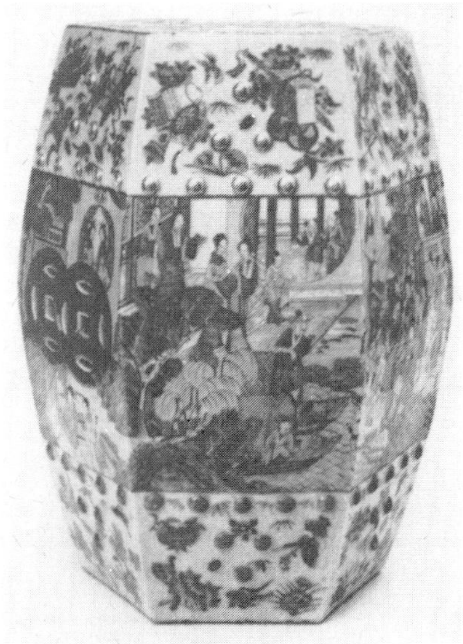

A Canton garden seat, with studded and painted body, 48.5 cm., late Daoguang or Xianfeng. **£750-880**

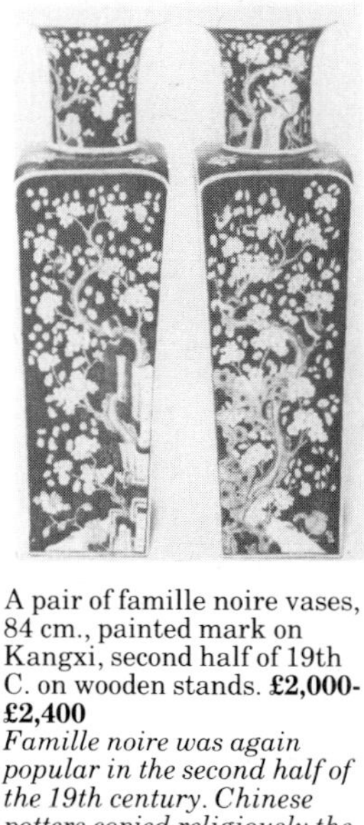

A pair of famille noire vases, 84 cm., painted mark on Kangxi, second half of 19th C. on wooden stands. **£2,000-£2,400**

Famille noire was again popular in the second half of the 19th century. Chinese potters copied religiously the wares of the Kangxi period such as the pair of vases illustrated here.

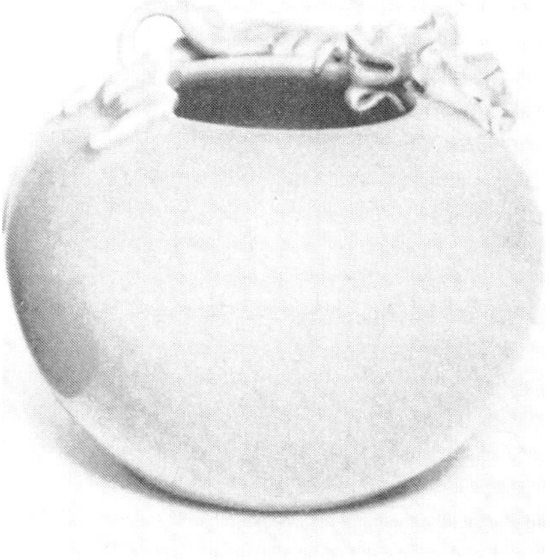

A powder-blue dragon bowl, applied around the rim with a dragon and a bat, claw chipped, 10 cm., seal mark of Yongzheng, 19th C. **£100-150**

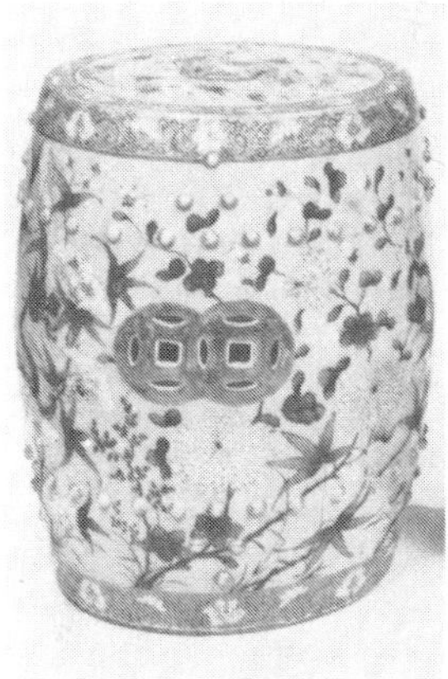

A pair of 'Empress Dowager' yellow ground barrel-shaped garden seats, painted in turquoise and white enamel, grisaille and gilt with dragons amongst camellia, magnolia and chrysanthemum, divided by pierced interlocking cash and bands of studs within floral borders, Guangxu, 18½ in. high. **£1,000-1,500**

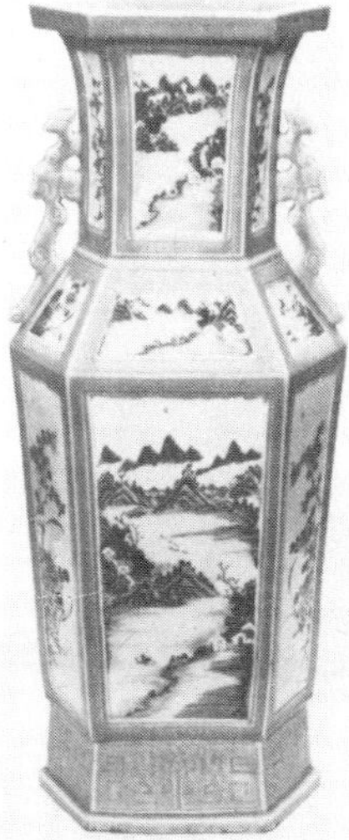

A celadon ground vase, each facet painted and underglaze with a landscape of a rural scene between key-fret borders, 86.8 cm., Guangxu. **£500-800**

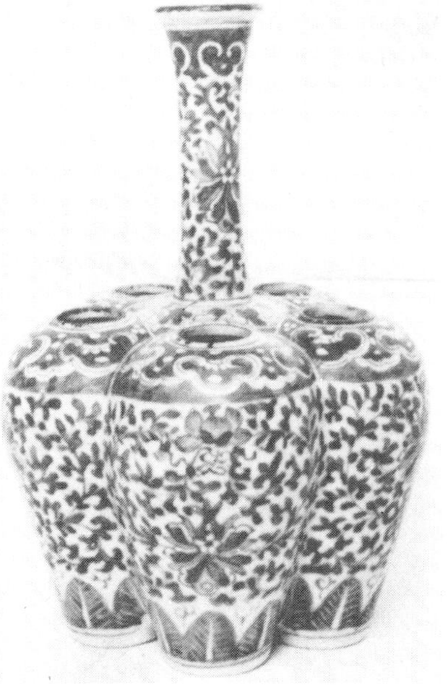

A blue and white vase, the lobed body painted with flowers and foliage, 26 cm., Guangxu. **£120-£150**

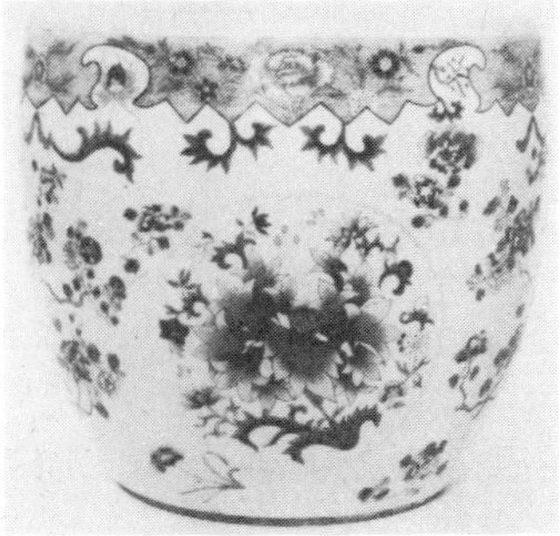

A famille rose jardinière, enamelled in red, blue and green with chrysanthemum and foliage beneath a geometric border, some enamel chipped, 41 cm., Guangxu. **£400-600**

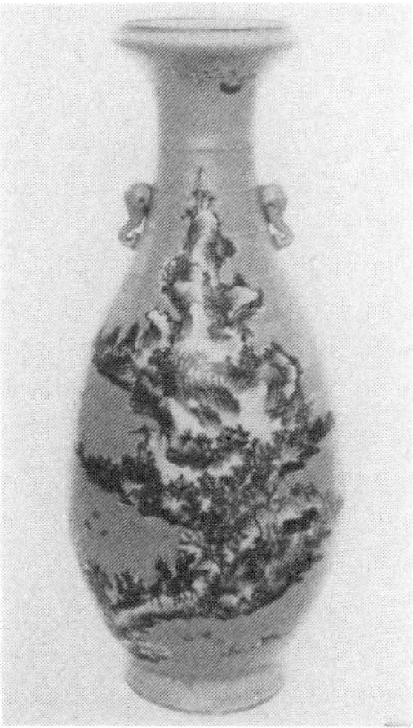

A celadon vase, decorated in low relief in blue and white with a landscape scene of figures, buildings and mountains, with mask and tongue handles, 60.5 cm., Guangxu. **£150-250**

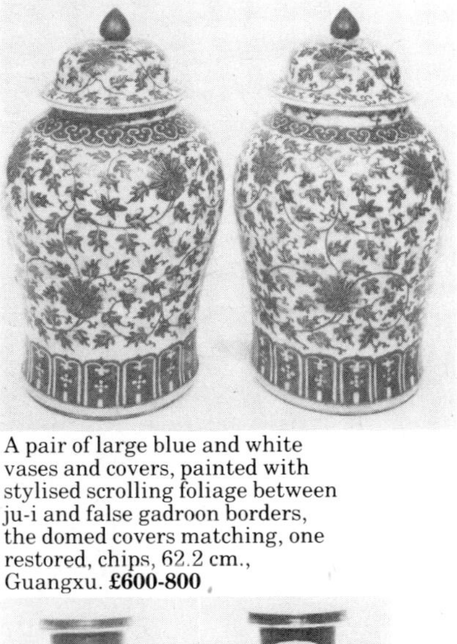

A pair of large blue and white vases and covers, painted with stylised scrolling foliage between ju-i and false gadroon borders, the domed covers matching, one restored, chips, 62.2 cm., Guangxu. **£600-800**

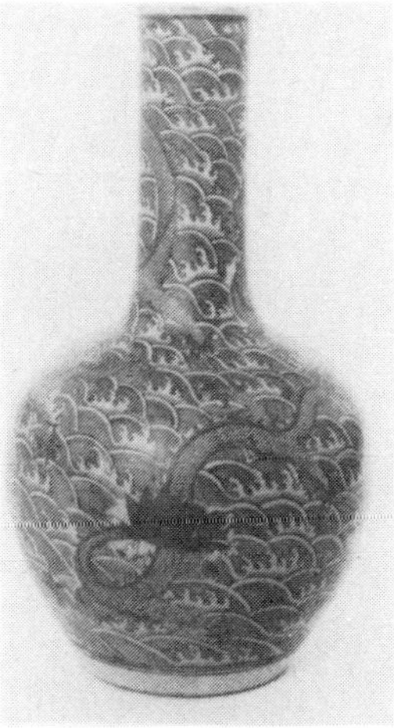

An underglaze-blue and white vase, painted in iron-red with numerous dragons above waves, rim slightly chipped, 48 cm., Guangxu. **£250-350**

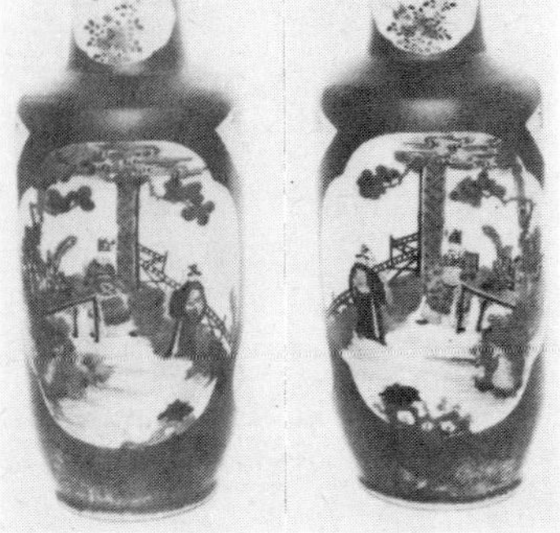

A pair of blue and white Rouleau vases, each painted with panels of courtiers on balconies and smaller foliate panels, on a powder-blue ground, 45 cm., Guangxu. **£250-350**
Based on Kangxi originals.

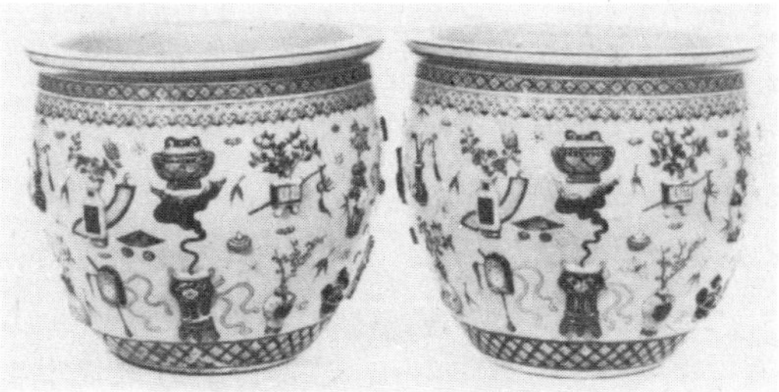

A pair of famille rose fishbowls, the interiors painted in iron-red with shibumkin, the exteriors enamelled and applied with vases of flowers, one with body crack, some chips, 41 cm., Guangxu. **£1,000-1,500**

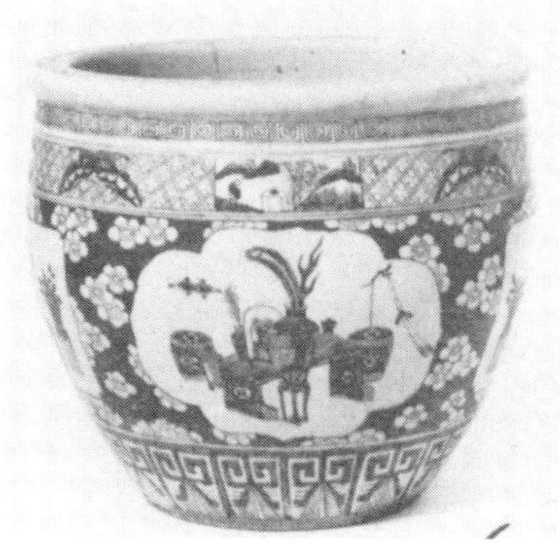

A blue and white jardinière, painted with panels of flower arrangements, the ground scattered with flowers above a formal border, 37 cm., Guangxu. **£300-400**

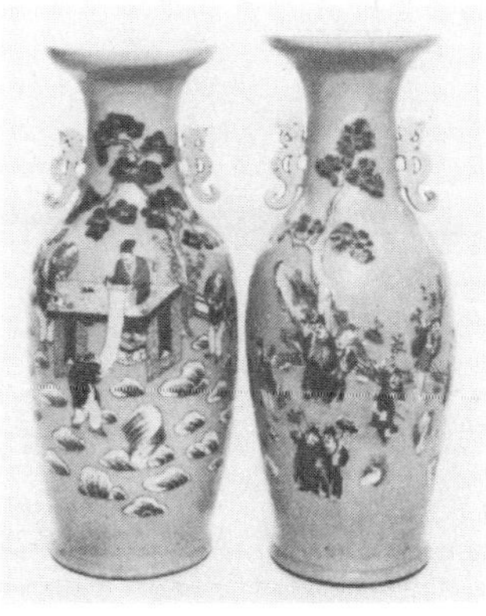

Two blue and white vases, one painted with a scribe writing at a table beneath a pine tree, the other with figures amongst rocks, on a celadon ground, 61 cm., Guangxu. **£350-450**

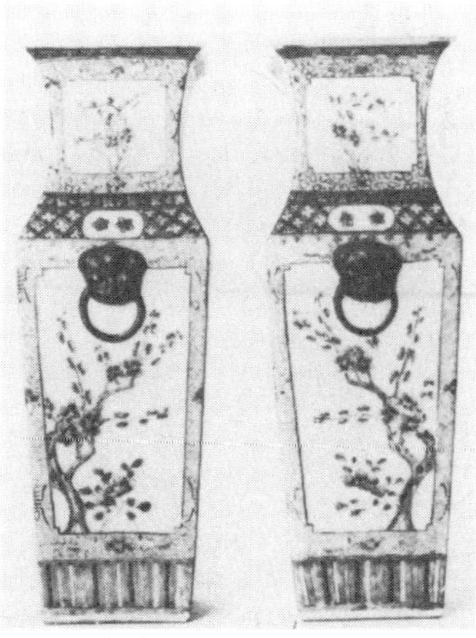

A pair of famille rose vases, each of square section painted with panels of flowers and foliage on a yellow ground between formal borders, 39.5 cm., Guangxu, on wooden stands. **£280-350**

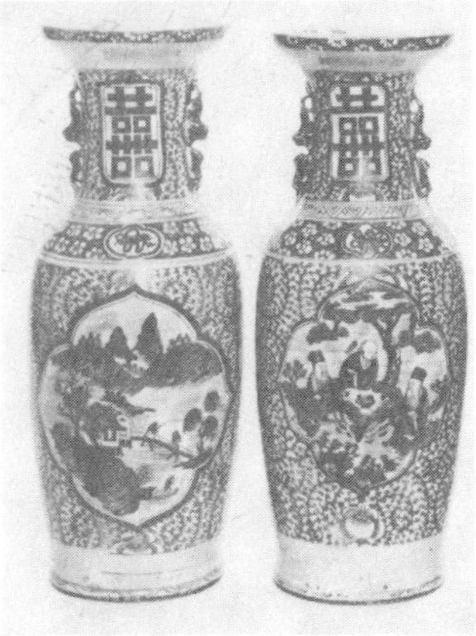

Two blue and white vases, each painted with panels of rural scenes on a scrolling foliate ground, painted with shou symbols, 61 cm., Guangxu. **£300-£400**

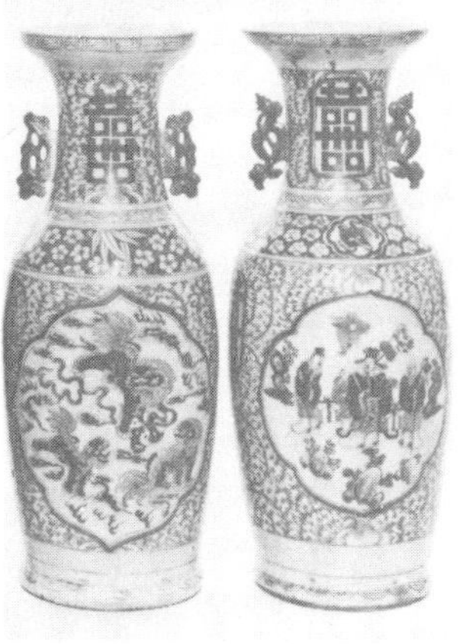

Two blue and white vases, each painted with panels of Buddhist lions and with shou symbols, 60 cm., Guangxu. **£300-400**

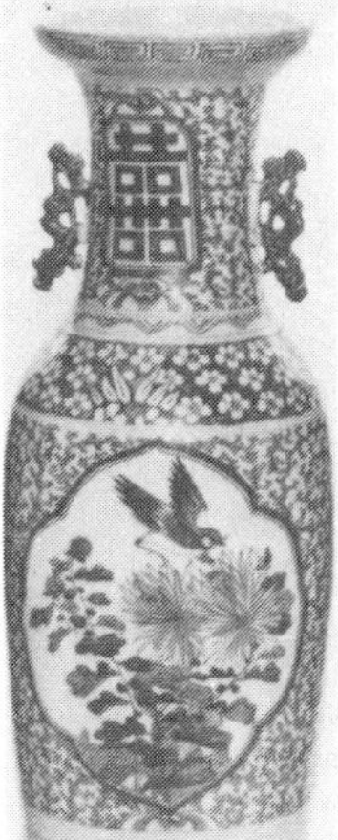

A blue and white vase, painted with panels of birds amongst flowers and foliage, 57 cm., Guangxu. **£150-200**

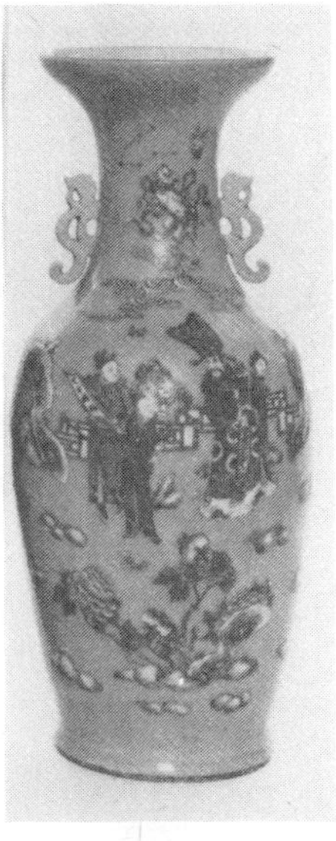

A blue and white vase, decorated in low relief with figures before a fence with rocks and clouds on a celadon ground, 59.5 cm., Guangxu. **£120-160**
A typical example of a late 19th century vase, both in form and decorative content.

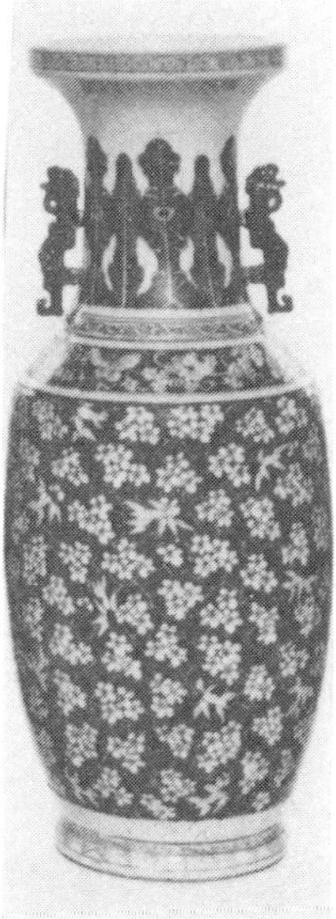

A blue and white vase, decorated with flowering cherry and bamboo leaves on an inky-blue ground beneath a leaf border, 61 cm., Tonghzi or later. **£250-£400**

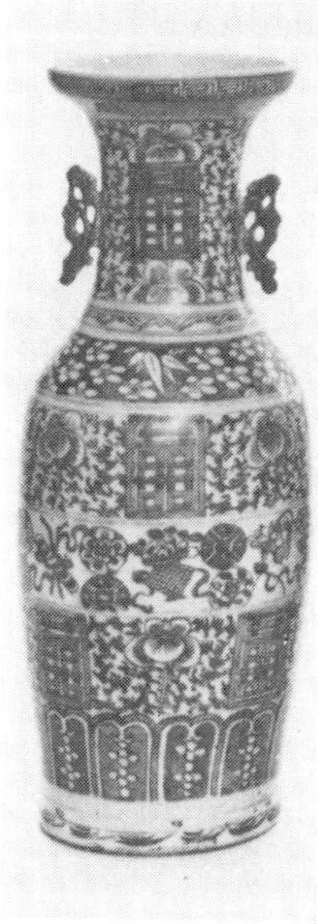

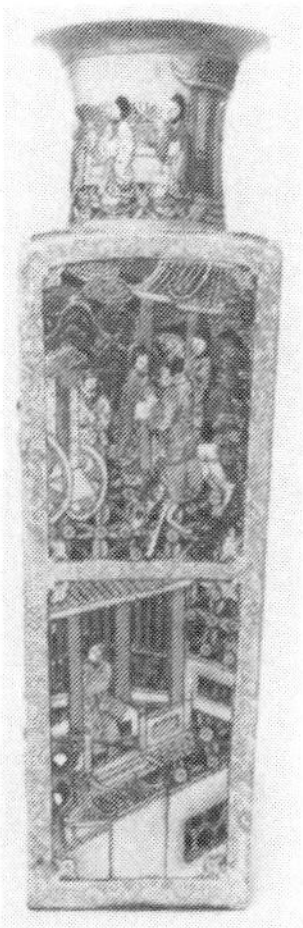

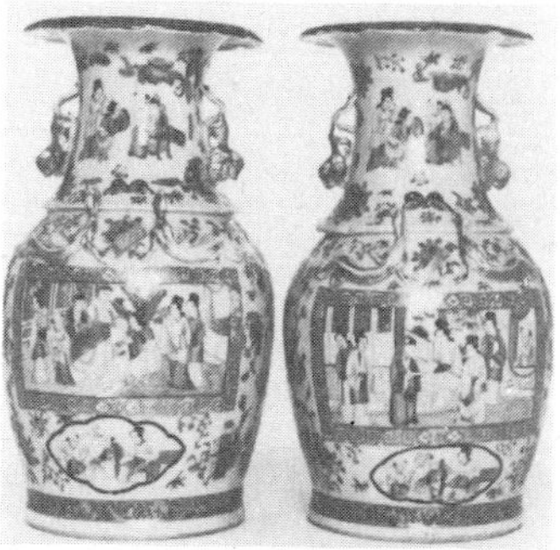

A pair of Canton vases, each painted and gilt, Guangxu, 33 cm. **£440-500**

A Canton vase, with pierced and enamelled decoration, impressed mark, Guangxu, 44 cm. **£450-£520**

A blue and white vase, painted with bands of precious objects, shou symbols, scrolling foliage and flowers above a false gadroon border, 60 cm., Guangxu. **£150-200**

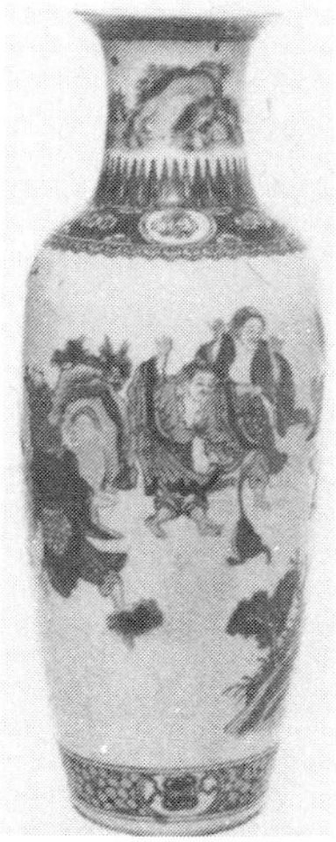

A famille rose vase, Guangxu, 45.5 cm. **£340-400**

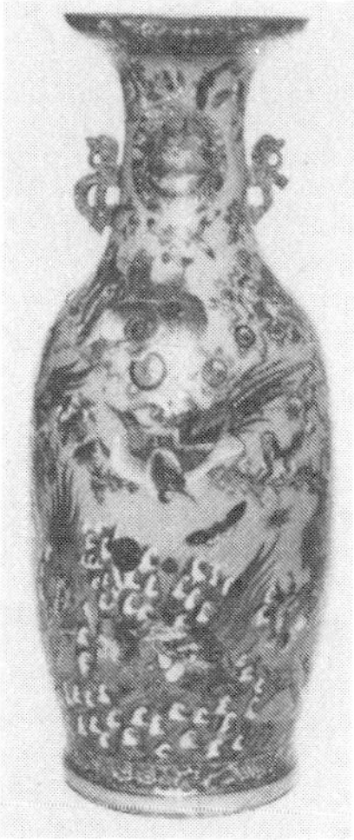

A Canton vase, brightly enamelled, Daoguang, 60.5 cm. **£370-420**

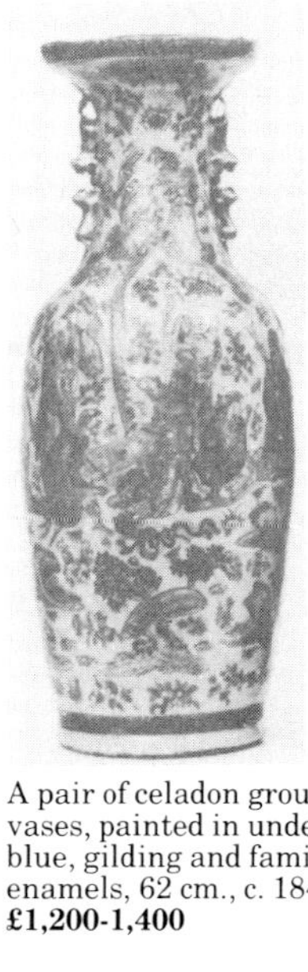

A pair of celadon ground Canton vases, painted in underglaze-blue, gilding and famille rose enamels, 62 cm., c. 1840-50. **£1,200-1,400**

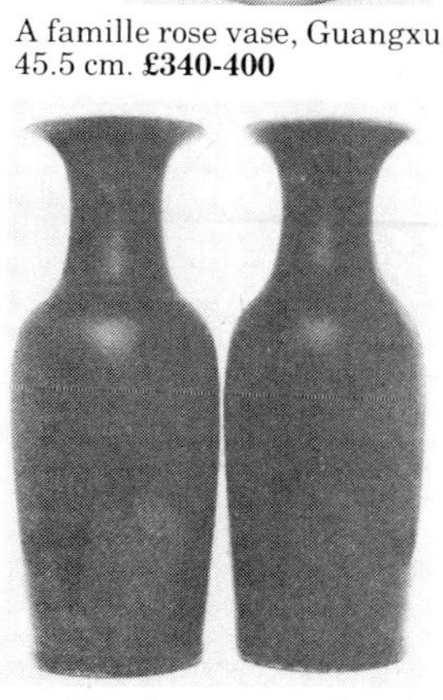

A pair of flambé vases, each with a sang-de-boeuf glaze, Guangxu, 57 cm. **£330-430**

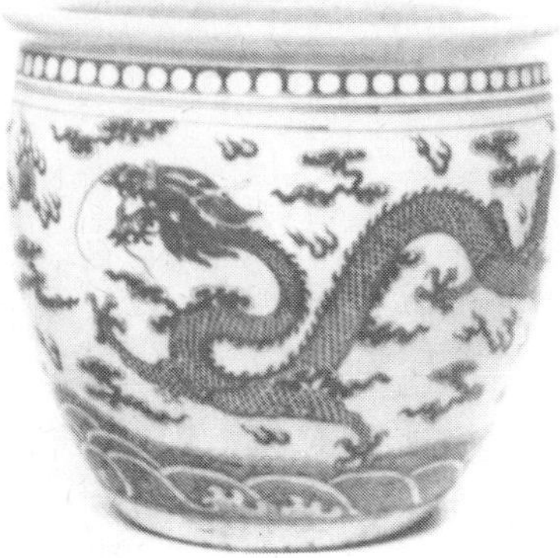

A blue and white jardinère, 36 cm., Guangxu. **£500-560**

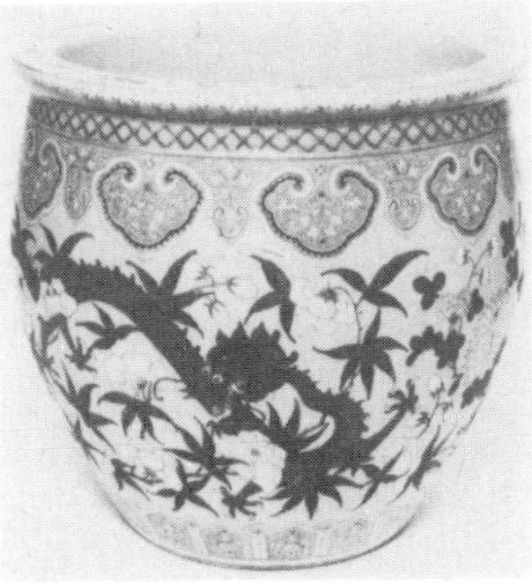

A famille rose fish bowl, the exterior with dragons amongst flowers on a yellow ground, thé interior with fish amongst water weed, 46.5 cm., Guangxu. **£850-£950**

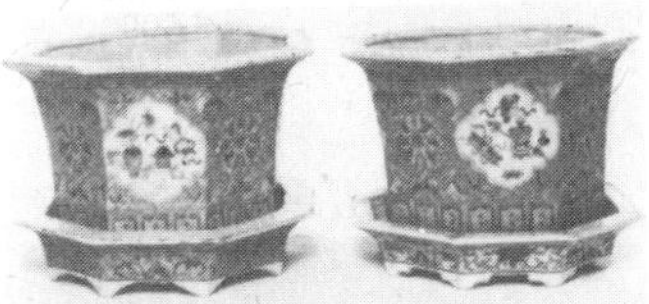

A pair of famille rose jardinères and stands, 19 cm., Guangxu. **£250-300**
Note the somewhat crowded appearance typical of late 19th century wares.

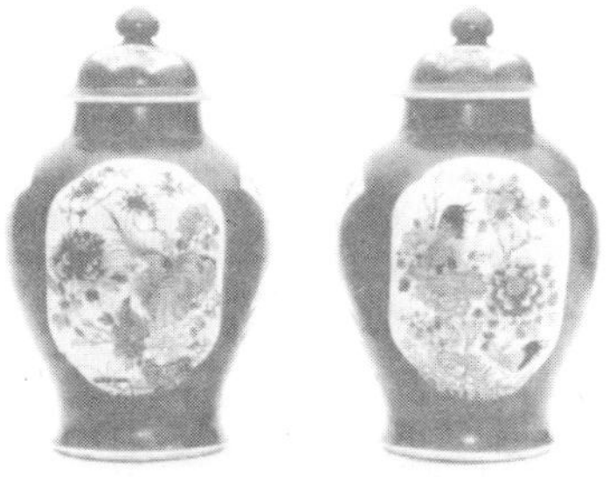

A pair of famille rose jars and covers, in bright enamel covers on a powder blue ground, 43 cm., mid 19th C. **£520-600**

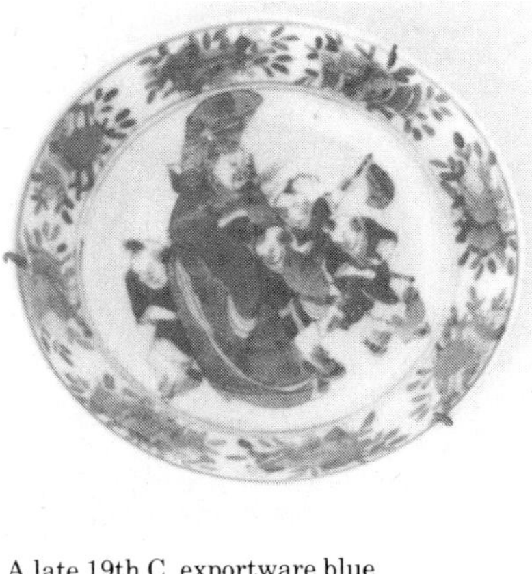

A late 19th C. exportware blue and white saucer, 6 in. diam. **£15-20**

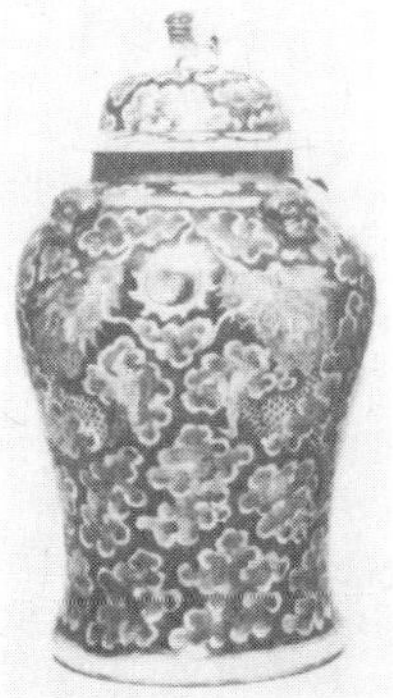

A pair of blue and white jars and covers, 40 cm., Guangxu. **£300-£350**

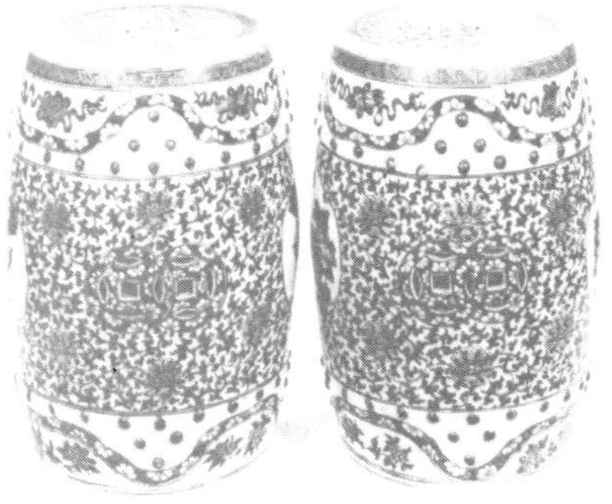

A pair of blue and white garden seats, with pierced top and sides, 48 cm., Guangxu. **£780-880**

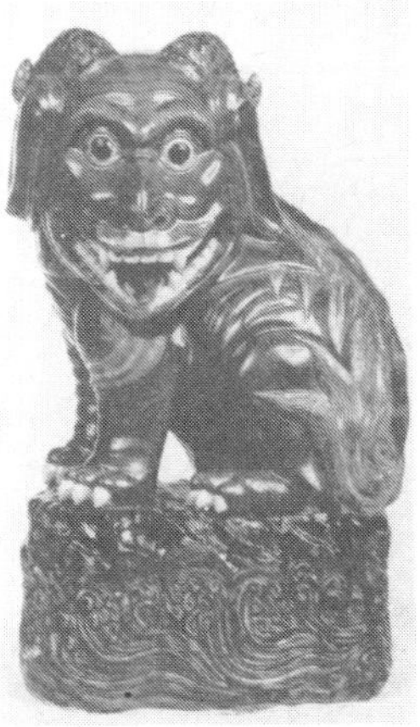

A pair of green, ochre and brown glazed figures, impressed Qianlong six-character seal marks, on wooden stands, 16¼ in. high. **£450-600**

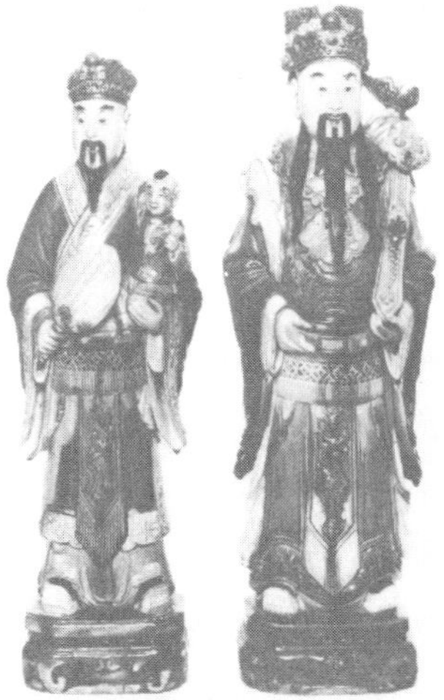

Two glazed biscuit figures of dignitaries, decorated in green, ochre and blue, 52 cm. and 48.5 cm., Guangxu. **£100-200**

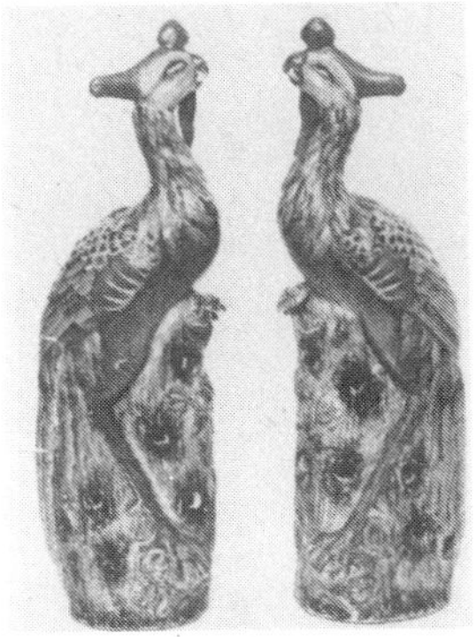

A pair of famille rose figures of phoenix, 47.5 cm., late 19th C. **£600-700**

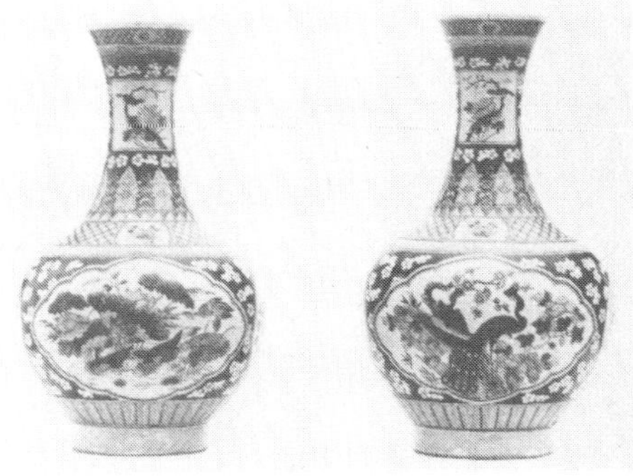

A pair of Canton vases, each body thickly enamelled, height 38.5 cm., late 19th C. **£180-220**

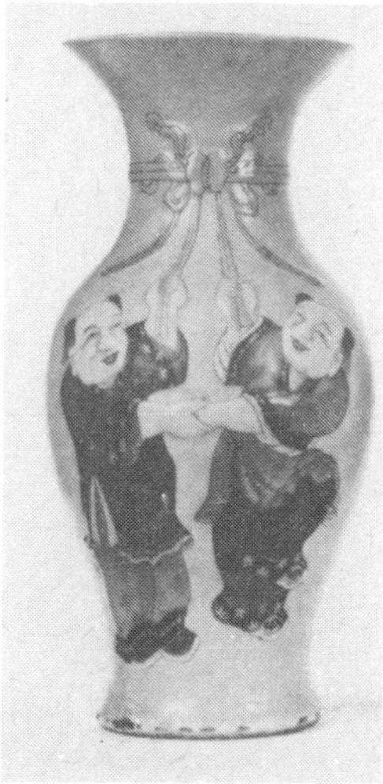

A pair of famille rose vases, reserved on a pink graviata ground, some restoration, 19th C., 17½ in. high. **£250-350**

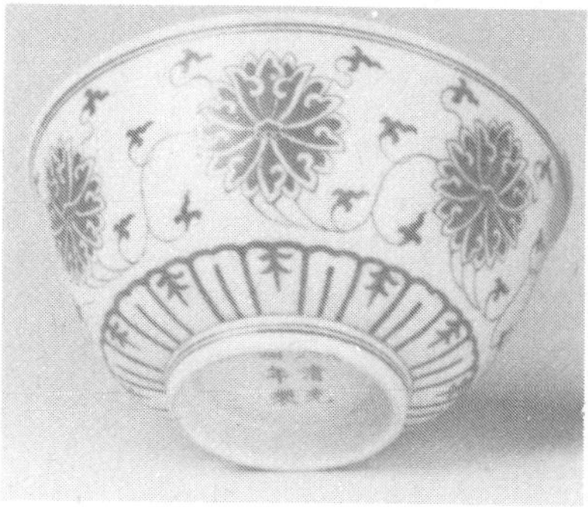

A pair of blue and white bowls, each painted in the interior with a formal chrysanthemum head and on the exterior with scrolling chrysanthemum above petal-shaped lappets radiating from the foot, encircled Guangxu six-character marks and of the period, 6½ in. diam. **£300-400**

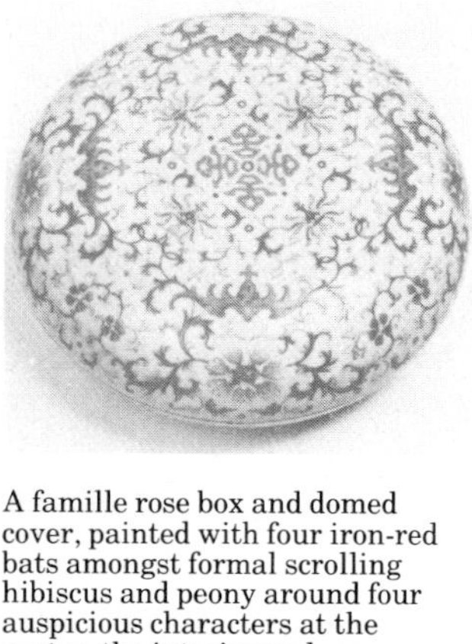

A famille rose box and domed cover, painted with four iron-red bats amongst formal scrolling hibiscus and peony around four auspicious characters at the centre, the interior under a turquoise glaze, minor chips, Guangxu, 14¼ in. diam. **£250-£350**

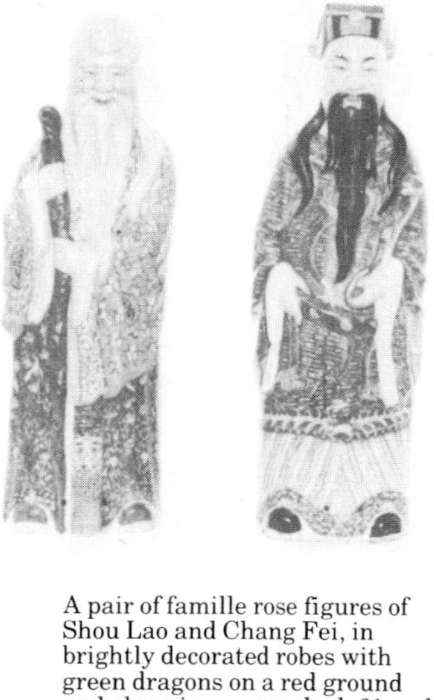

A pair of famille rose figures of Shou Lao and Chang Fei, in brightly decorated robes with green dragons on a red ground and phoenix, one cracked, 61 and 63 cm., impressed mark, 20th C. **£300-500**

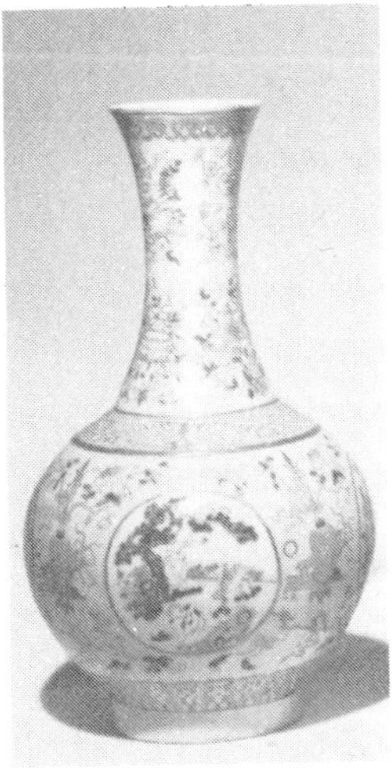

A pair of sgraffiato lemon-yellow ground globular vases, painted with roundels of deer and horned sheep below a pine, alternating with roses dividing vases of emblems, with eight Buddhist emblems on the waisted necks, one chipped, iron-red Guangxu six-character marks and of the period, 15½ in. high. **£700-900**

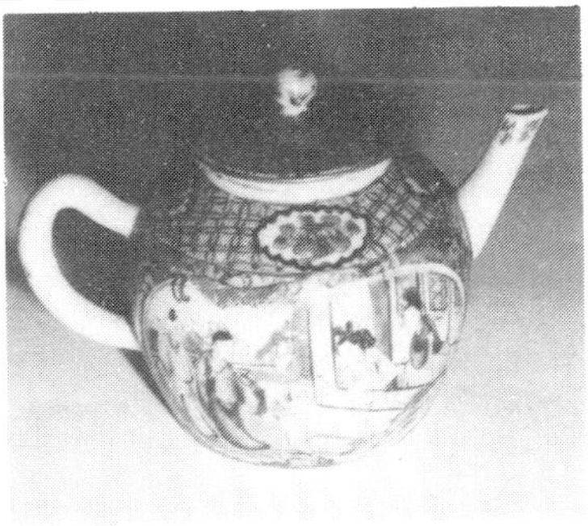

A Cantonese teapot, c. 1860. **£45-£50**

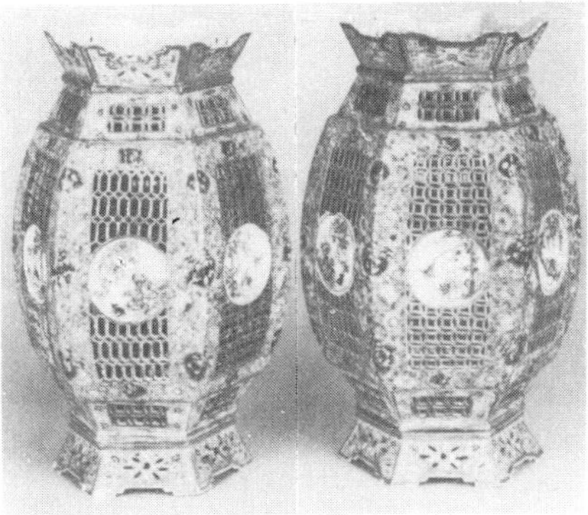

A pair of fine openwork hexagonal lanterns and stands, 29 cm., 19th C. **£200-300**

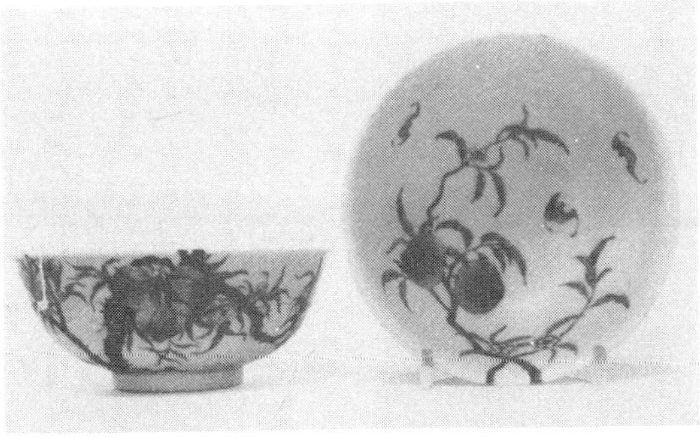

A good famille rose bowl, painted mark, Hongxian, 17 cm. **£400-450**

An example of Chinese taste porcelain, the design is typically restrained utilising pears and bats, both auspicious themes. This piece is of particular interest as the reign mark belongs to the President Yuan Shihkai, who created himself emperor in 1916 and who reigned for a few months only.

Chinese dynasties and marks

Earlier Dynasties

Shang Yin, c. 1532-1027 B.C.
Western Zhou (Chou) 1027-770 B.C.
Spring and Autumn Annals 770-480 B.C.
Warring States 484-221 B.C.
Qin (Ch'in) 221-206 B.C.
Western Han 206 B.C.-24 A.D.
Eastern Han 25-220
Three Kingdoms 221-265
Six Dynasties 265-589
Wei 386-557
Sui 589-617
Tang (T'ang) 618-906
Five Dynasties 907-960
Liao 907-1125
Sung 960-1280
Chin 1115-1260
Yüan 1280-1368

Ming Dynasty

洪武年製

Hongwu (Hung Wu)
1368-1398

永樂年製 永樂年製

Yongle (Yung Lo)
1403-1424

大明宣德年製

Xuande (Hsüan Tê)
1426-1435

大明成化年製

Chenghua (Ch'êng Hua)
1465-1487

大明正德年製

Zhengde
(Chêng Tê)
1506-1521

大明弘治年製

Hongzhi
(Hung Chih)
1488-1505

大明嘉靖年製

Jiajing
(Chia Ching)
1522-1566

大明隆慶年製

Longqing
(Lung Ching)
1567-1572

大明萬曆年製

Wanli (Wan Li)
1573-1620

大明天啟年製

Tianqi
(T'ien Chi)
1621-1627

崇禎年製

Chongzhen
(Ch'ung Chêng)
1628-1644

Qing (Ch'ing) Dynasty

大清順治年製

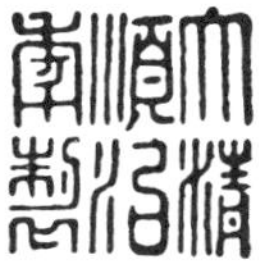

Shunzhi
(Shun Chih)
1644-1661

大清康熙年製

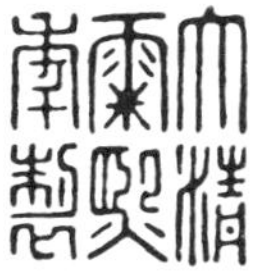

Kangxi (K'ang Hsi)
1662-1722

大清雍正年製

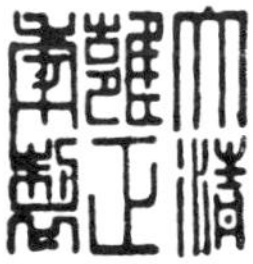

Yongzheng (Yung Chêng)
1723-1735

大清乾隆年製

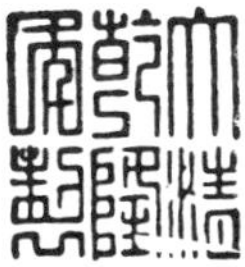

Qianlong (Ch'ien Lung)
1736-1795

嘉慶年製

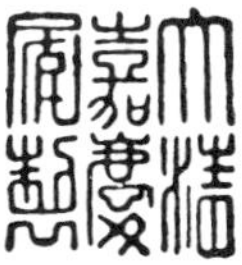

Jiaqing (Chia Ch'ing)
1796-1820

大清道光年製

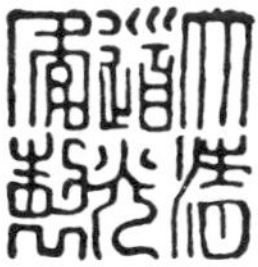

Daoguang (Tao Kuang)
1821-1850

大清咸豐年製

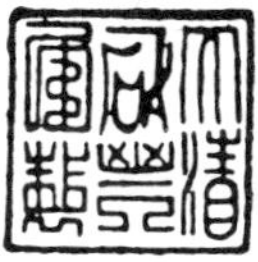

Xianfeng (Hsien Fêng)
1851-1861

大清同治年製

Tongzhi (T'ung Chih)
1862-1874

大清光緒年製

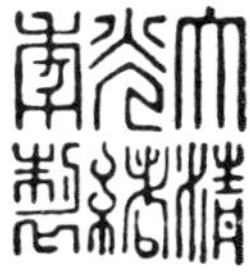

Guangxu (Kuang Hsü)
1875-1908

大清宣統年製

Xuantong
(Hsüan T'ung)
1909-1911

洪憲年製

Hongxian
(Hung Hsien)
1916

INDEX

P. Tito M

Cecilia Eusepi

Il sacrificio dei desideri

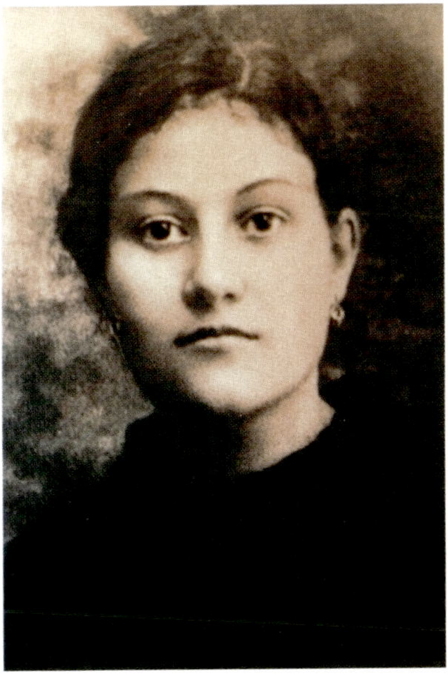

ELLEDICI
EDITRICE VELAR

Carissimi fedeli della Diocesi di Civitavecchia-Tarquinia,

la nostra Chiesa attende la Beatificazione di Cecilia Eusepi, nata a Monte Romano nel 1910 e morta appena diciottenne, come un dono dell'amore di Dio che ci sorprende e ci incoraggia, indicandoci ancora che la santità è la vocazione di ogni cristiano e il suo impegno quotidiano.

La storia di Cecilia è una bella storia di amore, quella dell'amore di Gesù che è riconosciuto e accolto negli avvenimenti ordinari e difficili di una povera famiglia, come tante del nostro territorio, e di una ragazza che coltiva grandi progetti di bene e li vede impediti da una terribile malattia. Ma è proprio l'amicizia di Gesù e la compagnia della Vergine Maria a sostenere Cecilia e a condurla verso le più grandi esperienze spirituali, fino all'offerta della sua vita, come risposta all'amore ricevuto.

Cecilia ci insegna a fidarci di Dio che, su strade diverse e a volte molto faticose, vuole portarci tutti alla salvezza; ai giovani, soprattutto, raccomanda di custodire la speranza e di fare scelte di generosità e di servizio.

A tutti voi affido questo testo del p. Tito M. Sartori che ci aiuterà a conoscere meglio Cecilia Eusepi, una santa che ci appartiene.

Con la benedizione del Signore

✠ Gino Reali
Amministratore Apostolico

Civitavecchia, 1 ottobre 2010

La vita

La fanciullezza

Superato l'arco che immette nella cittadina di Monte Romano (VT), in diocesi di Civitavecchia, si rimane colpiti nel constatare, nella vastità della piazza, tre elementi di spicco: la chiesa parrocchiale, il Municipio, e una lastra di marmo murata sulla parete di un edificio ubicato lungo la strada che fiancheggia la piazza stessa. Vi si legge un nome: Cecilia Eusepi. Verrebbe spontaneo pensare ad un personaggio che in qualche modo abbia avuto un impatto particolare sulla storia della cittadina. Ma i dati anagrafici lo escludono perentoriamente: ella nacque il 17 febbraio 1910 e decedette il 1° ottobre 1928. Il limite biografico, 18 anni e sette mesi, esclude qualsiasi possibilità di influsso decisivo sullo svolgersi delle vicende sociali d'allora.

Monte Romano (VT). *Panoramica di Monte Romano.*

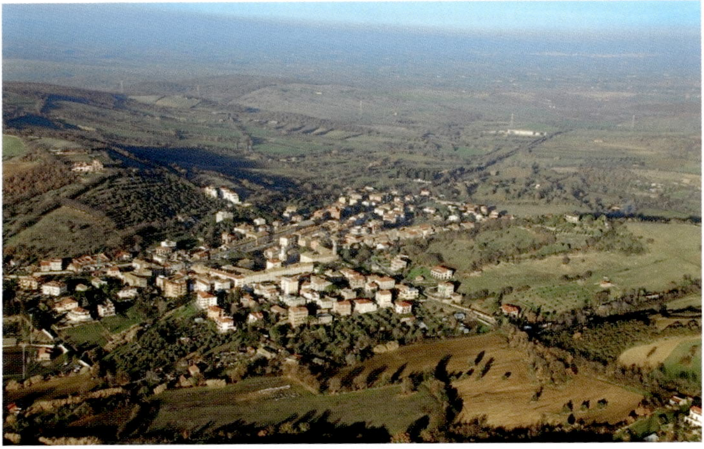

Infatti, Cecilia Eusepi ebbe sì i natali a Monte Romano, ma la sua vita si svolse altrove, soprattutto a Nepi, città della medesima provincia, elevata allora anche a Diocesi. Le ragioni del trasferimento in detta località emergono immediate alla lettura delle prime esperienze della bimba. Papà Antonio lasciò questa terra quando lei aveva circa 45 giorni. Sul letto di morte raccomandò al cognato Filippo Mannucci, fratello della moglie Paolina, di avere a cuore l'educazione della figlia. Egli sapeva bene di quale rettitudine brillasse la condotta severa della persona cui raccomandava tanto tesoro. Filippo, infatti, tenne fede alla parola data, sostenuto anche dall'affetto della sorella e dei nipoti Vincenzo e Giuseppina. Quest'ultima, di diciotto anni maggiore di Cecilia, lasciò presto la casa paterna e si trasferì con il marito Lucca-

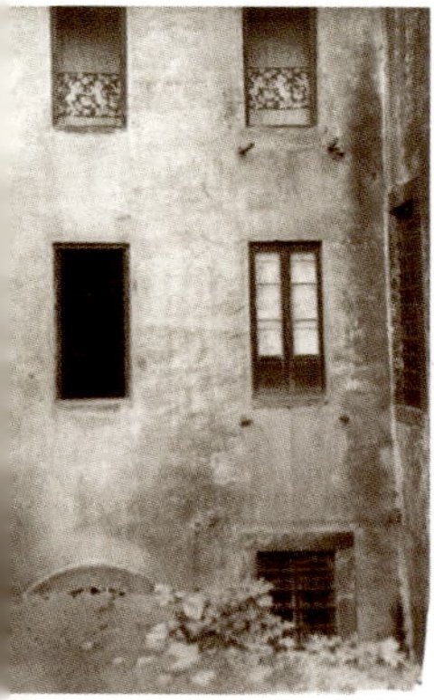

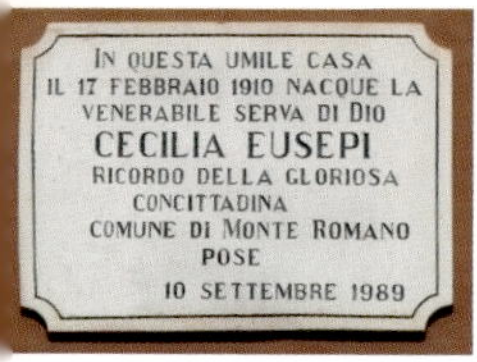

Monte Romano (VT).
Sopra:
Casa natale di Cecilia Eusepi. Finestre in alto con tendine.

Sotto:
Targa ricordo murata sulla facciata del medesimo edificio, ma dalla parte anteriore prospiciente la piazza cittadina.

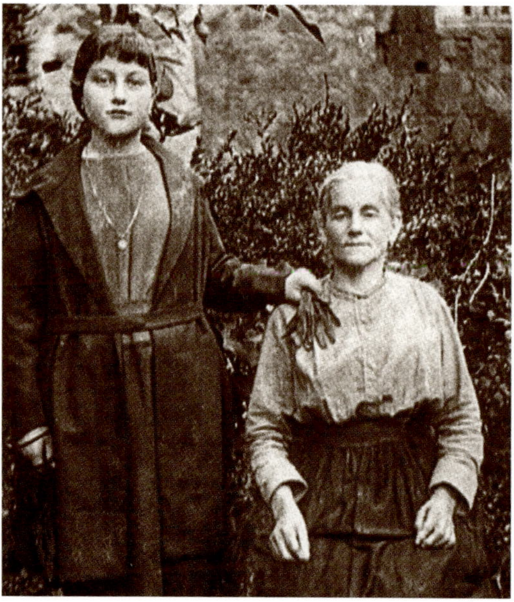

Mamma Paolina e Cecilia.

relli in provincia di Pesaro, a Secchiano di Cagli. Vincenzo, scoppiato il primo conflitto mondiale nel 1915, dovette partire per il fronte, rimanendovi colpito a morte il 30 maggio 1917. Gli altri otto figli che Paolina Mannucci dette alla luce, lasciarono questa terra ancora in giovane età.

Rimasta sola con Cecilia a Monte Romano, Paolina accettò l'invito del fratello Filippo, desideroso di averla presso di sé a Nepi alla fattoria *La Massa*, proprietà dei duchi Lante Della Rovere, residenti a Roma, che a lui avevano affidato la gestione amministrativa della vasta tenuta agricola. E così il 6 gennaio 1915 mamma Paolina condusse con sé la piccola Cecilia che, abbandonati i compagni della scuola materna del Paese natale, si trovò sola in mezzo alla campagna desolata, nel freddo gelido della campagna romana. Nel mese di agosto a farle compagnia verrà l'undicenne cugino Vittorio, figlio della zia Anna Rosa. Nei primi sette mesi ella avrà come quotidiani interlocutori soltanto mamma e zio.

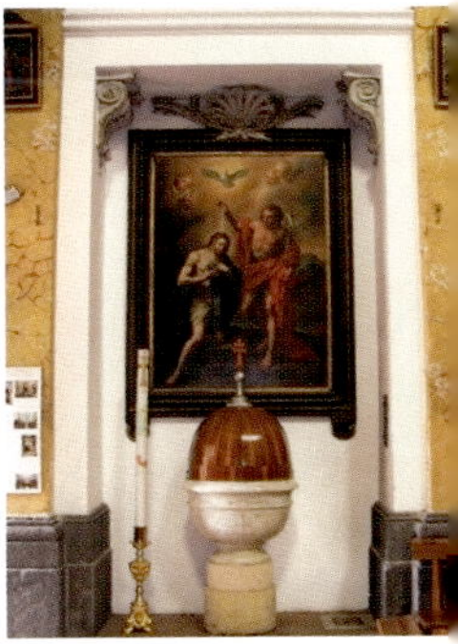

Monte Romano (VT). *Battistero della chiesa parrocchiale.*

Monte Romano (VT). *Chiesa parrocchiale e piazzale.*

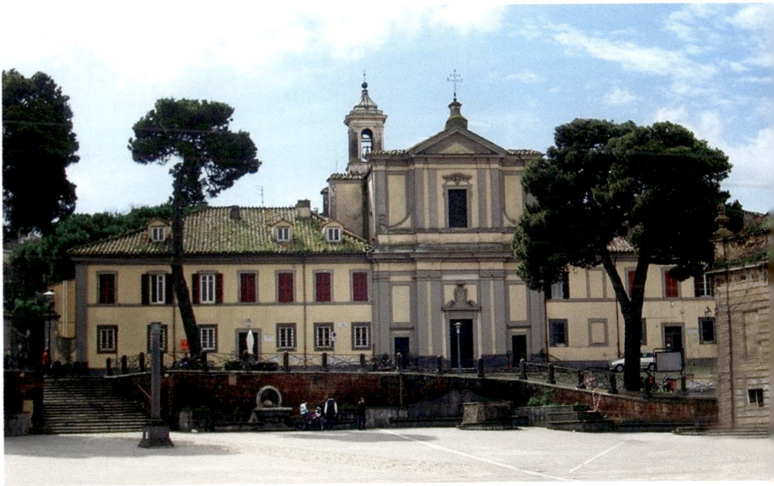

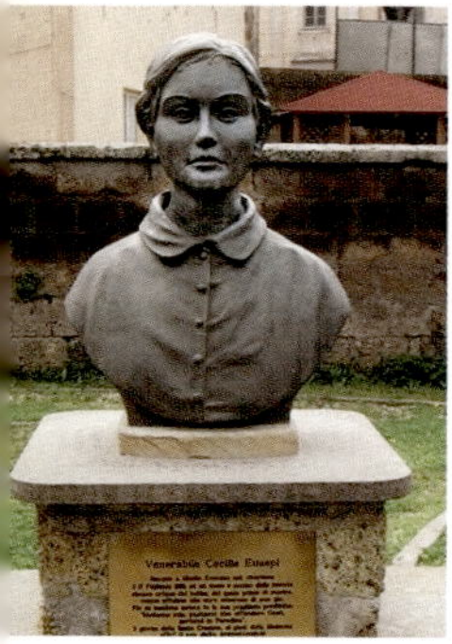

Monte Romano (VT).
Busto di Cecilia Eusepi collocato nell'omonimo "Largo".

Non è che si annoiasse molto, perché, essendo di straordinaria vivacità, ne inventava di continuo una dopo l'altra, correndo dappertutto, senza pericolo alcuno, dato che nel periodo invernale i lavori campestri sono praticamente inesistenti.

A settembre si pose con forza il problema dell'educazione della fanciulla. Mamma e zio, da mesi preoccupati per la presenza dei contadini e dei pastori non tutti religiosissimi come loro, e pertanto timorosi che discorsi e atteggiamenti un po' liberi potessero influire negativamente sulla piccola, decisero di affidarla alle Monache Cistercensi, il cui monastero, adiacente alla Chiesa parrocchiale dei SS. Romano e Tolomeo, era divenuto per tutti un punto di riferimento sicuro nell'opera educativa delle ragazze. L'attività da loro svolta era indirizzata non solo alle giovani di Nepi, ma anche a convittrici, provenienti da altri luoghi, alle quali le monache impartivano l'insegnamento delle scuole elementari.

Il 5 settembre 1915 mamma e zio affida-

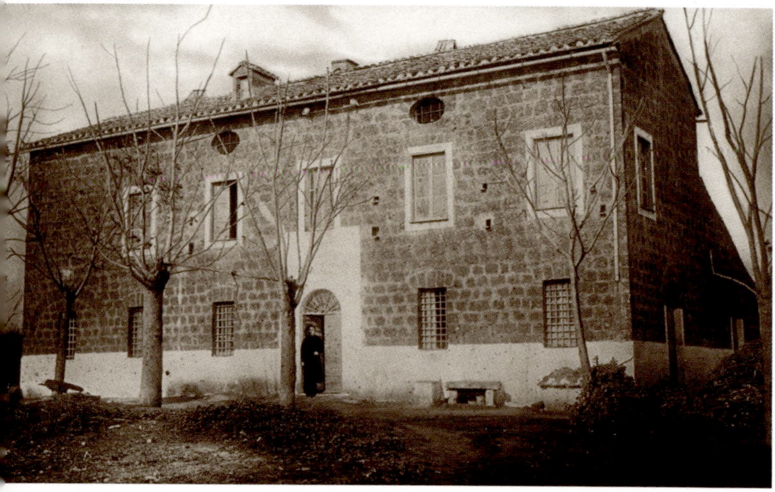

Nepi (VT).
Cecilia sulla soglia del casale "La Massa".

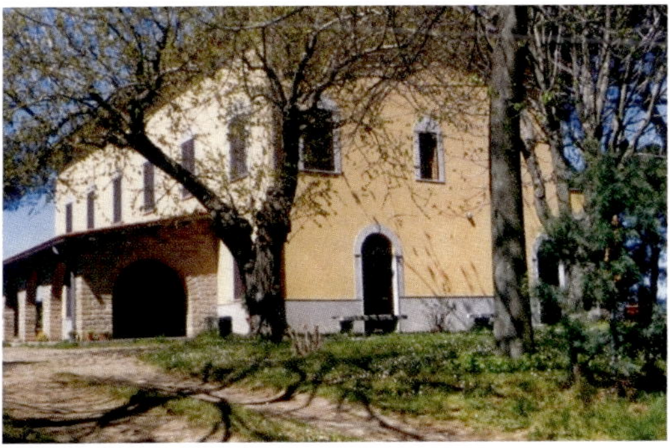

Casale "La Massa", oggi.

no alle Monache Cistercensi la loro piccola. Da quanto poi ci viene narrato da Cecilia, pare che lei non si sia affatto dispiaciuta di lasciare *La Massa*, e nemmeno di allontanarsi dalla mamma. Probabilmente il sollievo le veniva dal pensiero che ogni settimana la madre sarebbe venuta al monastero a portarle il bucato, approfittando della Messa da ascoltare nella chiesa parrocchiale, ubicata a circa 100 metri dal monastero.

Ma la sorpresa felice per lei fu quella di trovare altre amiche. A *La Massa* tale possibilità era inesistente, perché i tre chilometri che separavano quella località dalla cittadina di Nepi, per lei costituivano una lontananza insuperabile data l'età, unita, questa, al dovere di essere ovviamente accompagnata da qualcuno dei suoi.

E poi il vivere in mezzo alle monache si rivelò per la fanciulla una novità particolarmente gradita: tutte la guardavano, di lei si compiacevano, delle sue trovate e risposte si beavano. Tutto ciò risultava molto gradito all'orgoglio della bimba, che pur essendo ancor piccola, su questo versante era acutamente intuitiva.

A circa 20 mesi dall'entrata nel monastero, le monache la presentano al Vescovo di Nepi, il salesiano Mons. Luigi Maria

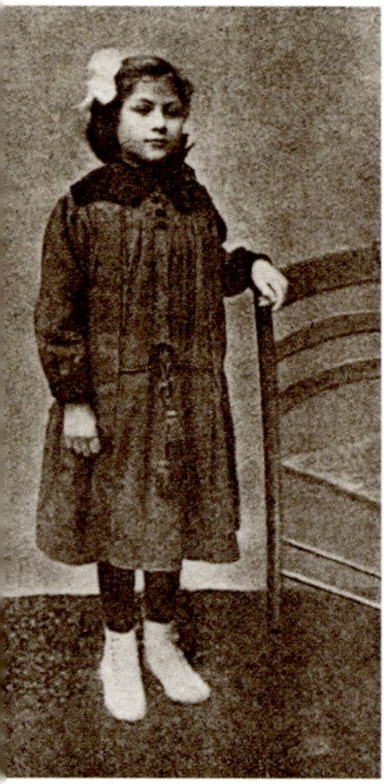

Nepi (VT). *Cecilia pochi giorni dopo la Prima Comunione.*

Olivares, il 27 maggio 1917, per il conferimento della Confermazione. La gioia della fanciulla fu talmente straripante che alla fine, dopo la partenza di mamma e zio, si recò tutta sola dinanzi all'altare della Madonna delle Grazie, per consacrarLe interamente il suo cuore.

Ma l'avvenimento che segnò a caratteri d'oro il suo rapporto con Dio, sarebbe accaduto pochi mesi dopo: il 2 ottobre 1917, giorno della Prima Comunione ricevuta dall'Abate Angelo Testa. Lei ne scrive con animo commosso nella *Storia di un Pagliaccio.* Col pensiero vi ritornerà sovente nel corso degli anni, perché quello non fu un giorno, ma "il" giorno più radioso della sua vita. Ne fu preparata con infinito amore dalle monache. La sera prima, l'Abbadessa, Donna Teresa, le si avvicinò mentre la fanciulla stava in giardino a contempla-

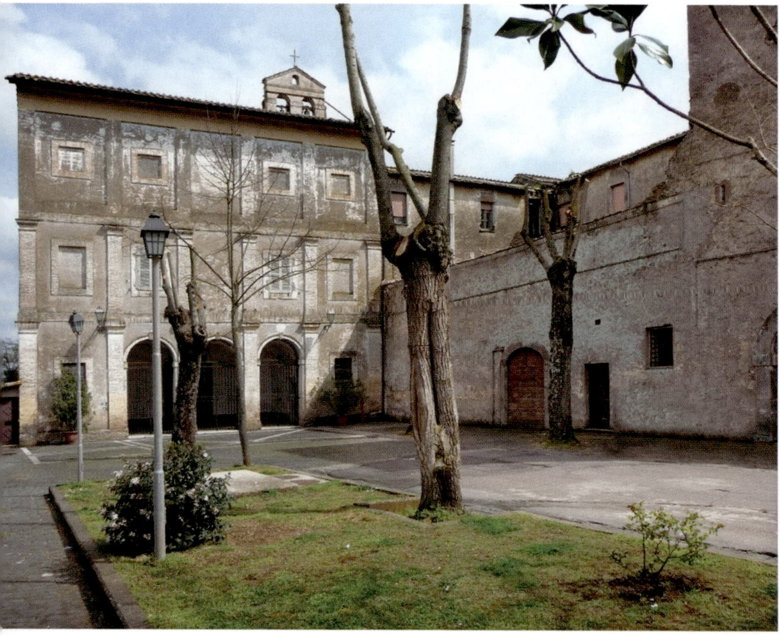

re il cielo stellato e con voce sommessa le disse: "Domattina riceverai nel cuore Colui che ha creato queste stelle". Bastava molto di meno per eccitare in lei ardenti sentimenti d'amore e di devozione!

Infatti, il giorno dopo, ricevuto Gesù Eucaristia, gli disse: *"Caro Gesù, piuttosto che offenderti, fammi morire. Gesù, te lo prometto, sarò tua, per sempre tua"*. Con queste parole ella intendeva significare al Signore la sua intenzione di consacrargli l'intera sua esistenza nell'intimità della vita claustrale. Vedremo che cosa invece accadrà.

La novità più interessante collegata con la Prima Comunione, fu la scoperta del significato della santità appreso dalla *Storia di un'anima* che le monache le posero tra le mani subito dopo l'accesso al Sacramento Eucaristico. Prima lei confondeva l'essere santa con il dire tante preghiere

Nella pagina precedente ed in questa:
Nepi (VT).
Monastero cistercense.

"[...] nelle notti in cui si vedeva la luna, mi divertivo a correre in giardino".
(Autobiografia, p. 14)

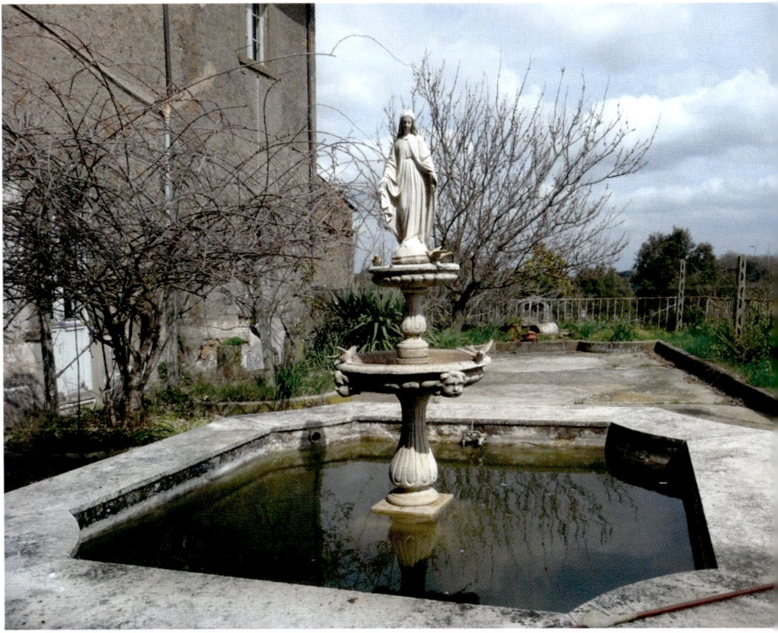

Giardino del monastero.

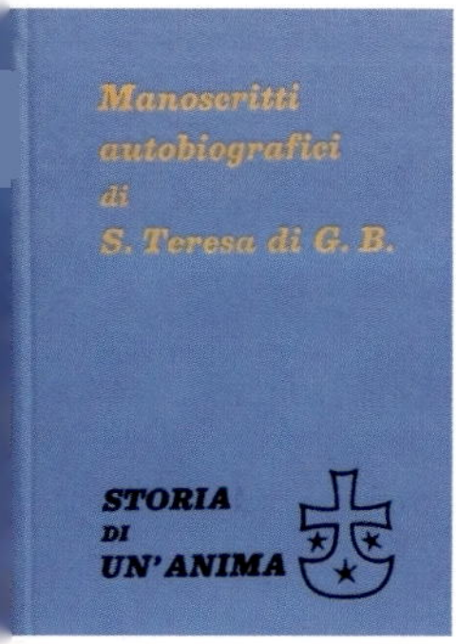

"Naturalmente leggevo vite di santi, la prima che lessi fu la vita di S. Teresa del Bambino Gesù".
(Autobiografia, p. 24)

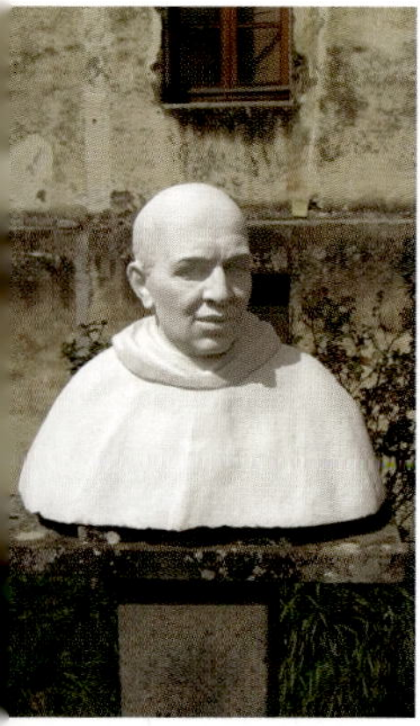

Padre Angelo M. Flamini, suo confessore e primo direttore spirituale.

sull'esempio che ammirava nella vita del monastero. Poi, invece, comprese, dietro la guida della Santa di Lisieux, che essere santi significava *"far bene tutte le nostre azioni ordinarie, anche minime, allo scopo unico di far piacere a Gesù"*. Che una ragazzina di otto anni giunga a simili conclusioni non può che destare profonda meraviglia per la maturità dimostrata.

Tra le varie letture cui si dedica a quel tempo, trova collocazione anche la biografia di San Gabriele dell'Addolorata, passionista. A colpirla fu soprattutto la constatazione che anche lui aveva attinto dal Terz'Ordine dei Servi di Maria, cui si era iscritto, la devozione alla Vergine dei Dolori, così com'era accaduto anche a lei fin dall'inizio nel suo ingresso al monastero, in un primo tempo spaventata di fronte alla solenne statua dell'Addolorata in cui si era imbattuta improvvisamente nella penombra del coro delle monache.

Oltre alla vita di San Gabriele, Cecilia lesse attentamente il libretto *Grappoli d'oro della mistica vite del Senario, ossia cenni biografici dei santi e beati dell'Ordine dei Servi di Maria.* Se ne innamorò, come capita facilmente a quell'età. Chiese pertanto di diventare pure lei Terziaria dell'Ordine servitano, ma essendo troppo giovane, dodicenne appunto, dovette chiederne l'autorizzazione al Padre Angelo M. Flamini, Priore provinciale della Provincia Romana dell'Ordine dei Servi di Maria, lui pure residente a Nepi e per di più direttore spirituale della stessa Cecilia.

Il 14 febbraio 1922 nella cornice del monastero cistercense e con immenso gaudio, Cecilia vestì, in qualità di novizia, lo scapolare e la cintura di Terziaria e assunse il nome Suor Angela Maria. Alla vestizione seguirà, pochi mesi dopo, la professione emessa il 17 settembre 1922, non più nell'ambito del monastero, ma nella Chiesa parrocchiale dei SS. Tolomeo e Romano. Ricorreva, infatti, quel giorno la terza domenica di settembre, dedicata alla solennità dell'Addolorata. Era stata Lei ad ispirare i Sette Mercanti Fiorentini il giorno dell'Assunta del 1233 a dare inizio ad una Famiglia religiosa – appunto l'Ordine dei Servi di Maria – dedita alla venerazione dei Dolori da Lei patiti sotto la Croce, mentre il Figlio agonizzava.

Come mai nella chiesa parrocchiale anziché nel monastero? Perché Cecilia quell'estate dovette, per la prima volta

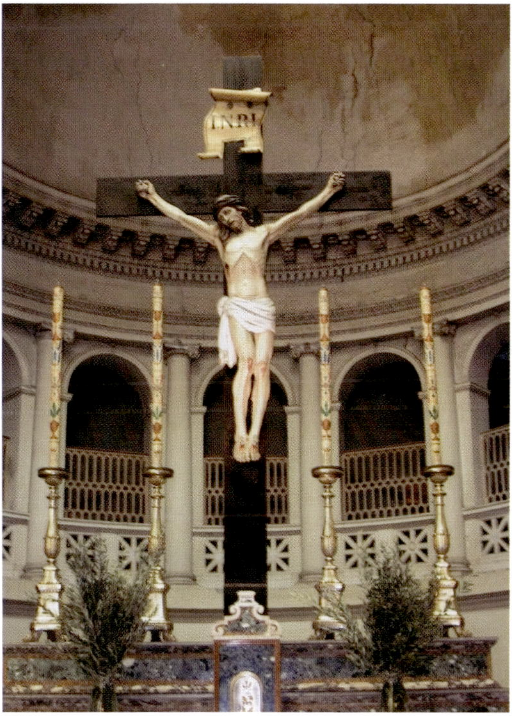

Nepi (VT). *Chiesa parrocchiale dei SS. Tolomeo e Romano, detta del "Rosario", dove il 17 settembre 1922 Cecilia emise la professione di Terziaria dell'Ordine dei Servi di Maria.*

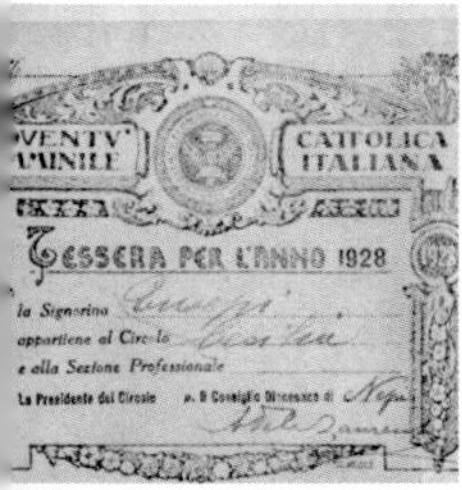

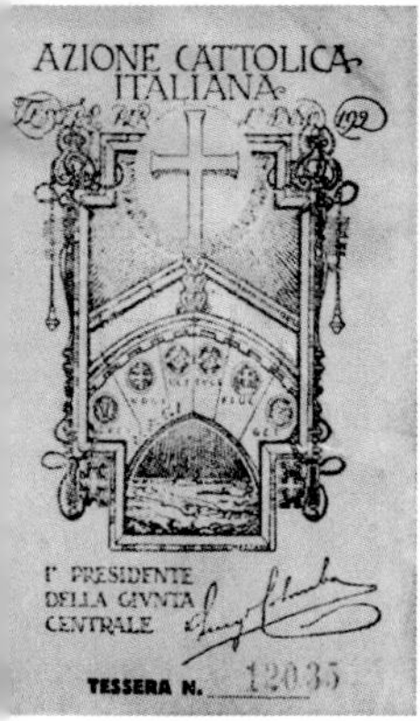

La prima iscrizione all'Azione Cattolica avvenne nell'estate del 1922.

dopo sette anni, ritornare a *La Massa*, per volontà dello zio Filippo a causa di una epistassi irrefrenabile che aveva colpito la giovane. A suggerirne il ritorno tra le pareti domestiche era stato il medico curante e lo zio non esitò ad eseguirne il suggerimento.

L'adolescenza

Quella domenica rimase nel cuore di Cecilia come un punto fisso: al mattino la Messa solenne, cantata dai giovani studenti e dai Frati Servi di Maria, la predicazione incentrata sulla Vergine Addolorata, i fiori, il suono dell'organo; al pomeriggio, la festosa cornice dei Vespri cantati, le luci, la folla numerosa, tutto un insieme che le sembrò trasfigurare l'evento in un momento radioso di grazia da conservare come ricco patrimonio spirituale. Quando il 1° novembre 1922, solennità di Tutti i Santi, Cecilia rientrò nel monastero per continuare gli studi, fu accolta con tanta felicità dalle Monache Cistercensi, che già la pensavano una di loro. Infatti non la misero tra le convittrici, ma nel reparto riservato alle novizie, con il compito di seguire, come responsabile, le altre convittrici tutte più giovani di lei. Questo nuovo ruolo le consentì di dar vita alla *Compagnia dell'Addolorata*, di cui addirittura scrisse una specie di Statuto.

In quei mesi però avvenne un fatto traumatico: la morte dell'Abbadessa Teresa Salvatori, che per Cecilia non era solo un'istituzione all'interno della vita monastica, ma la sua "mamma" nello spirito, colei che le aveva fatto amare Gesù fin da quando, bimba, aveva oltrepassato la soglia del monastero. Quel dolore profondo mise allo scoperto un sentimento che da qualche tempo le agitava il cuore: non si sentiva più attratta a monacarsi in quel luogo. L'attrazione verso la Vergine Addolorata, che lei chiamava il suo "cuore", la spingeva ad abbracciare lo stato di vita religiosa tra le Suore Mantellate Serve di Maria di Pistoia, che alla spiritualità dei Frati Serviti ispiravano la propria vita. L'occasione per realizzare tale aspirazione si presentò con forza il 28 marzo 1923 con il ricovero ospedaliero a Civita Castellana a causa di una pesante gastralgia, accompagnata da epistassi. Il ricovero si prolungò fino all'8 aprile.

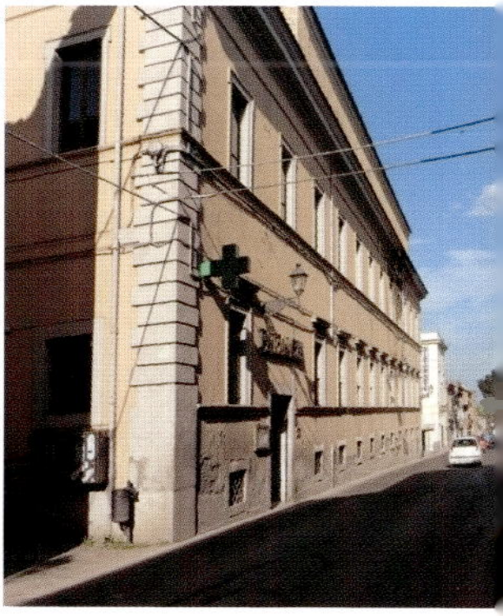

Civita Castellana (VT). *Ospedale Andosilla: Cecilia vi fu ricoverata dal 28 marzo all'8 aprile 1923.*

Nel dimetterla dall'ospedale, il dott. Ferretti le ingiunse di rimanere per sei mesi a *La Massa*, di fare delle passeggiate, di nutrirsi con cibi fortificanti. Così ebbero termine gli studi di Cecilia.

Soltanto alla domenica poteva recarsi a Nepi per assistere alla Santa Messa. Sprofondata nella solitudine della campagna com'era accaduto all'arrivo a *La Massa* nel 1915, la tredicenne malata poté contare sulla saltuaria compagnia di quattro amiche nepesine, tutte più anziane di lei, la cui età si aggirava tra i 22 della più giovane ai 40 anni dclla maggiorc! Lo sbalzo notevole di differenziazione anagrafica rivela quale straordinaria maturità fu da loro riscontrata nella persona dell'adolescente Cecilia.

Tra il mese di aprile e quello di settembre, l'Eusepi inizia una nuova attività, iscrivendosi tra le Aspiranti dell'Azione Cattolica. Così il suo recarsi domenicale a Nepi le permette di assistere i ragazzi,

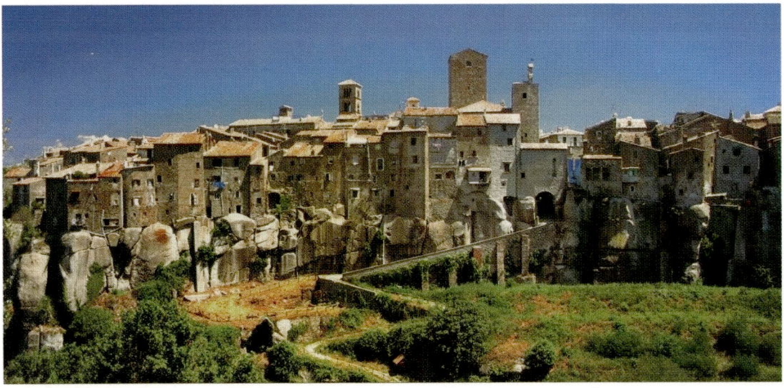

Vitorchiano (VT).

"[...] andammo a Vitorchiano dove ci fermammo parecchi giorni, in casa del Signor Francesco Menicucci intimo amico di zio Filippo".

(Autobiografia, p. 41)

di farli giocare e di condurli a confessarsi nel primo pomeriggio, realizzando il programma di fondo dell'Associazione: preghiera, azione, sacrificio.

Quei sei mesi tuttavia non trascorrono soltanto in passeggiate e in discorsi, ma le consentono di approfondire l'anelito che da tanto tempo le urgeva in cuore: quello di consacrarsi a Dio nella Congregazione delle Suore Mantellate Serve di Maria di Pistoia. Bisognava però rivelarlo alla mamma. E la mamma che cosa le risponderà? Negativamente. E lo zio? Anche lui negativamente, data l'eccessiva età giovanile di Cecilia. Ma lo zio farà un passo ulteriore: intende aprire gli occhi alla nipote, farle conoscere, per così dire, il mondo.

A settembre il proposito diviene realtà: lo zio conduce Cecilia in visita ad amici, a conoscenti e a parenti. Ne sono testimonianza i viaggi a Viterbo, prima città vista da Cecilia; a Vitorchiano da Francesco Menicucci, intimo amico dello zio, presso il quale si ferma alcuni giorni. Invece che divertirsi, Cecilia cercò invece di fare opera di apostolato nei confronti della diciottenne figlia dell'ospitante. Successivamente lo zio condusse la nipote a Macerata da una zia, dove il cugino Graziano, ventunenne ma già sindaco del paese e capo della milizia fascista, cercò di farla divertire, portandola all'inaugurazione del monumento ai caduti opera di lui, a quell'età già ingegnere.

Alla fine l'approdo fu a Cagli, dalla sorella Giuseppina, sposata Lucarelli , sostando, pure lì, alcuni giorni. Tutti si pronunciarono negativamente circa la vocazione religiosa della consanguinea. Lo zio, allo scopo di dare un assetto definitivo a tutti quei no, condusse Cecilia dal Vescovo di Cagli. E qui avvenne la sorpresa: quel vecchietto dette invece risposta positiva! "Fatti coraggio – le disse l'anziano Presule – se Gesù vuole, sarai accontentata". E per di più le regalò una medaglia di Santa Teresa di Lisieux con queste parole: "Tieni, raccomandati a questa santa, anche questa ha dovuto soffrir tanto per farsi monaca".

Il giro turistico non era ancora finito. L'ultima tappa fu a Secchiano (PU), sempre presso la sorella Giuseppina. Anche lì Cecilia stette alcuni giorni, godendo della bellezza del paesaggio, facendo delle splendide passeggiate. Il momento più pesante era quello della sera, quando la sorella le ripeteva la solita filastrocca: "Non devi farti suora, la tua salute non te lo permette, poi devi stare con mamma, da' retta allo zio, se no te ne pentirai". Questa raccomandazione gliela ripeterà anche anni dopo, ma torniamo al momento presente.

Nel tornare a Nepi s'imbattono in un Padre cappuccino, al quale lo zio si rivolge, raccontandogli il motivo di quell'ormai lungo errare. Ma il buon frate, dopo aver fissato Cecilia, gli risponde: "La lasci

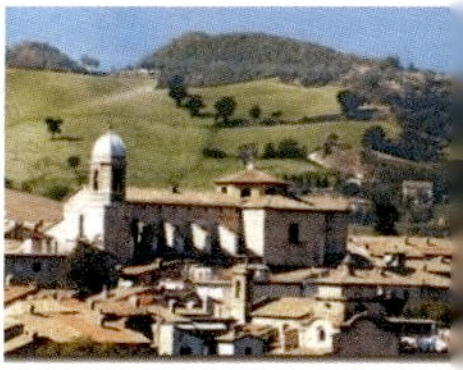

Cagli (PU).

"Di lì [Macerata, io e lo zio Filippo] andammo a Cagli, da mia sorella [Giuseppina] e lì pure ci fermammo alcuni giorni".
(*Autobiografia*, p. 43)

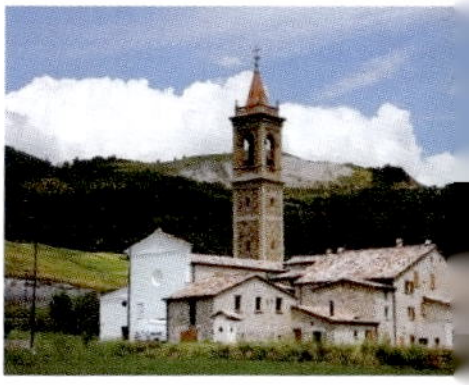

Secchiano (PU).

"Da Cagli andammo a Secchiano, piccolo paesello posto a metà di un monte, sotto il quale scorre un fiumicello".
(*Autobiografia*, p. 44)

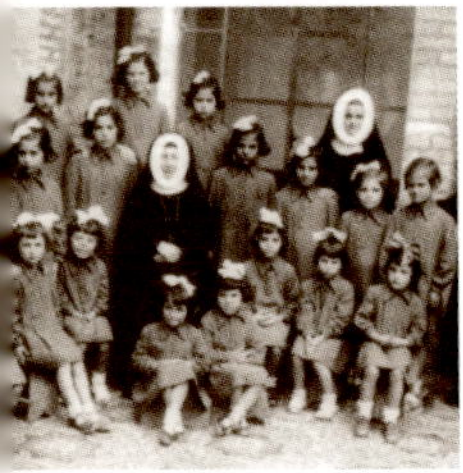

Cagli (PU).

"Di lì [ossia dal Vescovo di Cagli] andammo a far visita alle suore del Preziosissimo Sangue, dove si recavano a scuola i miei nipotini".

(Autobiografia, p. 44)

fare, non ha l'età, ma comprende il passo che vuol fare, altrimenti un giorno potrà pentirsene amaramente". Questo consiglio, unito all'altro del Vescovo di Cagli, troverà completezza nell'incontro successivo con il Vescovo di Nepi, il salesiano Mons. Luigi Maria Olivares, oggi Servo di Dio, che persuaderà lo zio ad acconsentire al desiderio di Cecilia. E così il 16 novembre 1923 Cecilia parte per Roma, due giorni dopo prosegue per Pistoia per raggiungere la Casa Madre delle Suore Mantellate Serve di Maria. Poco dopo l'arrivo a Pistoia le si presenta una giovane, lei pure collegina, di nome Clara Laffi, sorellastra di Padre Bernardino M. Piccinelli, religioso dei Servi di Maria, la cui causa di Beatificazione oggi è presente presso la Congregazione dei Santi.

Clara diverrà l'amica del cuore di Cecilia, che solo a lei permetterà l'accesso al *Libro dei segreti,* nel quale l'autrice usava segnare le sue esperienze spirituali. Clara Laffi sarà altresì la sua compagna di studi, perché, come Cecilia, dovette prepararsi all'esame di quinta elementare sotto la guida di suor Guglielma Borsari, che diventerà, qualche anno dopo, Superiora generale della Congregazione. All'insegnamento scolastico suor Guglielma univa l'insegnamento spirituale con opportune e sante ammonizioni, aprendo cuore e mente al contatto con Dio. Nulla di meglio per Cecilia e, di riflesso, anche per la sua compagna. A luglio entrambe le studenti superano l'esame di ammissione alla 1ª Complementare.

Nei mesi estivi Cecilia è mandata ad assistere i bambini dell'asilo di Quarrata. Non è un bel modo per rifarsi dalle fatiche degli studi e dall'onere degli esami, ma questa è la prassi di fatto allora seguita. Tra i bimbi dell'asilo di Quarrata, paese agricolo del pistoiese, Cecilia trascorre i mesi estivi in preparazione degli Esercizi Spirituali che agli inizi del mese di ottobre precederanno la sua partenza per Zara (Croazia), fissata per il 22 ottobre di quel mese con arrivo il giorno appresso, dopo 31 ore di viaggio. Ambedue le amiche inizieranno quasi subito il 1° anno delle Complementari.

È talmente esemplare la condotta dell'Eusepi che la Direttrice – una religiosa Serva di Maria – le assegna il compito di "guida" delle sue compagne, incarico che le procurerà umiliazioni e sofferenze. Ciò nonostante, Cecilia con tanto garbo riesce ad ottenere dalle compagne l'adesione alle sue proposte di impegno spirituale: ogni sera riunione sotto forma di "capitolo delle colpe" con penitenza fatta insieme e assegnazione di un certo numero di "fioretti" che ciascuna di loro si impegna a compiere nel giorno successivo.

Pistoia. *Casa Madre della Congregazione delle Suore Mantellate Serve di Maria.*

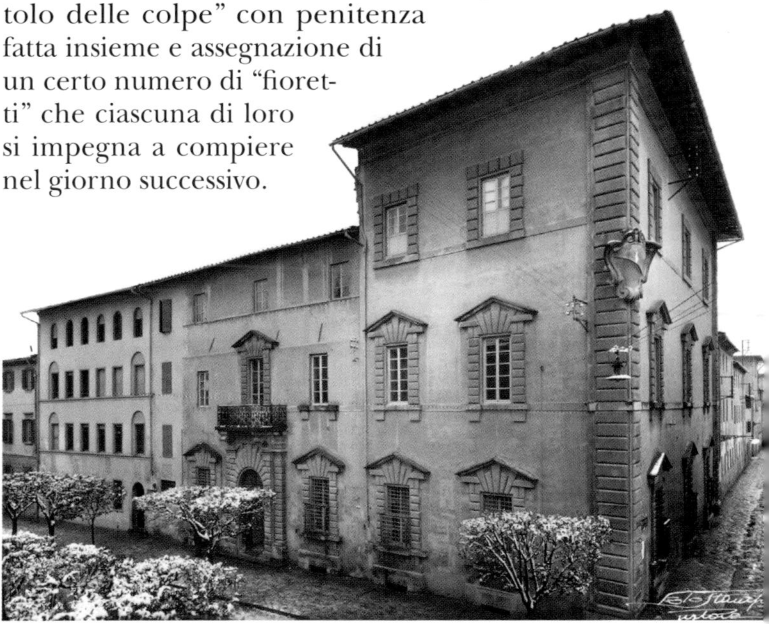

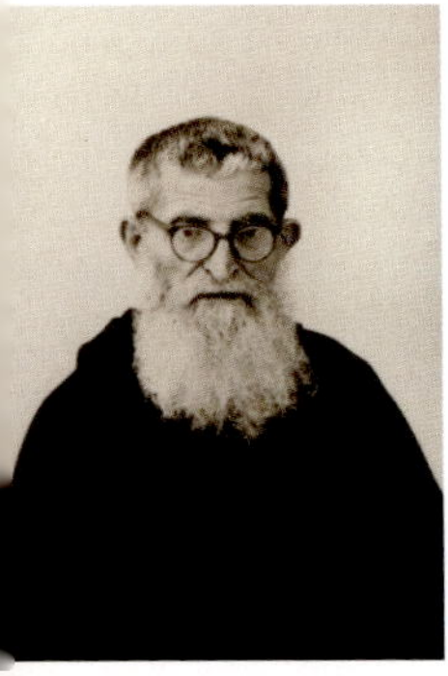

P. Agostino M. Fagiolo. Alle ore 4,30 Cecilia si comunicò alla Chiesa del Rosario. "Il P. Agostino [Fagiolo] m'accompagnò fino alla porta di chiesa, qui mi benedì e mi disse: 'Va angioletto e ritorna angelo'".
(Autobiografia, p. 46s)

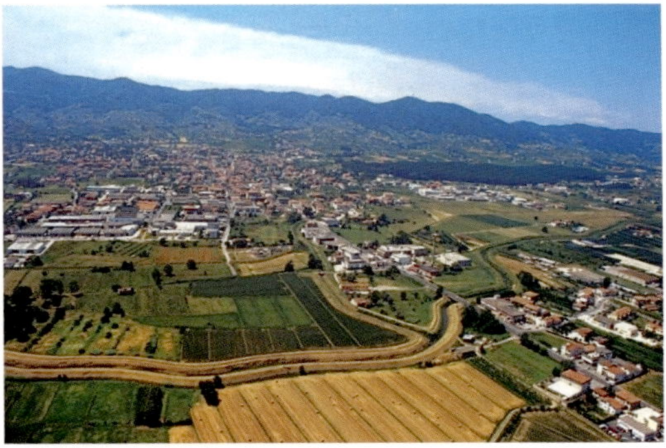

Quarrata (PT).

"La Madre Generale mi mandò a passare le vacanze a Quarrata, piccolo paese dei dintorni di Pistoia".
(Autobiografia, p. 52)

La giovinezza

Nell'anno scolastico 1924-25 lo stato di salute di Cecilia accusò degli alti e bassi. Il momento peggiore avvenne durante il mese di maggio 1925, quando fu colpita da febbri altissime che toccarono i 40 gradi. Il medico le prescrisse di cambiare aria, ossia di lasciare Zara, luogo per lei insalubre. Rimessasi, ritornò tra i banchi di scuola, nel mese di luglio affrontò gli esami riportando ottime valutazioni. Giunse però per lei un ordine amaro: doveva ritornare in Italia e ripetere, durante l'estate, l'esperienza di Quarrata vissuta l'anno precedente. Nel lasciare Zara, Cecilia, che nel mese precedente aveva confidato a Clara Laffi l'anelito di consacrarsi a Dio con il voto di vittima, raccomandò all'amica di fare altrettanto. Il 12 luglio 1925, giorno della partenza, le consegnò un biglietto sul quale aveva scritto delle parole ritenute come le più preziose sia per lei che per Clara: *"Gesù, fa' di me quello che vuoi, sono pronta a tutto, basta che tu mi dia la forza necessaria per sopportare con forza e pazienza qualunque sia la croce"*.

A Quarrata (PT), tutto procede come prefissato. Ad ottobre ritorna a Pistoia per frequentare il 2° corso delle Complementari; l'amica Clara rientra invece in Dalmazia.

Nel cuore della giovane persiste l'anelito a emettere il voto di vittima, mai a lei concesso dal confessore. In sostituzione di quel voto, la notte di Natale del 1925, rifacendosi all'esempio di Santa Teresa di Lisieux, Cecilia si offre come pallina nelle mani di Gesù, perché sia lui a gestire la sua vita.

Da quel momento inizia il travaglio che la condurrà alla tomba: mancanza di appetito, un non sentirsi bene che culmina in primavera nelle febbri intestinali, relativa degenza a letto per 21 giorni a cominciare dal 27 marzo. Si rimette in sesto, termina studi ed esami, e il 31 luglio viene rimandata a Quarrata per la terza volta. Vi rimane però poco tempo, perché avendo chiesto, l'anno precedente, di indossare la *mantellina*, ossia di passare dal rango di collegina a quello di probanda, il 16 agosto viene richiamata a Pistoia, le viene posta sulle spalle la surriferita mantellina e la si assegna alla Comunità di Maresca (PT) – un borgo montano a circa 800 metri s.l.m. – con il compito di fare il doposcuola a 21 ragazzi appartenenti alle prime quattro classi elementari.

Pochi giorni dopo essere giunta a Maresca, Cecilia accusa una temperatura febbrile di 38 gradi, causata, a giudizio del medico, da morbo intestinale. Viene rimandata a Pistoia, dove, oltre alla predetta malattia, le vengono diagnosticate peritonite e infiammazione ai polmoni. Il male si aggrava, Cecilia giunge in fin di vita. Una novena indirizzata a suor Bertilla Boscardin le ottiene un momentaneo superamento del

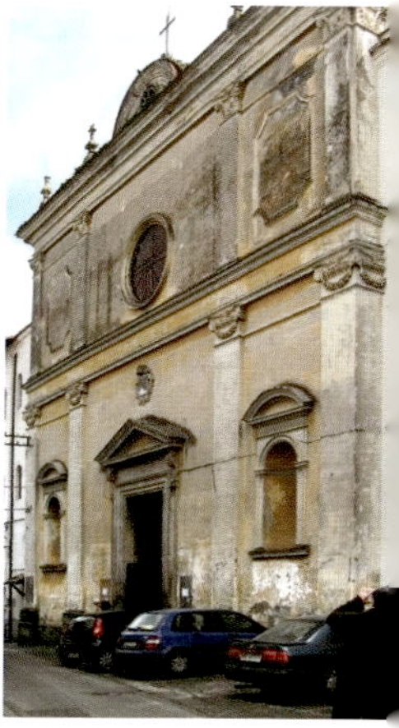

Nepi (VT). *Facciata della Chiesa dei SS. Tolomeo e Romano.*

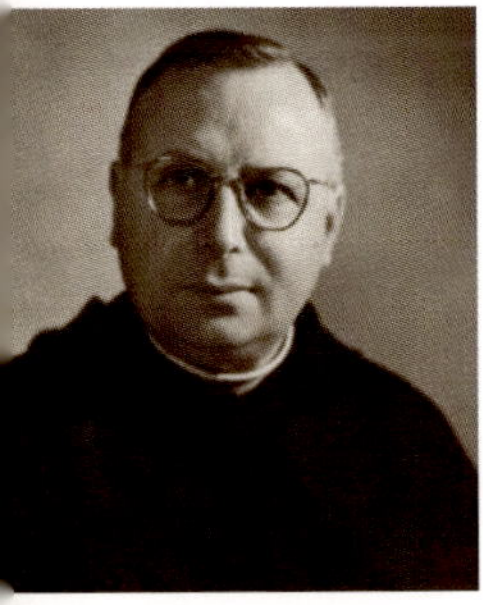

P. Gabriele M. Roschini. La sera del 25 ottobre 1926 P. Gabriele andò a "La Massa".

"[…] Gesù stesso l'ispirò a promettermi di venire più spesso che le fosse stato possibile, a portarmi Gesù". (*Autobiografia, p. 65*)

male. Dopo 40 giorni di degenza a letto, il medico le prescrive "aria nativa", la ricetta allora in uso in questi casi.

Con grande dolore, lunedì 10 ottobre, Cecilia parte per Nepi accompagnata da madre Gioacchina Passaglia. Giunte sul tardi nella cittadina laziale, pernottano in paese e il mattino seguente, 11 ottobre, ascoltano la Santa Messa nella Chiesa dei SS. Tolomeo e Romano. Alla colazione, loro offerta dal Padre Angelo M. Flamini, Priore provinciale, è presente anche un giovane sacerdote, Padre Gabriele M. Roschini. Cecilia viene accompagnata a *La Massa* da madre Gioacchina, dove mamma Paolina e il cugino Vittorio sono ad attenderle con trepidazione ed affetto. Per tre giorni rimane in compagnia di Cecilia anche madre Gioacchina.

La partenza di quest'ultima chiude la felice parentesi di Cecilia con le Suore Mantellate Serve di Maria di Pistoia e suggella pure un sogno di consacrazione grandemente accarezzato dall'Eusepi.

Dal 14 ottobre alla sera del 25, Cecilia trascorre giorni pesantissimi, oppressa non solo dalla solitudine in cui si vede precipitata – lei abituata da anni alla condivisione di ideali e di vita con delle coetanee – ma soprattutto dal dolore di non poter ricevere Gesù Eucaristia e di non poter accedere al sacramento della Confessione. Ad alleviare tanta sofferenza giunge, la sera del 25 ottobre, come un raggio di luce in fitta tenebra, il Padre Gabriele M. Roschini, di soli 10 anni maggiore di lei. La visita inaspettata del Padre Gabriele M. Roschini probabilmente fu suggerita dal Padre Angelo M. Flamini, che ben conosceva la sensibilità della sua figlia spirituale. Comunque l'incontro si rivelò provvidenziale. Padre Gabriele intuì il travaglio e i bisogni interiori di Cecilia e le promise di portarle il giorno seguente la Santa Comunione. Infatti, come ben disse l'Eusepi, la Comunione del 26 ottobre 1926 costituì un momento particolarmente significativo, tanto da scrivere: *"L'anima mia in quel giorno subì una trasformazione meravigliosa; cominciò ad irrobustirsi, fino al punto che nulla può più abbatterla"*.

Il desiderio di ritornare tra le Suore Mantellate continuava a persistere in lei, tuttavia lo stato precario di salute non le consentì nemmeno di recarsi a Nepi durante il mese di novembre fino al 10 del successivo dicembre. Ci fu però una parentesi meravigliosa: il giorno della solennità dell'Immacolata, il Padre Gabriele non solo le porta la Comunione, ma l'autorizza ad emettere i voti privati di povertà, castità, obbedienza, quei voti che da anni ormai rappresentavano il sogno della sua consacrazione a Gesù.

L'andata a Nepi il 10 dicembre con pernottamento presso le suore Dorotee e partecipazione alla Messa di domenica 11 presso la Chiesa parrocchiale dei SS. Tolomeo e Romano, non prelude a guarigione. Seguirà un attacco di pleurite, con allettamento anche durante il periodo natalizio, al punto che Cecilia sarà costretta a rinunciare all'invito del 13 gennaio 1927 della Madre Generale delle Suore Mantellate, che la pregava di rientrare nell'Istituto e prestare servizio a Fara Sabina. Tale stato d'infermità continua fino ad aprile. Per poter comunicarsi più agevolmente, Padre Gabriele le ottiene dalla Santa Sede, il 24 febbraio 1927, la dispensa dal digiu-

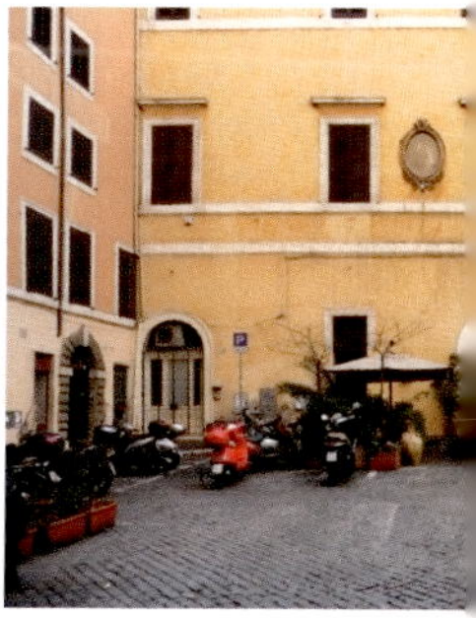

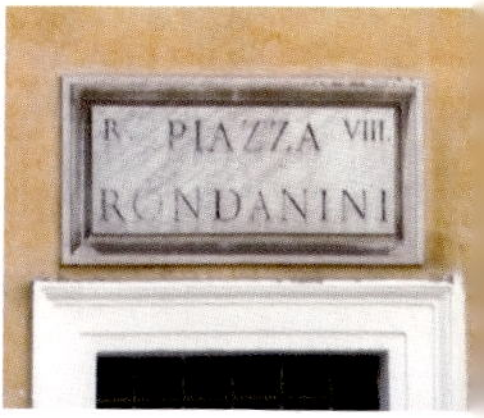

Roma.
Sopra: *Piazza Rondanini, dov'era ubicata la Curia Generalizia delle Suore Mantellate di Pistoia.*
Sotto: *Targa di Piazza Rondanini.*

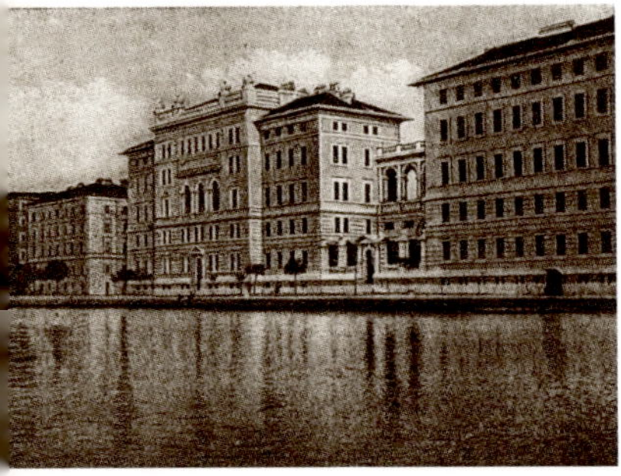

Zara (Croazia). *Istituto S. Demetrio: "Arrivammo a Zara alle 10 di sera, così, il mio desiderio di andare lontano lontano fu appagato".* *(Autobiografia, p. 52)*

no eucaristico, potendo usufruire di alimenti presi *ad modum potus.*

Dall'11 aprile, Lunedì Santo, a tutto il mese di luglio 1927 si nota un miglioramento nello stato di salute di lei. Può infatti partecipare alle solenni funzioni della Settimana Santa; compiere, nel mese di maggio, gli Esercizi Spirituali sotto la guida del Padre Roschini. Ad iniziare dal 29 maggio redige le sue memorie dietro richiesta del Padre Gabriele. In un mese traccia il racconto della sua vita nelle pagine della *Storia di un Pagliaccio*, che consegna al direttore spirituale il 29 giugno 1927. Da questa data fino al 12 settembre 1928 scriverà il Diario, la cui redazione fu suggerita al Padre Gabriele dal Card. Alessio M. Lépicier, in risposta allo sconcerto dimostrato dal Padre Roschini di fronte alla straordinaria maturità spirituale riscontrata nella giovane nepesina.

Dal mese di agosto 1927 la salute di Cecilia peggiora. Le viene interdetto l'accesso a Nepi. Deve rimanere confinata a *La Massa.* L'itinerario spirituale è registrato nelle pagine del diario, nelle quali si legge il travaglio della notte dello spirito subita da Cecilia nel dicembre 1927 con la massima punta di sofferenza interiore raggiunta nel periodo natalizio. Le pare che anche il direttore di spirito non riesca a capirla.

Ai problemi suoi, si aggiungono, soprattutto nei mesi invernali del 1928, le calunnie che serpeggiano in paese in riferimento alla sua famiglia, zio e cugino Vittorio compresi. Nel mese di maggio 1928 interviene anche la duchessa Lante Della Rovere, che impone l'allontanamento da *La Massa* dei due cugini Vittorio e Cecilia, ad iniziare dal mese di ottobre.

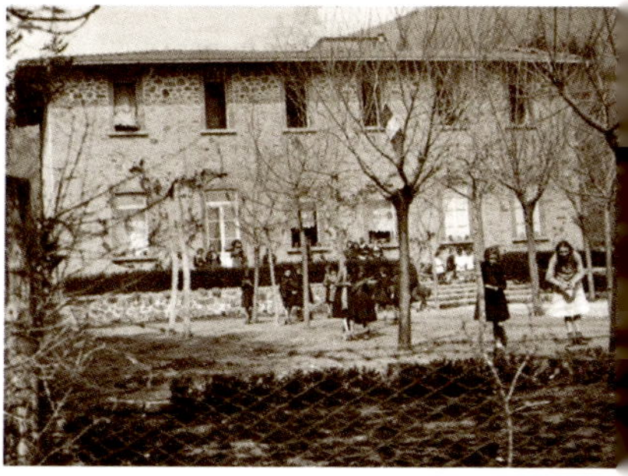

Maresca (PT). *Asilo infantile delle Suore Mantellate: "Infatti, alle 5 insieme alla Madre Agnese [Andreani], ex Madre Generale, partii per Maresca".* (*Autobiografia*, *p. 59*)

In risposta, Cecilia indirizza alla duchessa una lettera chiarificatrice, ma non risulta che la missiva ottenga dei significativi cambiamenti rispetto alla decisione precedente.

Nel mese di giugno 1928 Cecilia chiede alla mamma che le venga preparato il vestito delle Suore Mantellate Serve di Maria di Pistoia, che lei intende indossare al momento del rito funebre. Viene accontentata.

Il 29 luglio finalmente Cecilia emette il voto di vittima autorizzata dal Padre Gabriele M. Roschini. Altro sogno rivelatore della sua prossima dipartita è registrato nel diario del 12 agosto. Lei ormai sente prossima la fine; il 23 agosto 1928 desidera salutare per l'ultima volta le persone e i luoghi che a Nepi le furono tanto cari. Il 3 e 4 settembre altra visita a Castel Sant'Elia per salutare la mamma di Padre Gabriele M. Roschini.

Nel mese di settembre, deposta la penna il 12, detta le ultime lettere al cugino Vittorio. Il Padre Gabriele M. Roschini descrive nella *Storia di un giglio* le ultime giornate di Cecilia, riportandone gli episodi più significativi. Il 1° ottobre, come predetto nelle visioni sia del 30 settembre 1927 che del 12 agosto 1928, Cecilia lascia l'esilio terreno per ricongiungersi con Gesù e con l'Addolorata sua Madre, nel regno dei cieli.

La dottrina spirituale

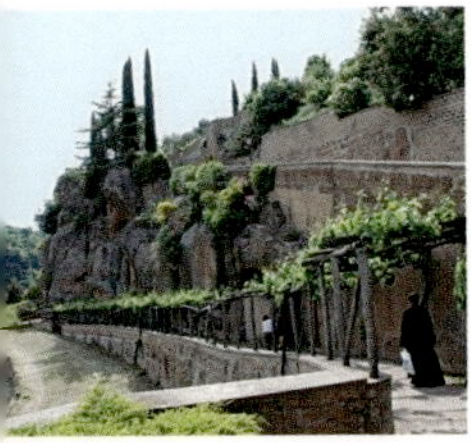

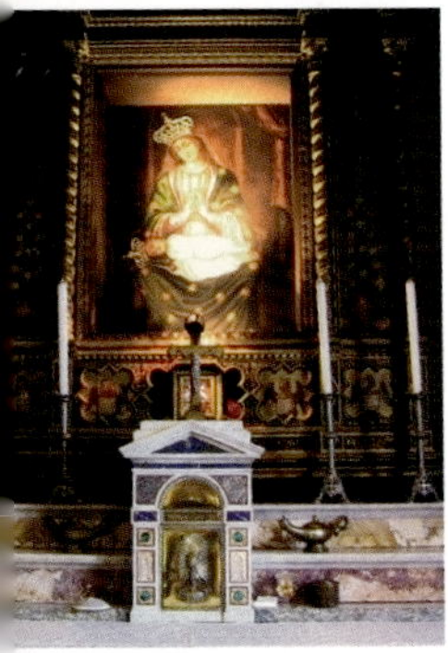

Castel S. Elia (VT).
Visione panoramica.

"[…] e in casa di Mamma Marietta ho aspettato il Padre [Gabriele M. Roschini] per fare la S. Comunione".
(Diario, p. 499)

Non accade quasi mai che una dottrina spirituale possa ascriversi ad una ragazza che si spenga a 18 anni e sette mesi. Meraviglia pertanto che ciò sia potuto accadere nel caso di Cecilia Eusepi.

Tuttavia delle spiegazioni ci sono. Quali? Che lei, stranamente, all'età di cinque anni abbia potuto entrare entro le mura claustrali di un monastero cistercense e abbia in esso trascorsi sette interi anni senza mai uscirne. Perciò, nell'età della maggiore assimilazione della realtà esteriore, appunto la fanciullezza, convisse con persone adulte, ne recepì l'influsso al punto tale da maturare, in un'età incredibilmente tanto inadatta, opinioni, pensieri, prassi di vita che era – e rimane – consentanea soltanto a persone mature. Perfino le letture sue, mi riferisco alla *Storia di un'anima* di Teresa di Lisieux, alla biografia di San Gabriele dell'Addolorata scritta da Padre Germano di San Stanislao, verterono su esempi adulti prospettati in quel momento come modelli di ordinaria vita cristiana, perciò ben lontani dalla psicologia di una ragazzina.

La conseguenza fu che lei, quando all'età di 13 anni lasciò il monastero, ebbe, per interlocutori, persone adulte, la cui età si aggirava da un minimo di 22 anni ad un massimo di 40, come già dicemmo! L'abbattimento della barriera anagrafica rivela, ancor oggi, l'eccezionalità della maturazione umana e spirituale di Cecilia Eusepi.

L'entrata tra le Suore Mantellate Serve di Maria di Pistoia le aperse lo sguardo interiore su altre prospettive, che non erano tuttavia in contrasto, ma in linea di continuità con quanto precedentemente appreso. Il suo *vademecum* rimase sempre la *Storia di un'anima* di Teresa di Lisieux, al quale lei ricorreva in continuazione, come per abbeverarsi a sorgente fresca e limpida di energia spirituale. Da supporto al testo della Carmelitana rimanevano le letture ruminate del libretto *Grappoli d'oro della mistica vite del Senario, ossia cenni biografici dei santi e beati dell'Ordine dei Servi di Maria*, che costituiva per lei come il completamento ideale degli insegnamenti appresi dalla biografia citata di San Gabriele, lui pure Terziario dell'Ordine servita prima di entrare fra i Passionisti.

"Questa mattina credevo proprio che Gesù non venisse per la gran pioggia. [...] mi è dispiaciuto tanto che al Padre sia costato molto sacrificio [...]". (*Diario*, p. 377s)

Nepi (VT). *Convento dei Servi di Maria.*

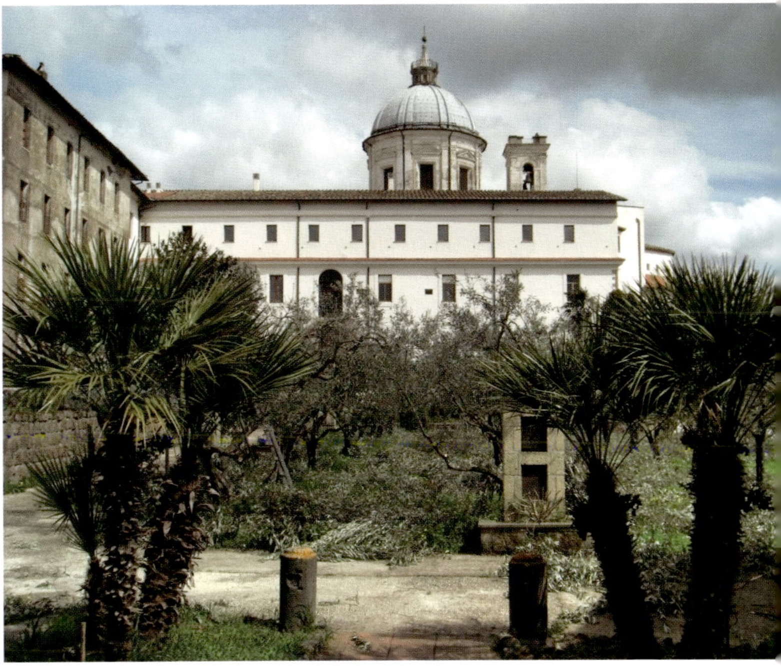

Dalle Suore Mantellate Cecilia apprese un'apertura straordinaria allo spirito missionario. Infatti detta Congregazione fin dal 1922 mandò Suore missionarie in Swaziland (Africa del Sud). Quando nel 1923 Cecilia Eusepi entrò nell'Istituto, l'entusiasmo per le missioni registrava allora punte massime di adesione e questo aggiungerà ulteriore motivo di interesse per lei, che dalle pagine di Teresa di Lisieux aveva appreso la grande apertura del cuore e della mente allo spirito missionario.

Nepi (VT). *Facciata del monastero cistercense.*

"La visitina alle Monache mi ha fatto piacere". *(Diario, p. 46)*

Tornata, inferma, a Nepi nell'ottobre 1926, nell'arco di tempo giugno-settembre 1927 Cecilia legge la vita di Santa Gemma Galgani, ne imita il rapporto con il Padre Germano di San Stanislao, chiamando a sua volta "babbo" il Padre Gabriele M. Roschini. A noi interessa cogliere, in queste sue appassionate letture, i principi spiri-

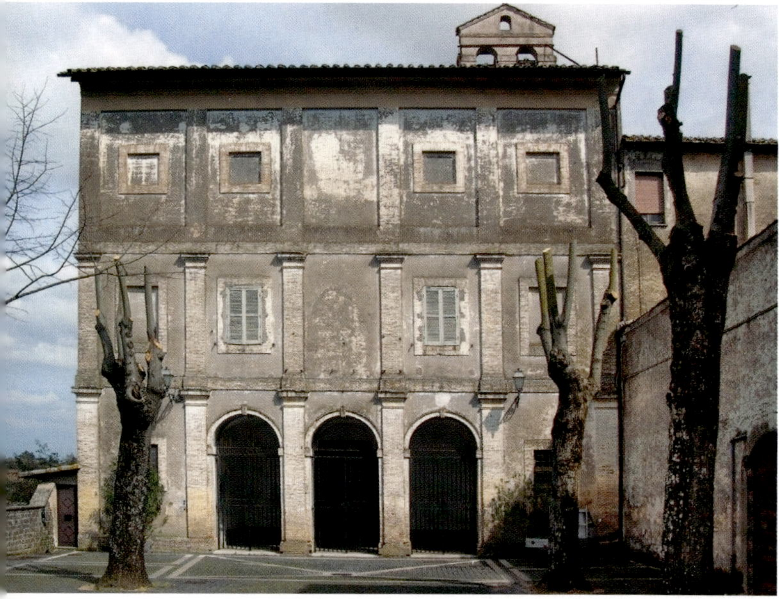

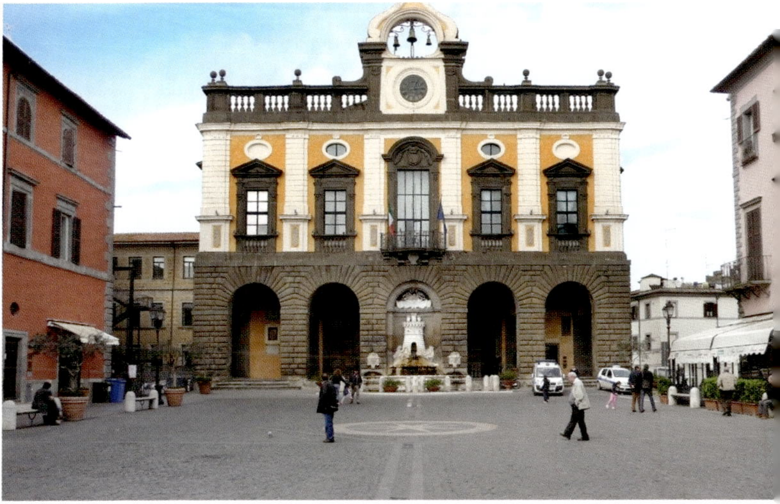

tuali ai quali lei si rifà nell'esporre quelle idee e quei sentimenti che oggi formano come un tutt'uno dottrinale in parte riferito ai nomi citati, ma in parte frutto di sue personali riflessioni ed esperienze interiori.

Coglieremo queste caratteristiche esponendo il concetto del nulla di sé, della complessa natura dell'amore, del desiderio di Dio, della conformità alla volontà divina, del rapporto con i nemici, della devozione alla Vergine Addolorata.

Nepi (VT). *Piazza principale.*

"M. Scevola e Tutina sono venute ad accompagnarmi [...] finché non siamo arrivate quasi in piazza". *(Diario, p. 490)*

Relazione nulla-niente-debolezza

Nei mesi estivi del 1927, ad iniziare dal 20 agosto, Cecilia è costretta a rinchiudersi a *La Massa* a causa dell'aggravarsi del male. Per supplire l'assenza del Padre Roschini, partito, nel mese di settembre, per un corso di predicazione, viene ogni domenica a portarle la comunione il Padre Lorenzo Luccatelli, confratello del Padre Gabriele. Sull'onda di pensieri da tempo

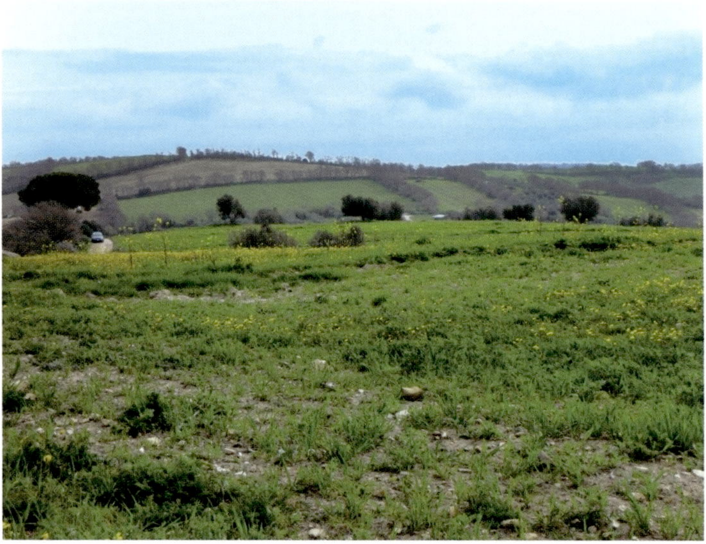

Monte Romano (VT). *Località Buffolareccia. Luogo dove si trebbiava il grano.*

coltivati ed espressi nel diario fin dal 24 luglio, Cecilia si intrattiene con lui sull'argomento del Tutto di Gesù che nell'Eucaristia è ricevuto dal *nulla* di lei. A commento, il Padre Lorenzo le dà addirittura la qualifica di "Piccolo Niente". Lei, ricevuta con gioia tale qualifica, ritorna su di essa per approfondirne il significato. E conclude così:

Il Piccolo Niente è tutto di Gesù, anche i peccati io ho offerto a Gesù, se mi lasciassi quelli, non sarei più un niente, perché il niente non ha niente (Diario, 15 ottobre 1927).

Stupendo questo pensiero dell'offerta del "peccato" come unica realtà di cui lei è proprietaria, offerta che prelude a quel totale spogliamento del proprio io di cui parla Gesù nel vangelo, riferendosi alla necessità di "perdere la propria vita" per poterla salvare (*Mt* 16,25). Lei comprende che l'unico modo che le rimane per realizzare pienamente l'unione con Gesù, consiste nel donargli tutto:

Gesù si è degnato farsi conoscere alla povera anima mia. Conosco Gesù, per questo sono felice. Prima mi agitavo per ogni mia infedeltà, adesso no, se mi agitassi, non conoscerei la mia debolezza, e la bontà del buon Dio. Quando la volontà non vuole offendere Gesù, l'offesa mi sembra che non sia più offesa, ma frutto della mia debolezza. Gesù non se ne può offendere, perché Egli sapeva prima ancora di crearmi che io l'avrei offeso senza volontà di offenderlo, ma che la mia debolezza sola sarebbe stata la causa del mio deviamento. Se queste debolezze gli dispiacessero, allora non avrebbe chiesto con tanta insistenza il nostro amore, ma lo avrebbe chiesto agli Angeli. Certo però, che se noi lasciamo correre, anzi chiudiamo gli occhi su queste debolezze, senza riconoscere e riparare l'offesa fatta a Gesù, con un atto di umiltà e di amore, Gesù ne rimarrebbe offeso (Diario, 15 ottobre 1927).

Monte Romano (VT). *Località Buffolareccia. Strada sterrata dove avvenne l'investimento.*

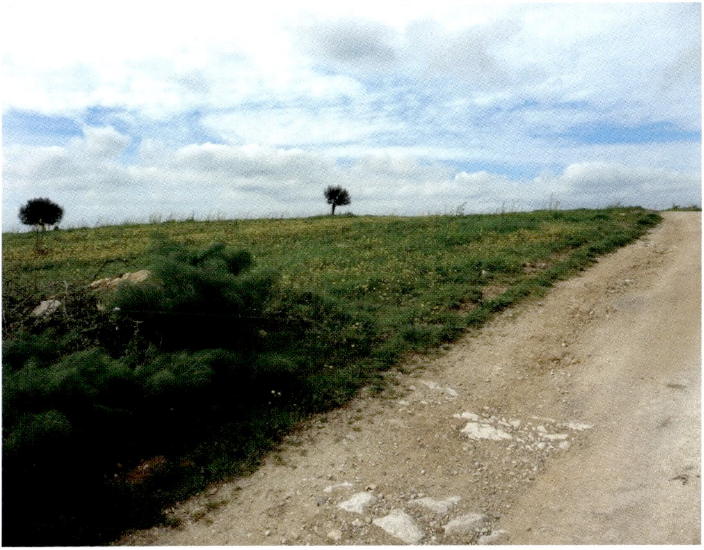

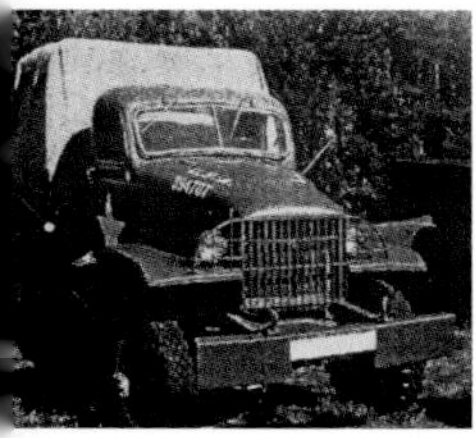

Lo Chevrolet, tipo di camion investitore.

Tommaso Ricci, l'investito.

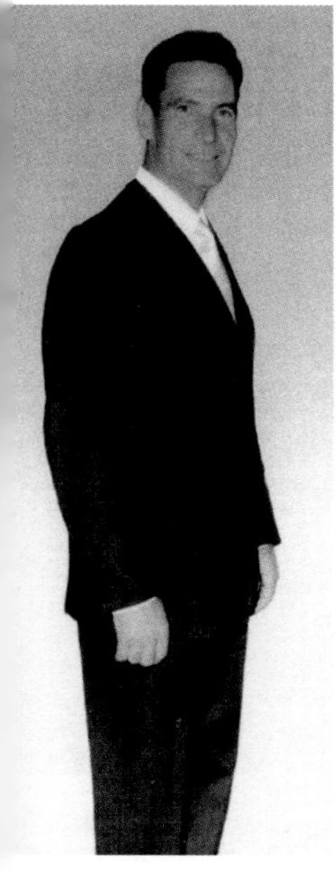

Ci si trova di fronte a due situazioni paradossali: da un lato l'affermazione della propria libertà di poter decidere di non voler offendere Dio; e dall'altra, la constatazione che, ciò nonostante, di fatto tale offesa avviene. Come risolve tale problema Cecilia? Lei non cita San Paolo, ma ne ripete il principio: "Con la mente, servo la legge di Dio, con la carne invece la legge del peccato" (*Rm* 7,25).

La novità riguarda la valutazione delle cosiddette "debolezze", che nel pensiero di Cecilia risultano rientranti nel piano divino della creazione dell'uomo contrapposto, come creatura dotata di materia e spirito, alla natura angelica costituita solo dall'elemento spirituale. In tale differenza strutturale l'Eusepi, all'età di 17 anni, fa convergere la sua e la nostra attenzione, ritenendo la debolezza umana un qualcosa di cui non ci si deve preoccupare più di tanto: *"Se queste debolezze gli dispiacessero, allora non avrebbe chiesto con tanta insistenza il nostro amore, ma lo avrebbe chiesto agli Angeli"*. Tuttavia, quasi ad attenuare la forza propositiva dell'affermazione, vi aggiunge la necessità di chiederne comunque perdono a Dio con un atto di "umiltà e amore". Quale la conclusione? Che la debolezza è da Dio permessa al fine di indurre ciascuno ad essere consapevole della propria miseria creaturale, assumendo pertanto l'atteggiamento del "povero in ispirito".

La complessa natura dell'amore

Le considerazioni fin qui condotte dovrebbero ingenerare un senso di frustrazione derivante dall'imperfezione cui si è di fatto condannati. Tuttavia, Cecilia è convinta che il Signore ci abbia chiesto di amarlo per farci felici e non per rattristarci. Tutto ciò lo esprime con chiarezza solare:

Vorrei che tutti conoscessero il segreto della felicità: l'amore. Tante anime forse lo conoscono, ma non sanno come darsi all'amore (anche questo io ho provato), perciò desidererei dire a queste come ho fatto io: ho riconosciuto il mio nulla, anzi ho amato il mio nulla, riconoscendo me stessa ho conosciuto Dio, la Sua bontà, la Sua misericordia, il Suo amore, la Sua giustizia. Tutto in Dio mi è sembrato amore, anche la Sua giustizia. Dio l'ho conosciuto in me, in tutti i doni, le grazie, i privilegi di cui mi ha abbellita, con questi ha riempito il mio nulla. La conoscenza del mio nulla mi ha portato alla conoscenza di Dio, e questa conoscenza mi ha spinto ad amarlo. Vedendolo tanto amabile, l'amarlo è diventato per me un bisogno, un martirio, una gioia, sento d'amarlo tanto, tanto, tanto. No, non m'inganno, sono pronta a tutto per il mio Dio, credo che sulla terra non si possa amare più di così (Diario, 8 febbraio 1928).

È impressionante che una ragazza così giovane, senza alcuna preparazione teologica specifica, giunga ad impostare tutto il discorso della relazione con Dio soffermandosi sul principio dell'Amore come unico punto di riferimento. Infatti, Dio è amore, come asserisce San Giovanni (*1Gv* 4,8). Amore che crea, amore che redime e salva.

Il sapore pascaliano della dottrina impartita da lei è tuttavia nelle seguenti parole: "La conoscenza del mio nulla mi ha portato alla conoscenza di Dio, e questa

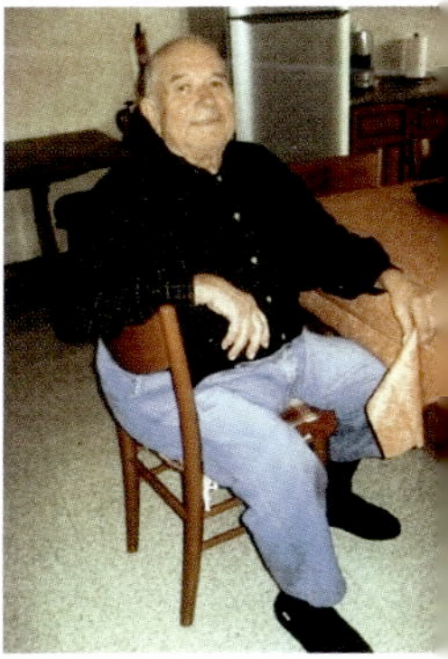

Domenico Cavanna, che trasportò il Ricci all'ambulatorio medico.

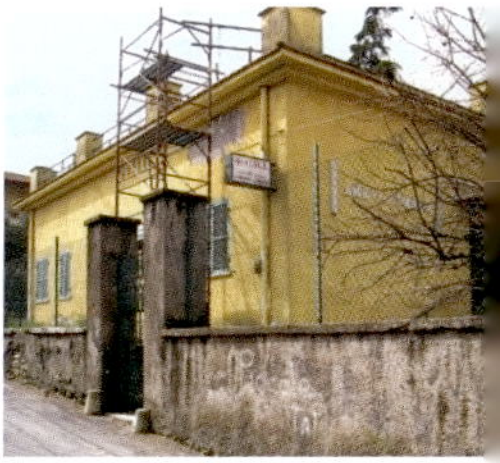

Monte Romano (VT). *Ambulatorio del medico condotto.*

conoscenza mi ha spinto ad amarlo". Cecilia non parte dalla creazione, come solitamente si fa per dimostrare il Dio esistente; lei parte dall'esistenza del suo nulla, che trova però ricolmo di doni non originati dall'azione sua, ma ricevuti da Altro da sé e a quest'Altro da sé lei attribuisce il titolo di Dio. È indubbiamente un modo originale di leggere la presenza divina nell'universo.

Che cosa sviluppa tale constatazione? Il senso della riconoscenza per tanto bene ricevuto, e in questa riconoscenza si radica la gioia dell'anima, che si sente proiettata interiormente verso il Donatore con anelito irrefrenabile. Di qui la gioia, la felicità causata dall'amore.

Ad oscurare questo sentimento intimo non v'è nulla, perché anche la giustizia divina in tale contesto assume la connotazione del dono ricevuto. Tradotto, significa che anche la sofferenza della croce acquisisce nel Cristo la colorazione del gaudio interiore.

Non si tratta di un'allusione generica, ma di una constatazione sperimentata da lei e così tratteggiata nel diario dell'8 febbraio 1928:

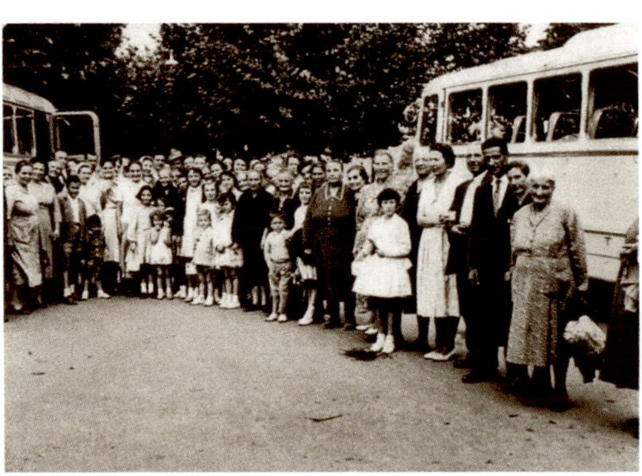

Pellegrinaggio del 27 settembre 1949 dei Monteromanesi alla tomba di Cecilia, a Nepi, per ringraziarla.

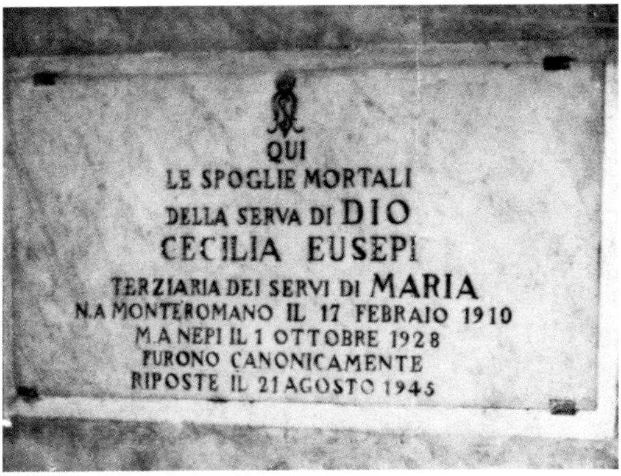

Nepi (VT). *Convento dei Servi di Maria. Targa tombale inserita nel muro del corridoio del convento, dove le spoglie mortali di Cecilia Eusepi, esumate il 16 marzo 1944, furono traslate due giorni dopo.*

Ecco, io soffro, tanto fisicamente quanto moralmente, ma amo tanto la sofferenza. È tanta la soddisfazione che provo soffrendo, che vorrei soffrire di più, vorrei soffrire tanto. Questo desiderio stesso mi fa soffrire, e nel sacrificarlo a Gesù, trovo la felicità, una grande soddisfazione. Non è vero che questa vita è triste, no, basta conoscere il segreto di convertire tutte le amarezze in gioia, per godere continuamente. Con tutta verità, quando morirò, potrò dire a Gesù che io sono abituata a godere e quindi mi metta per tutta l'eternità a godere. Questa gioia della quale io parlo, non toglie l'amarezza al sacrificio, è l'amore, l'amore solo che addolcisce tutto: questo è il segreto. Più uno si abbandona all'amore, più si dà in braccio al dolore e più il dolore diventa gioia. Il mio amore non è sensibile, e ne ringrazio di tutto cuore Gesù. Fin da bambina cercavo, domandavo cos'era l'amore, come si amava, perché sentivo che l'amore sensibile, i trasporti non erano per me. Finalmente Gesù mi ha fatto conoscere quel che io cercavo, ho compreso che amare vuol dire abbandonarsi al dolore, fidandomi di Gesù, che è la mia forza, e diffidando di me. Conoscendo benissimo la mia debolezza, mi sono abbandonata all'amore (Diario, 8 febbraio 1928).

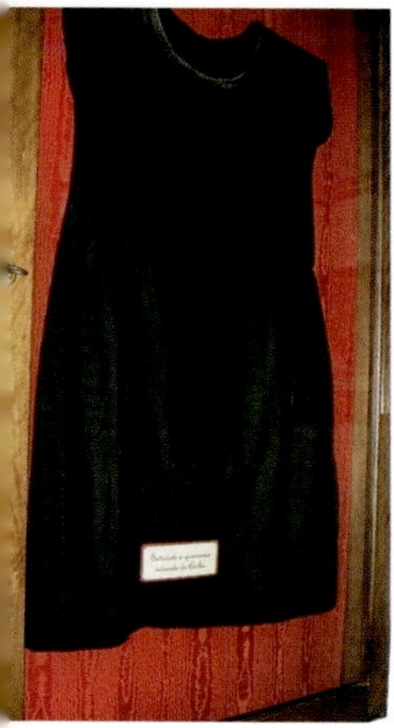

Veste di Cecilia sostituita con quella delle Suore Mantellate nella seconda esumazione del 20 agosto 1945.

È difficile per chiunque riuscire a cogliere il rapporto amore-dolore così come illustrato dall'Eusepi. Lei tuttavia ne parla per esperienza e distingue nettamente la concezione dell'amore sensibile, da quello che lei sperimenta e che differisce profondamente dall'esperienza e dal giudizio comune. Infatti la *"gioia della quale io parlo* – precisa Cecilia – *non toglie l'amarezza al sacrificio"*.

Finora abbiamo parlato del rapporto amore-dolore. Cecilia legge nell'amore un ulteriore aspetto che lei nel diario mette bene in luce, riferendosi alla natura contraddittoria dell'amore stesso. Lei vi legge, come intrinseca legge operativa, due mondi opposti: da un lato il desiderio di essere posseduti dall'Amato; dall'altro, la disponibilità ad allontanarsi da lui per sempre, se l'essergli vicino dovesse dispiacergli. Il riferimento è alla Santa Comunione. Lei vorrebbe ricevere spesso Gesù sacramentato, ma ciò non è possibile, anzi talvolta le pare che lo stesso Gesù non voglia venire da lei, perché non sopprime impedimenti a tale riguardo da lui facilmente risolvibili,

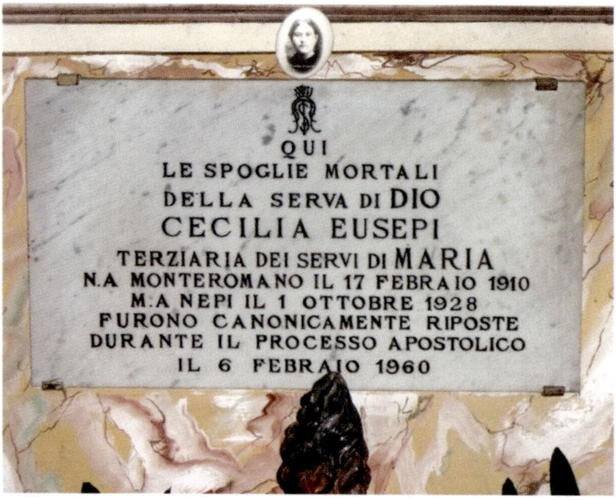

Nepi (VT). *Chiesa dei SS. Tolomeo e Romano. Ultima targa sepolcrale apposta durante l'Inchiesta diocesana del febbraio 1960.*

come, per esempio, impedire la pioggia che rende difficile al Padre Gabriele Roschini, per l'impraticabilità del sentiero, l'andare a *La Massa*:

Amare vuol dire sacrificare a Gesù la nostra propria volontà, i nostri desideri anche ottimi, dimenticare noi stessi, anzi obliare noi stessi per seguire la Sua SS. Volontà. Gesù, da chi lo ama, vuole il sangue del cuore, che io credo sia ben più doloroso del sangue del corpo. Preferirei mille volte, farmi staccare la testa dal busto, che vedermi priva della Comunione quotidiana, eppure, se amo Gesù, devo accettare con gioia questo sacrificio, ed offrirgli col sorriso sulle labbra, il sangue del cuore (Diario, 10 giugno 1927).

Quello che lei asserisce nei confronti dell'Eucaristia, l'estende anche allo spegnersi della vita. Malgrado la giovane età, Cecilia affronta il tema della precarietà dell'esistenza considerata nel suo specifico carattere di esilio dalla patria definitiva, mettendo in luce i due amori corrispondenti: l'amore alla vita presente e quello alla vita futura. Le sue parole acquistano particolare rilievo, perché a pronunciarle è una persona consapevole di essere colpita da malattia letale:

Dico solo questa contraddizione che sento in me; non amo l'esilio, poiché per me è un vero esilio, non mi ha dato e non mi dà che dolore, ma nello stesso tempo sento di amarlo tanto, perché mi dà tante occasioni di dimostrare a Gesù il mio amore, di sfogliarmi ai Suoi piedi, è tanto bello dare, dunque ecco la contraddizione, amo e nello stesso tempo non amo l'esilio, anche questa contraddizione nasce forse dall'amore? (Diario, 4 aprile 1928).

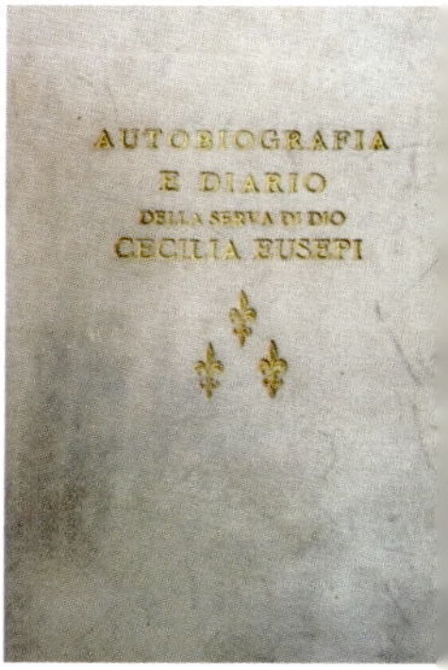

Autobiografia e Diario.

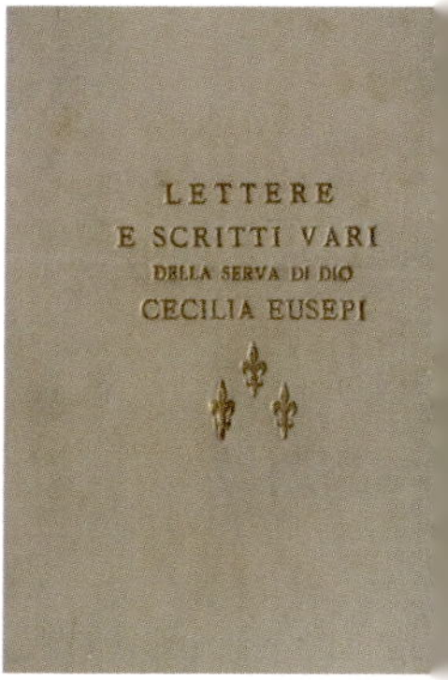

Lettere e scritti vari.

È per lo meno singolare che una giovane riesca ad esprimere concetti così alti e al contempo così umanamente difficili come quelli da lei manifestati nei confronti di quella realtà vitale che definiamo "amore", da lei considerata come in filigrana sullo sfondo della Croce.

Il desiderio di Dio

Che cosa sta alla radice di simili atteggiamenti se non il desiderio di entrare nel possesso definitivo dell'Amato? Il desiderio di Dio contraddistingue il rapporto di lei con il Signore, ne segna le tappe progressive di avvicinamento al congiungersi ultimo con Lui.

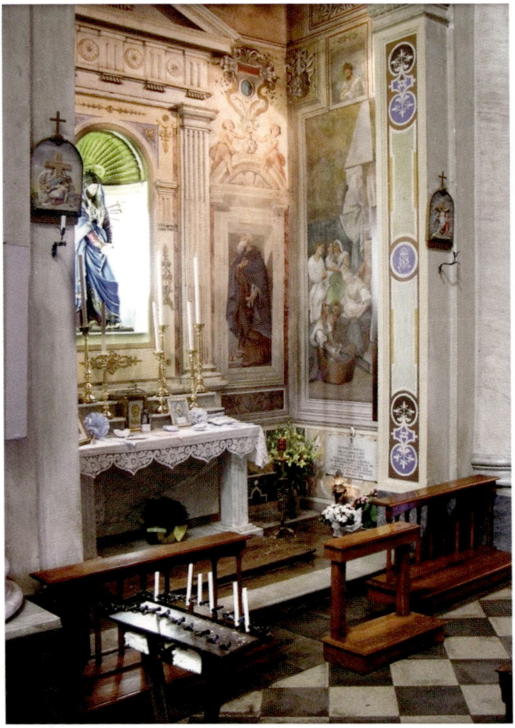

Nepi (VT). *Chiesa dei SS. Tolomeo e Romano. Altare dell'Addolorata dove sono tumulate le spoglie mortali di Cecilia Eusepi.*

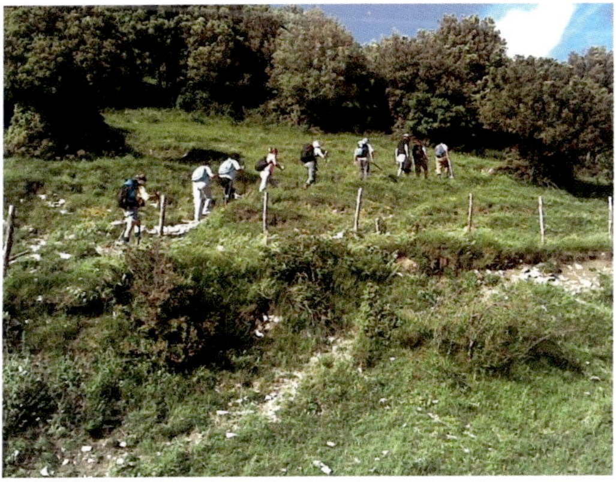

Sul tema dell'esilio di cui ho appena detto, Cecilia ritorna ripetutamente. Oppressa dalle calunnie che le amareggiarono gli ultimi mesi di vita, l'Eusepi manifesta un distacco totale dalle cose terrestri, spinta dal desiderio intenso di Dio:

Ho detto tante cose a Gesù, e la principale questa, che mi dia la follia dell'amore, che si prenda tutto questo mio cuore piccolo, ma pur tanto grande, poiché soltanto Dio lo può riempire, saziare. Gli ho detto che mi faccia morire piuttosto che dare uno solo dei palpiti del cuore alle creature senza aver Lui di mira. Ho dato tutto a Gesù e sono felice, mi sento leggera leggera, tanto che, se anche dovessi morire in questo momento, sarei felice, lascerei l'esilio senza rimpianti, poiché non ho niente che mi attira quaggiù, solo il dolore, perché soffrendo si ama, si danno prove d'amore a Gesù, questo sì mi dispiace un po' lasciarlo (Diario, 25 marzo 1928).

Si noti la singolarità: solo il dolore l'attira quaggiù, perché il dolore è la prova del suo amore al Signore! Lei infatti ha piena consapevolezza che solo Dio può

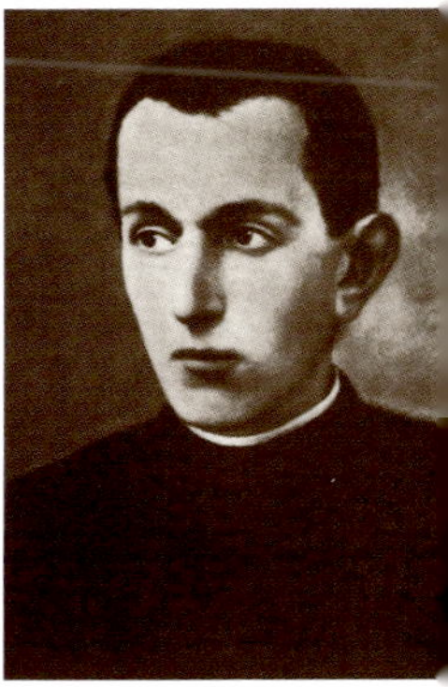

Ven. Andrea Beltrami.

"Un pensiero dello scrittore della vita di Don Beltrami, mi ha molto colpita: [...] per certe anime, non c'è via di mezzo: o eroi o reprobi, o santi o nemmeno buoni".
(Diario, p. 463)

Cagli (PU). *Sentiero montano.*

"Desidero stare unita a Gesù, [...] quando vado col pensiero, al Tabernacolo, mi sembra di stare proprio vicina a Gesù, non sento più la distanza che mi separa da Lui".

(Diario, p. 366)

Pistoia. *Cecilia in preghiera dinanzi al tabernacolo.*

riempire il suo cuore, saziarne la brama ardente. Come realizzare tale brama? La modalità per Cecilia è evidentissima: la Comunione!

Domattina io lo riceverò, lo desidero ardentemente. Io non comprendo un amore che non senta attrattiva per il tabernacolo, dove vive, ama Gesù. Che bella cosa è la comunione, unirsi a Lui intimamente! Non è un miracolo quello di unirsi così intimamente col fuoco divino Gesù, e non sentirsi bruciare? Sì, è un miracolo, il miracolo della umana freddezza. Io non sento dolcezza, non sento ardore, nella preghiera ed anche nella comunione, ma non mi affliggo, il mio amore sarà più forte e disinteressato, non sarà un amore egoista (Diario, 7 dicembre 1927).

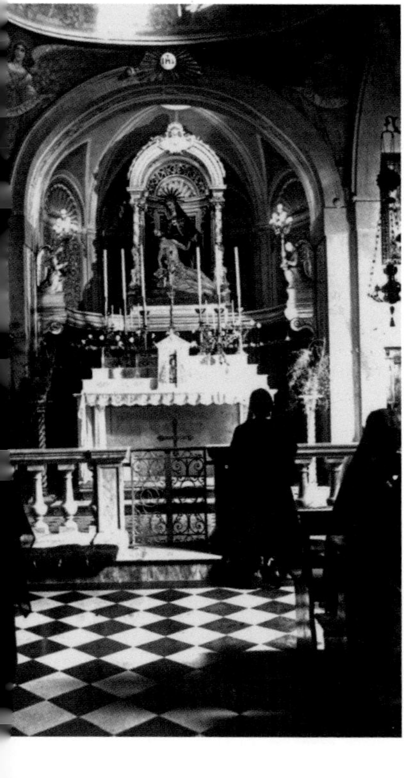

L'aspetto di maggior rilievo concerne l'amore volitivo da cui è animata Cecilia, che confessa sinceramente di non avvertire in lei la presenza dell'amore emotivo, ossia quella dolcezza sensibile verso la quale tutti siamo portati nel desiderio di sentirci anche spiritualmente appagati. L'assenza dell'amore emotivo esprime a chiare lettere il distacco totale da se stessa e da qualsiasi personale compiacimento, tutto orientando verso l'Amato per esserne posseduta e interiormente vivificata.

Non si tratta di episodi isolati, ma di situazioni spirituali talvolta persistenti, come appare anche dal testo seguente:

Domani verrà Gesù, qui, nel mio cuore, non vedo l'ora, io amo Gesù ma non sento nessun trasporto, quando prego sono continuamente distratta, non sento più quel fervore che sentivo una volta, non penso più tanto spesso a Gesù. Eppure io vorrei pensarci non ogni minuto, ma ogni secondo. Però mi consolo pensando che, essendomi offerta a Gesù, anche non pensando a Lui, io lo amo. La mia vita è una continua preghiera, tutti i palpiti del mio cuore, i battiti del mio polso, i miei respiri, intendo siano tanti atti d'amore. E non è dunque questo un continuo pregare, un continuo amare?
(Diario, 15 ottobre 1927).

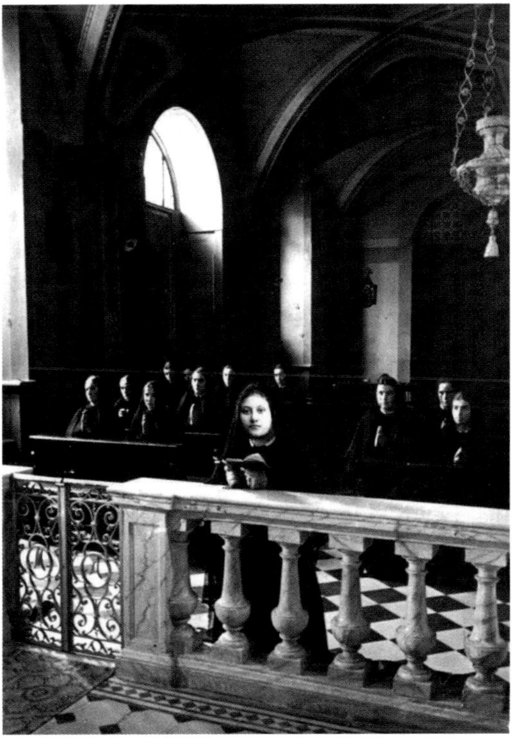

"Aveva ragione S. Filippo di chiamare il Crocifisso Suo libro, è lì che viene descritta, o meglio, è lì che si apprende la scienza dell'amore".
(Diario, p. 344)

Pistoia.
Cecilia guida la Via Crucis.

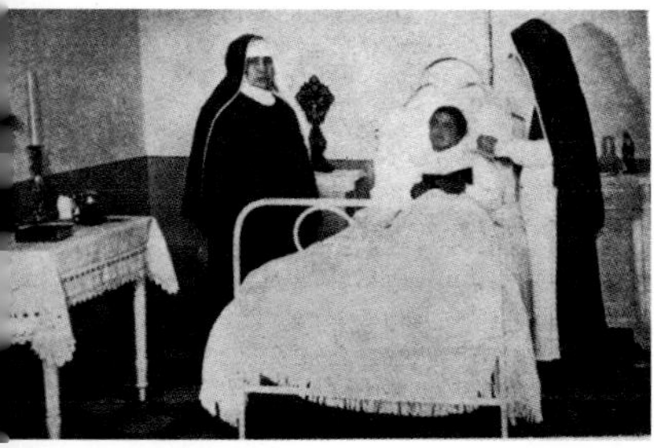

I particolari emergenti dal testo, ora riportato, fanno rientrare la psicologia della Eusepi entro i parametri comuni a tutti noi soggetti a distrazioni e ad assenza di trasporti emotivi particolari. Colpisce tuttavia la conclusione che lei ne trae, che parrebbe contraddittoria: *"La mia vita è una continua preghiera"*.

Nepi (VT). *Fattoria [ossia il Casale] "La Massa".*

L'abito delle Mantellate: "Mamma ha detto al Padre il desiderio che ho di cucirmi il vestito da Mantellata per quando muoio". *(Diario, p. 444)*

La conformità alla volontà divina

Alla luce di questa confessione di Cecilia, è possibile riassumere le tappe progressive del suo abbandonarsi alla volontà divina, prima come celata nei desideri suoi: essere Monaca Cistercense, poi Suora Mantellata, quindi dedita all'apostolato soprattutto missionario e, alla fine, inferma di malattia letale.

Fin dal luglio del 1925 lei manifesta la disponibilità a compiere la volontà di Dio qualsiasi questa possa essere, come appare dalla risposta data alla Priora di Zara che la invitava a pregare Gesù per guarire e divenire Suora Mantellata delle Serve di Maria di Pistoia: *"Madre, pregherò volentieri, affinché il Signore mi dia la forza di fare sempre e in tutto la sua SS.ma Volontà"*.

Questo atteggiamento culminerà nell'offerta di sé a Gesù come "pallina", come già scrissi a proposito del Natale 1925. Ma il momento più alto Cecilia lo raggiungerà nel voto di vittima del 29 luglio 1928 a pochi mesi dal decesso:

Voglio proprio farmi santa, e se il Padre lo permette, prenderò per base questa massima: "Non farò niente che piace a me, ma tutto ciò che mostra più amore a Gesù". Ho paura a scrivere queste parole, ho paura di essere poi infedele a questa mia promessa, per la mia estrema debolezza, ma a Gesù non è nulla impossibile, anzi si confonde con le anime più deboli e miserabili, purché queste, diffidando di loro stesse (ciò non è difficile, quando Gesù si degna mostrarci il nostro nulla), si abbandonino e confidino pienamente in Lui, e ciò lo fa con le anime deboli, appunto, per mostrare la Sua grande misericordia (Diario, 29 luglio 1928).

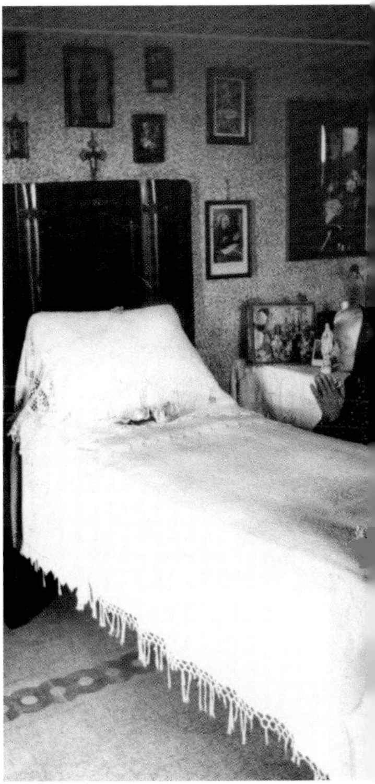

Mamma Paolina prega sul letto della figlia defunta.

Nel "non farò niente che piace a me, ma tutto ciò che mostra più amore a Gesù" è racchiuso l'atto di eroico abbandono di Cecilia Eusepi alla divina volontà: da questo momento lei è solo e unicamente nelle mani di Dio.

Il rapporto con i nemici

Il più alto traguardo raggiunto da Cecilia Eusepi nel conformare la sua alla volontà divina, è certamente raggiunto da lei nel rapporto intercorso con coloro che l'hanno non solo calunniata, ma addirittura voluta allontanare da *La Massa* nel momento più tragico della sua vita di inferma e questo alla vigilia, per così dire, della morte.

Lei infatti non si limita a perdonarli, pur racchiudendo simile gesto un atto di grande amore cristiano; lei fa molto di più, come appare dalle seguenti parole:

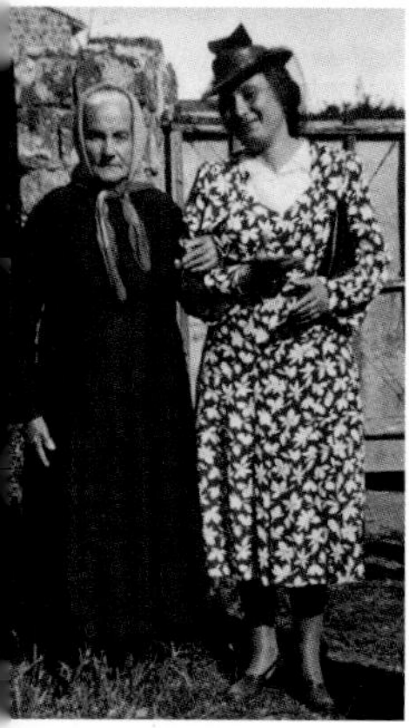

Mamma Paolina con la sorella Anna Rosa, zia di Cecilia.

[...] *è tanto bella la legge del perdono! Piuttosto che perdonare i miei nemici, io mi sento l'obbligo di ringraziarli, poiché mi hanno dato e mi danno ancora tante belle occasioni di cantare il mio amore a Gesù. La mia riconoscenza per questi sarà eterna, prego sempre per la santificazione delle loro anime. In Paradiso poi, farò di tutto per tirarli su. Se loro non vogliono venire, io sono pronta, per quanto è possibile, di strascinarceli* (Diario, 19 luglio 1928).

I nemici, lei, non solo li perdona, ma li ringrazia, per l'occasione offertale di dimostrare, attraverso il perdono per la cattiveria subita, il suo amore a Gesù. Addirittura giunge a parlare, nei loro confronti, di riconoscenza. È incredibile e inimmaginabile che al perdono si aggiunga la riconoscenza!

La devozione alla Vergine Addolorata

Sullo sfondo di un simile comportamento leggiamo, come in trasparenza, la figura della Vergine Addolorata. Il nucleo fondamentale dell'amore verso Dio di Cecilia si articolava in due realtà soprannaturali straordinarie, da lei definite "Tesoro" e "Cuore": l'Eucaristia e le sofferenze redentrici della Madre. Il primo per lei rappresentava la sorgente cui attingere in continuazione forza e vita e pertanto giustamente considerato il "tesoro" prezioso dell'Essere: "Chi mangia la mia carne e beve il mio sangue rimane in me e io in lui" (*Gv* 6,56). Il secondo, per Cecilia costituiva il rifugio sicuro cui approdare nei momenti difficili dell'esistere. Ne aveva avuto esperienza fin da bambina:

Da piccola ricordo che mi nascondevo in coro, sotto l'altare della Madonna Addolorata, chiudevo gli occhi e mi rappresentavo all'immaginazione tutta la passione di Gesù, e piangevo tanto, nello stesso tempo godevo, provavo una gioia che non so esprimere. Allora ero piccola, non pensavo che tutto quel dolore era causato dal peccato e dall'amore, e così le mie non so se chiamarle meditazioni, non producevano in me che la compassione, ma adesso, uno sguardo solo al Crocifisso, basta per accrescere in me l'orrore al peccato e l'amore a Gesù. Quelle piaghe, quelle lacrime della Mammina, hanno un linguaggio troppo potente per non udirlo (Diario, 10 febbraio 1928).

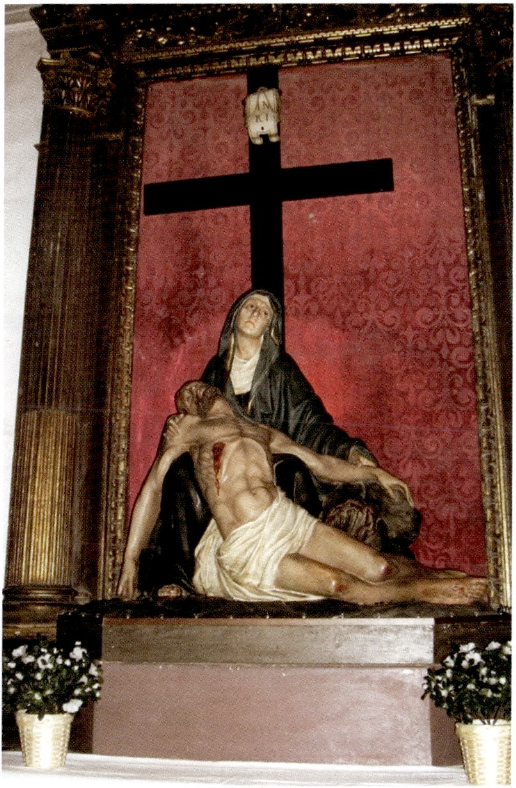

Nepi (VT). *Chiesa dei SS. Tolomeo e Romano. Statua dell'Addolorata.*

"Mio Dio ti offro i miei dolori uniti a quelli della tua passione, e al dolore immenso della mia Mammina Addolorata". *(Diario, p. 166)*

Le lacrime della Madonna sono, per Cecilia, linguaggio d'amore, amore pertanto che sanguina, che lacrima. La Vergine Madre piange infatti per il Figlio ucciso e per i figli uccisori, ossia per noi. Ecco perché Cecilia definisce Maria "modello perfetto di carità", perché Lei abbraccia nel suo dolore tutti: il Dio che si spegne sul Legno e gli uomini che quel figlio inchiodano con il loro peccato!

È possibile riassumere il duplice dolore materno? Sì, afferma Cecilia. Lei lo vede racchiuso sul Tesoro deposto, morto, sul grembo della Madre ai piedi della croce. Magnifica immagine che solo l'amore appassionato di Cecilia poteva intuire:

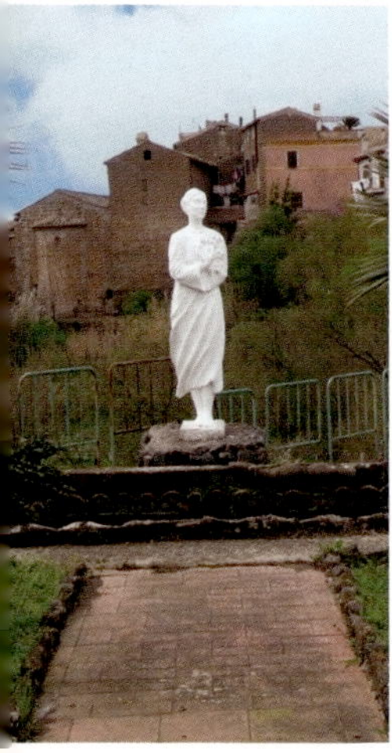

Nepi (VT). *Convento dei Servi di Maria. Statua di Cecilia nel giardino.*

Questa mattina ho letto il sesto dolore della Madonna, povera Mamma mia quanto hai sofferto! Come non ti devo amare? Tu sei la Mamma mia, io t'amo tanto, tanto, tanto, vorrei asciugare a una a una tutte le tue lacrime. Con che amore e riverenza ricevesti il corpo di Gesù fra le tue braccia. Ebbene, per le tue lacrime e i tuoi dolori concedimi la grazia di accostarmi a Gesù nella Santa Comunione con lo stesso amore, fa' che io l'ami tanto tanto, fino a morire d'amore (Diario, 24 novembre 1927).

Anche Cecilia, la mattina del 30 settembre 1928, dopo aver ricevuto Gesù Eucaristia, volle cantarGli l'inno che accompagnò la sua Prima Comunione: "Morir d'amore". Fu l'ultimo canto suo, prima che, verso le 15,00, perdesse conoscenza e poi, alle 3,10 del 1° ottobre, reclinasse per sempre il capo sul cuore della Vergine Madre finalmente davvero incontrata nella luce folgorante della Gloria divina.

Sulla via della beatificazione

Negli anni 1939-1942 il Ven. Mons. Luigi Maria Olivares istruì il processo ordinario a Nepi con l'audizione di 46 testi. Nel timore che lo spostamento del fronte di guerra potesse causare la distruzione della tomba della Serva di Dio, il 16 marzo 1944 si procedette ad una prima esumazione delle sue spoglie mortali, allora praticamente intatte, tumulandole nel corridoio del convento dei SS. Tolomeo e Romano in Nepi. Concluso il conflitto bellico, ebbe luogo una seconda esumazione il 20 agosto 1945, durante la quale il corpo della Serva di Dio venne rivestito dell'abito delle Suore Mantellate Serve di Maria di Pistoia e definitivamente tumulato nella Chiesa parrocchiale a lato dell'altare dell'Addolorata "in cornu epistulae".

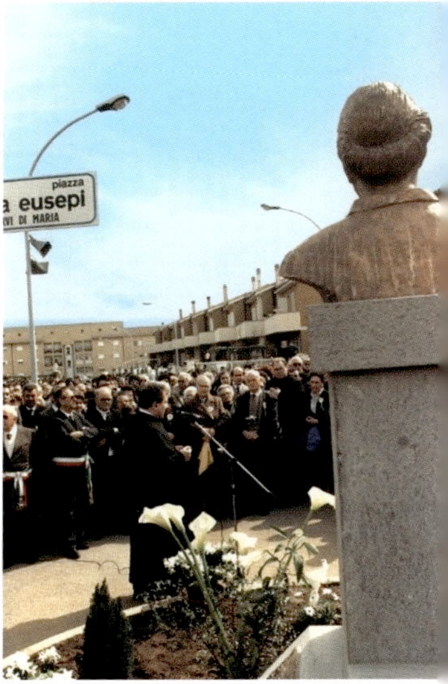

Nepi (VT). *Inaugurazione della piazza intitolata a Cecilia Eusepi.*

Nel 1957 si aprì il processo apostolico a Lucca con l'audizione di sette testi. Nel 1958 il processo apostolico fu aperto a Nepi, con l'ascolto di 39 testimoni, dei quali 2 *ex officio*. A chiusura dell'Inchiesta Diocesana si procedette, nel febbraio 1960, alla terza esumazione.

Il 1° giugno 1987 fu emanato il Decreto papale che riconosce l'eroicità delle virtù esercitate dalla Ven. Cecilia Eusepi.

Lo scampato pericolo di morte di Tommaso Ricci, investito il 4 agosto 1959 a

Monte Romano (VT), dalla ruota di un camion Chevrolet sulla quale gravava un peso di oltre 1.000 kg. – grazia ottenuta per intercessione dell'Eusepi – fu con Decreto papale riconosciuto come prodigioso in data 1° luglio 2010, riconoscimento che aprì la porta alla Beatificazione della giovane nepesina.

Le Suore Mantellate Serve di Maria di Pistoia

La Congregazione delle Suore Mantellate Serve di Maria di Pistoia , riconosciuta di diritto pontificio con decreto della Santa Sede dell'11 febbraio 1909, fu fondata a Treppio (PT) il 6 ottobre 1861 da due Terziarie dell'Ordine dei Servi di Maria: suor Filomena Rossi e suor Giovanna Ferrari. Il 16 novembre 1868 la comunità di Treppio fu aggregata all'Ordine dei Serviti, aggregazione estesa poi a tutta la congregazione in data 20 luglio 1879. Nel 1920, sotto il pontificato di Papa Benedetto XV, furono approvate le prime Costituzioni e il 14 giugno del 1980 la Congregazione romana competente approvò le Costituzioni rinnovate secondo le indicazioni del Concilio Vaticano II.

Nella sua attività apostolica la Congregazione s'ispira costantemente all'umile servizio svolto dalla Madre di Dio, l'Ancella del Signore. Esso si esplica nella promozione e nell'educazione, particolarmente della donna; nella cura degli infermi e dei bisognosi di umana solidarietà. Attualmente opera in Italia, negli Stati Uniti, in Swaziland, in Spagna, in Uganda.

PREGHIERA PER LA CANONIZZAZIONE DELLA BEATA CECILIA EUSEPI

O Gesù, che nel cuore verginale di Cecilia Eusepi suscitasti l'ardente desiderio di essere una sola cosa con Te e con la Vergine Tua Madre, dolente ai piedi della Croce, fa' che ne imitiamo l'abbandono alla Tua Volontà, la fede umile e costante, la disponibilità al sacrificio, l'affidamento a Te di tutta la nostra vita. Ti preghiamo di concedere a lei la glorificazione in terra e a noi la grazia particolare che invochiamo.

Pater, Ave, Gloria

(Con approv. Eccl.)

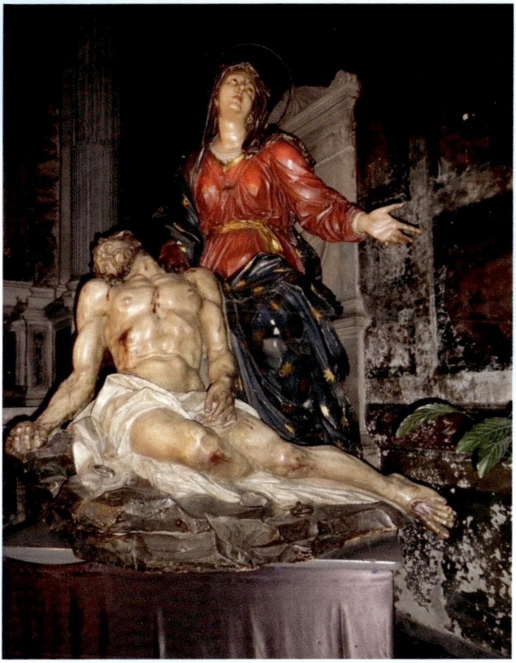

Roma. *Chiesa di S. Marcello.*

"Ho pensato parecchio al Tesoro che questa mattina avrei ricevuto, ed anche alla cara Mammina Addolorata, anzi, mi sembrava proprio di vederla vera con Gesù morto sulle braccia ed io che le stavo vicina".

(Diario, p. 507)

Indice

Giungerò
a Gesù per
un piccolo
sentiero, breve,
molto breve,
tracciatomi
dalla piccola
Teresa del B.G.
Eccolo:
umiltà,
abbandono,
amore.
(Storia di un
Pagliaccio,
p. 8 sg.)

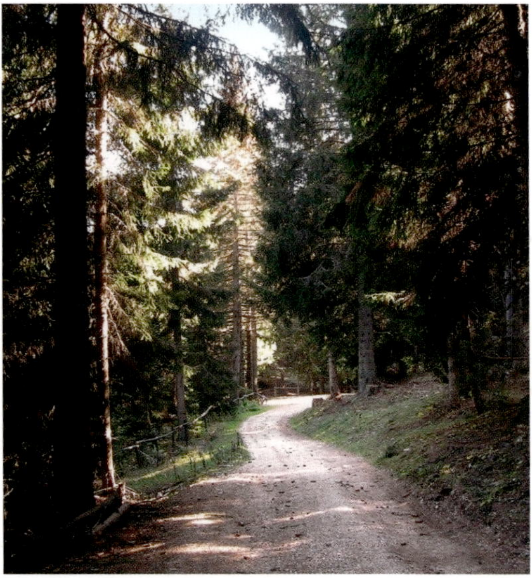

DIOCESI DI
CIVITAVECCHIA-TARQUINIA

Piazza Calamatta, 1
00053 Civitavecchia (RM)

e-mail: curia@civitavecchia.chiesacattolica.it